What people are saying about this book

The nation's future depends on a highly educated workforce. The Career Pathways reforms provide the means to equip our country's young people for the high-skill, high-wage jobs of the new century. I hope educators, employers, community leaders, and others will consider implementing the Career Pathways strategies.

Mike Huckabee, Governor of Arkansas
Chairman, National Governors Association

Career Pathways: Education with a Purpose hits precisely on the issues we as a nation must confront right now. Our economic vitality—and I would even suggest our national security—depends on preparing our people to meet the challenges of the global marketplace.

Mark R. Warner, Governor of Virginia

As Co-Lead Program Officer for the National Science Foundation's Advanced Technological Education program since its inception, I have learned that many of the long-term occupations from which employees can derive satisfaction and a good lifestyle require more than a high school education, but do not require a four-year college degree. Students in middle and high schools need realistic and consistent guidance so that they will pursue a course of study that does not foreclose options. Employers want and need technicians who can bring value to their enterprise. They expect technical competence; but they also emphasize, more than higher education, the need for employees who also excel at the "soft" or employability skills of working in teams, communication, critical thinking, problem solving, and a knowledge of business. These skills need to be consciously taught in schools, but teachers will require professional development to do so. This book discusses practical solutions to these issues.

Gerhard Salinger

I highly recommend this book to all state and local leaders, policymakers, and practitioners. The authors show how Career Pathways can be used to invigorate CTE by creating seamless programmatic connections to postsecondary learning and the world of work. With its strong emphasis on the need for greater collaboration across the learning levels and with the business community, *Career Pathways: Education with a Purpose* points the way to more effective whole school reform and higher achievement for every student.

Katharine M. Oliver
Assistant State Superintendent
Division of Career Technology and Adult Learning
Maryland State Department of Education
Chair, National Association of State Directors of Career Technical Education Consortium

---

There is not a better book in the field that has captured the true meaning of "partnership" to ensure there is a plan for student success. Perhaps the most useful book for educational leaders and policymakers to understand the need for systemic change. Excellent information to assist with collecting reliable and valid data for continuous pathway improvement.

Sheila Ruhland
President, National Association for Tech Prep Leadership (NATPL),
Vice President of Instruction, Clatsop Community College, Oregon

---

Text provides a common sense, pragmatic philosophy, an overall framework, and suggested strategies for those who currently work with Tech Prep designs and who are looking to build on the Tech Prep model through Career Pathways. The text is important as it continues to focus on improvements needed, designs, and strategies to educate well the *neglected majority*—the group targeted in Parnell and Hull's earlier writings.

Richard L. Lynch, Professor of Education
Director, Occupational Research Group
University of Georgia

Career Pathways: Education with a Purpose presents a compelling vision—and the means—to improve our educational system. Deeply researched and carefully presented, a must read for education reformers.

Compelling and thoughtful. For anyone who wants to understand AND take action, this book gives a thorough roadmap for success.

Mark N. Turner
Learning, Training and Development, The Boeing Company

In an environment where the high school experience is receiving increasing scrutiny, CORD has offered an important perspective. Rather than the common and traditional focus on trying to make all students follow the path of the minority of students that have always "succeeded" by attending and graduating from four-year colleges, CORD calls for a radical change in high schools. This book offers a realistic plan for coupling rigorous academic course work with preparation for future success for all students through Career Pathways. Perhaps the most important insight offered is the critical role of the community colleges as education partners with today's high schools, which is often overlooked or discounted by those who cannot see beyond the early 20th century model that pervades education policy.

George D. Nelson
Director of Science, Mathematics, and Technology Education
Western Washington University

Career Pathways: Education with a Purpose presents a compelling case for the urgency of repairing our "broken" secondary education system. The authors make specific recommendations for strategies and systemic changes that require the active cooperation of policymakers, employers, community leaders, and educators at both the secondary and postsecondary levels. If we are to keep students in school and set them on the paths that prepare them for the careers of the twenty-first century rather than a life of dependency, we must break down the current barriers to real reform al all levels. *Career Pathways: Education with a Purpose* is the book to read for those who are committed to improving education and ensuring the future economic competitiveness of our country.

George R. Boggs
President and CEO
American Association of Community Colleges

Career Pathways: Education with a Purpose is likely to become a key reference in the national dialogue on education reform and college transitions. It's a must read, for both policymakers and practitioners.

Ron Kindell, Director
Miami Valley Tech Prep Consortium
Sinclair Community College, Dayton, Ohio

Since the early 1990s, Tech Prep has been a driving force in improving career and technical education, and Dan Hull has been instrumental in providing a vision for Tech Prep. In *Career Pathways: Education with a Purpose*, Dan provides a challenging framework that ensures Tech Prep's continued role as a critically important facet of the American educational system. This book presents proven methods that promote effective Tech Prep programs and enable students to achieve success both in the classroom and in the workplace. As a result, Tech Prep remains a catalyst for change, providing a sound structure of quality education that addresses the needs of the evolving workforce.

Elizabeth C. Brown
Director of Federal Vocational Education
North Carolina Community College System

The book provides a comprehensive look at the issues related to Career Pathways. It is a primer for individuals to better understand the Career Pathways emphasis on transitions found in the Perkins reauthorization bills before Congress.

John M. Townsend
Executive Director, Tech Prep
Tennessee Board of Regents

For many years, Tech Prep consortia have been paving the way and building the foundations to improve the high school experience by engaging secondary and postsecondary educators and the local business community. We've been successful with bits and pieces and articulated or aligned lots of courses, but it's now time to rise to the next level and this "how to" guide provides the framework for moving from a "graduation requirements focused" educational system to a "career focused" system that will contribute to the economic prosperity of our great nation.

Kathy Jo Elliott, Manager
Program Development & Transition
Career, Technical & Agricultural Education
Georgia Department of Education

CAREER PATHWAYS: EDUCATION WITH A PURPOSE

Compiled and Coauthored by Dan M. Hull

CORD

Leading Change in Education

www.cord.org

For additional copies, contact:

CORD Communications
601 Lake Air Dr.
Waco, Texas 76710
254-776-1822
800-231-3015
Fax 254-776-3906
www.cordcommunications.com

For additional information on implementing Career Pathways, contact:

Teemus Warner, Career Pathways Liaison
601 Lake Air Drive
Waco, Texas 76710
254-772-8756 ext 437
Fax 254-772-8972
twarner@cord.org
www.cord.org

Printed April 2006

ISBN 1-57837- 408-1

CONTENTS

FOREWORD

If there's one thing I've learned in my years of sharing *Chicken Soup for the Soul* around the world, it's that everyone—and I do mean *everyone*—has dreams. Dreams of creating personal success. Dreams of a fulfilling career. Dreams of making the world a better place. Dreams of a better lifestyle, a way out of poverty, a way to support their family and afford the life they want. This is especially true of young people. They're eager, enthusiastic, and searching for ways to live out their dreams.

Isn't that what our education system should be about, shepherding our children towards their life goals? Yes, academic knowledge is important—who can survive today without a good grounding in math, science, reading, writing, technology and computer literacy?—but shouldn't the academic knowledge we teach be couched in what makes it useful in our kids' future life and work? Haven't we seen enough kids so turned off by school that they drop out and give up on their dreams? And haven't we seen how motivated young people can become when they see that what they are learning is helping them reach for the job they want, follow the career they seek, and fulfill the ambitions they have to change their world?

I strongly believe—and I've said it many, many times—that living your dreams is always the result of information, inspiration and perspiration. I also believe that if our schools provide the information and the inspiration, our students will provide the perspiration. And that's why I am so excited and honored to be asked to write a Foreword for this important book. I sincerely believe that the Career Pathways approach is the best way schools can impart both the information *and* the inspiration.

A few years ago I had the privilege of speaking to over 3000 practitioners at the National Tech Prep Network conference in Nashville. I personally met many of these outstanding educators and was inspired by how passionate they were to make a difference for their students. I learned a great deal about the Tech Prep reform program and have watched with interest and admiration as educators have carried out this hard but worthwhile work. It is clear to me that Career Pathways builds on what Tech Prep has learned over the years and can help schools restructure themselves to offer this wonderful new "information+inspiration" educational opportunity to all of their students.

I encourage you to read this book carefully and thoughtfully. And as you do, I encourage you to think about the effects Career Pathways can have on students. I urge you to put these changes into effect in your school, your community, and your district. I am convinced that if you do, you will be sharing "chicken soup for your students' souls" for generations to come!

Love to you!

—Jack Canfield
Co-creator of the #1 NY Times
best-selling book series
Chicken Soup for the Soul®

INTRODUCTION

As high schools move to the forefront of education reform, policymakers and practitioners from the national level to the local level are looking for ways to improve student achievement, high school graduation rates, and the career and college prospects for high school-aged young people. Research indicates that high school students need and want learning opportunities that challenge and engage them and that allow them to develop supportive, caring relationships with adults. Within this broad outline, there are many ways to design schools to help every young person be successful and ready to pursue postsecondary education or a career.

As policymakers and practitioners consider reform strategies, career and technical education (CTE) is often omitted from the discussion. This is not because policymakers don't think CTE is important. Indeed, most policymakers I know strongly believe that CTE supports economic development and the preparation of a skilled workforce needed to meet the demands of today's labor market. Unfortunately, however, debates about career preparation and high school reform are often held in distinct and separate spheres.

Dan Hull and his colleagues included in this book know that these conversations must be brought together — not only to ensure that we have a highly skilled labor force, but also to make sure we are providing an education that is relevant and meaningful to young people. According to several recent national polls, a significant majority of teens say they are not challenged academically and that they find high school boring and irrelevant. As we think about how to remake high schools to improve academic outcomes and ensure that our students can compete in the labor market against students from any other developed country, we also need to ensure that classes are engaging and that students are motivated to learn because they see a pathway to their future.

The chapters in this book provide a framework for helping policymakers and practitioners, particularly at the state and local levels, think about how to redesign high schools to make them academically challenging and engaging, as well as allowing for the creation of meaningful student-adult relationships. The Career Pathways concept outlined by Dan Hull and supported by a host of nationally known education experts, policymakers, and practitioners is one strategy for recreating high schools that are rigorous and relevant and that provide smaller learning communities allowing for stronger relationships between adults and students.

Career Pathways ensure that all students have a strong academic foundation in English, math, social studies, and science, linked to state standards, and that courses are taught in the context of careers to make them more relevant to students. Career Pathways also allow students to build a smoother transition to postsecondary education in their chosen fields by encouraging them to take postsecondary education courses and earn college credit while in high school. Career Pathways continue the CTE focus on helping students connect to the real world of work through hands-on work experience.

The Career Pathways framework builds on the foundation laid by the Tech Prep program over the past two decades. Like Tech Prep, Careers Pathways help the "neglected majority" of high school students see a purpose in what they learn and gain needed skills for the labor market. Career Pathways are an updated version of Tech Prep, building on what we have learned from research and the innovative practices of state and local policymakers, secondary and postsecondary educators, and employers around the country.

Dan Hull helped to lead the Tech Prep reforms of the 1990s with his vision and determination. Along with his coauthors, he is making another significant contribution with this well-timed book, which demonstrates the power of Career Pathways in reforming high schools.

Betsy Brand, Director
American Youth Policy Forum
September 2005

ACKNOWLEDGMENTS

This is a book about *partnerships:* how to build them, what to do with them, and how to sustain them. It is therefore fitting that I did not try to write this book alone. The collective vision, wisdom, and experience of my more than twenty collaborators and coauthors amount to far more value than I could ever have hoped to collect and write on my own. The policymakers, state and institutional leaders, researchers, practitioners, and wonderful CORD staff members who are listed on the following pages and at the ends of chapters are the experts who know how to do Career Pathways. I am so thankful that I was just smart enough — and fortunate enough — to find them and persuade them to help me create this "how about" and "how to" manual.

Mostly, what we created were "diamonds in the rough." These required considerable cleaving, polishing, and setting properly to let our thoughts and ideas shine through. The "jeweler" who refined our every word is our amazing editor, Mark Whitney. Mark is far, far more than an editor; he is indeed a quiet coauthor of every chapter in this book. He has taken our ideas and our experiences, and he has helped to place them in a logical, coherent, and understandable narrative that is both pleasant to read and well worth your efforts to study and put to use. When our writings needed more rationale, supporting references, or research, Mark saw the need and provided them. Thank you, Mark!

Two other persons require my very special thanks. First — as in all things — is my wonderful (and patient) wife, Rita, who has been my source of encouragement for over 45 years. And last I acknowledge my indebtedness to my very good friend and colleague Dale Parnell, whose suggestions and inspiration have contributed so much to every book I have attempted to write.

Dan Hull
September 2005

CONTRIBUTORS

JUNE ST. CLAIR ATKINSON, Ed.D., is the State Superintendent of Public Instruction in North Carolina. During her thirty-three years in education, she has been a public school teacher, community college instructor, and state administrator. As a member of the North Carolina Department of Public Instruction, she has been a Chief Consultant, Assistant State Director, Director of Vocational-Technical Education, and Director of Instructional Services. Dr. Atkinson has also served as President of the National Business Education Association and the National Association of State Directors for Career-Technical Education Consortium.

DEBRA D. BRAGG, Ph.D., is a Professor and Coordinator of the Community College Executive Leadership Program in the Department of Educational Organization and Leadership at the University of Illinois at Urbana-Champaign. For the past fifteen years she has led national studies funded by the U.S. Department of Education's Office of Vocational and Adult Education on high-school-to-college transition, including career and technical education, Tech Prep, and dual credit programs. As director of the Office of Community College Research and Leadership, Dr. Bragg also directs research for the Lumina Foundation for Education, The Boeing Company, and state agencies.

BETSY BRAND is the Director of the American Youth Policy Forum (AYPF), a nonpartisan professional development organization providing learning opportunities for national, state, and local policymakers working on education and youth issues. Before joining AYPF in 1998, Ms. Brand's career in education policy included serving as a professional staff member on the U.S. Senate Labor and Human Resources Committee, as Assistant Secretary for Vocational and Adult Education at the U.S. Department of Education, and as director of the consulting firm Workforce Futures, Inc.

DAVID BOND, Ed.D., is Director of the National Tech Prep Network and also CORD's Vice President for Education and Employer Partnerships. He has been with CORD and NTPN since 1993. Prior to that, Dr. Bond served as a U.S. Army officer and as an administrator for Baylor University. Besides directing NTPN, Dr. Bond has been involved in numerous evaluation projects and legislative activities.

DAVID BUNTING is the Executive Director of Secondary Programs for Kirkwood Community College. In this role, he provides leadership for the development of partnership programs with over forty area high schools. Programs include the Career Edge Academies and other college credit opportunities for high school students. In addition, he provides feedback to local districts on the academic preparation and ongoing success of local high school graduates who attend Kirkwood.

M. ELIZABETH CREAMER is the Director of Postsecondary Perkins and Tech Prep for the Virginia Community College System (VCCS). She also serves as the state administrator for Career Coaches, a new partnership initiative of the VCCS and Virginia Department of Education. Additionally, Ms. Creamer is the principal investigator for a VCCS National Science Foundation project named "Creating Pathways for the New IT Professional." Ms. Creamer was formerly Director of the Virginia Peninsula Tech Prep Consortium at Thomas Nelson Community College and Coordinator of Academic Programs for Paul D. Camp Community College.

JAMES R. (BOB) COUCH, Ed.D., is currently the State Director of Career and Technical Education for South Carolina. His twenty years of experience in education include serving as a teacher and career center administrator as well as a college administrator at both two-year and four-year institutions. Throughout his career, he has made major contributions to educational reform legislation.

KATHY D'ANTONI, Ed.D., is Vice Chancellor for the West Virginia Community and Technical College System. Her career in education includes teaching positions as well as working with the Tech Prep initiative at Marshall University and serving as West Virginia's State Director for Tech Prep. Dr. D'Antoni has worked extensively with curriculum alignment and development projects and is the past president of the National Association for Tech Prep Leadership. She has authored numerous articles on effective transitions from public schools to higher education.

ROBERT FRANKS is Director of Perkins Grants Administration for the Texas Higher Education Coordinating Board. He has been active in Tech Prep at the local, state, and national levels since 1991 and is past chairman of the research committee for the National Association for Tech Prep Leadership. Prior to taking his current position, Mr. Franks spent fifteen years in business as an engineer, chemist, and manager, and twenty-two years in education, teaching science and serving as a local and state Tech Prep director in Texas.

JANICE FRIEDEL, Ph.D., leads the Division of Community Colleges and Workforce Preparation for the Iowa Department of Education. In this position, she has statewide responsibility for the oversight and leadership of Iowa's 15 community colleges, secondary vocational education, adult education and family literacy, and veterans' education. Dr. Friedel previously served as President of Lexington Community College and has held a number of administrative and academic positions with the Eastern Iowa Community College District.

KIMBERLY A. GREEN is Executive Director of the National Association of State Directors of Career Technical Education consortium (NASDCTEc). Over the past thirteen years, she has worked extensively on federal legislation impacting career technical education, including Perkins III, the Workforce Investment Act, and the No Child Left Behind Act. She represents NASDCTEc on national boards such as the U.S. Chamber of Commerce's Employment and Training Committee and the National Center for Education Statistics' Technical Review Panel on Career Technical Education, in addition to providing leadership for the States' Career Clusters Initiative.

SANDRA HARWELL, Ph.D., is Vice President for Professional Development for CORD. Before joining CORD in 2001, she served as Director for Workforce Development and Adult Education at the Suncoast Area Center for Educational Enhancement at the University of South Florida. In previous positions, she has served as a local Tech Prep coordinator, High Schools That Work coordinator, health occupations instructor, adult basic education instructor, and university faculty member.

KATHERINE HUGHES, Ph.D., is the Assistant Director for Work and Education Reform Research at both the Institute on Education and the Economy and the Community College Research Center at Teachers College, Columbia University. Dr. Hughes specializes in research on education reform and on changes in the nature of work, including studies on employer involvement in high schools, work-based learning, the restructuring of vocational education, and career academies. Her current research focuses on secondary-to-postsecondary transitions, particularly the potential of credit-based transition programs (such as dual enrollment) in preparing underachievers for college.

DANIEL HULL has spent over thirty years leading education reform efforts across the United States and internationally. He is widely acknowledged as one of the founding architects of Tech Prep and is among the nation's foremost experts on technical education and workforce development. Mr. Hull is President and CEO of CORD, a national nonprofit organization providing innovative changes in education to prepare students for greater success in careers and higher education. A registered professional engineer, Mr. Hull received the National Association of State Directors of Career Technical Education's Distinguished Service Award and is the author of four books on Tech Prep and contextual teaching.

MELINDA KARP is a Research Associate at both the Institute on Education and the Economy and the Community College Research Center at Teachers College, Columbia University. Ms. Karp's research interests include the transition from school to work and from secondary to postsecondary education, particularly for disadvantaged youth. Her recent research includes studies of dual enrollment and credit-based transition programs and an investigation of state policies supporting Career Pathways.

LINDA KOBYLARZ is a career development consultant providing program design, staff development, evaluation, and research services to schools, federal and state agencies, and business. She is lead consultant for the National Career Development Guidelines Revision Project, funded by the U.S. Department of Education. Ms. Kobylarz was a contributing author for *The National Career Development Guidelines Handbook K–Adult, Managing Your School Counseling Program: K–12 Developmental Strategies,* and *School Counseling: New Perspectives and Practices.* She is past president of the Connecticut Counseling Association and has served on the board of directors for the National Career Development Association.

EDWIN R. MASSEY, Ph.D., has thirty-four years of experience in education at the high school, community college, and university levels. He has been a teacher, researcher, administrator, and, for the last eighteen years, President of Indian River Community College. Dr. Massey has won several state and national awards for his part in improving articulation and accountability in community colleges and was responsible for establishing the Treasure Coast Educators Coalition, which resulted in a national award-winning Tech Prep program. Most recently, he has led an initiative designed to change the culture of his institution through enhanced communication, leadership and staff development, and shared success at all levels.

HANS K. MEEDER is President of the Meeder Consulting Group, LLC, a firm offering assistance in education and workforce policy analysis, leadership development, and governmental relations. His extensive career in education policy includes serving as Deputy Assistant Secretary for Education in the U.S. Department of Education's Office of Vocational and Adult Education, policy and outreach director for the House of Representatives Committee on Education and the Workforce, Senior Vice President for Workforce and Postsecondary Education at the National Alliance of Business, and Executive Director of the 21st Century Workforce Commission.

DEBRA F. MILLS serves as Director of Partnerships for CORD, focusing on transitions from secondary to postsecondary experiences. Prior to her work at CORD, Ms. Mills served as a classroom teacher, a workforce development grant administrator, and Tech Prep Director for Danville Area Community College in Danville, Illinois, an award-winning Tech Prep consortium. She is the author of *Tech Prep: The Next Generation Planning Guide*, a strategic planning reference tool used in Tech Prep consortia across the country.

DALE PARNELL, Ed.D., has served as a university professor, college president, and President and Chief Executive Officer of the American Association of Community Colleges. He has been a high school teacher, principal, school superintendent, and state superintendent of public instruction in his native state of Oregon. His book *The Neglected Majority*, a classic in education literature, served as the foundation for the development of the Tech Prep/Associate Degree national initiative. Recognized as a pioneer in the field of career education, Dr. Parnell is also the author of *Why Do I Have To Learn This?* and *Contextual Teaching Works*.

JOHN J. SBREGA, Ph.D., is President of Bristol Community College in Fall River, Massachusetts. Dr. Sbrega has committed his entire career to community college teaching and leadership, actively promoting student success through instruction, instructional support, and workforce development. A trained historian, he has written four books and numerous articles on U.S. foreign policy.

PAT SCHWALLIE-GIDDIS, Ph.D., is a national leader in school counseling and a recognized expert in career development. She serves as an Associate Professor at George Washington University in Counseling and Human and Organizational Studies and as the Director of Graduate Programs. Her past positions include serving as an executive staff member for the Association for Career and Technical Education (formerly AVA) and the American Counseling Association, and as a teacher, counselor, district-level administrator, and State Program Director for Career Development in her native state of Florida. She has coauthored three books on counseling and career development.

JEAN C. STEVENS currently serves as Assistant Commissioner, Office of Curriculum and Instructional Support for the New York State Education Department (NYSED). Her responsibilities include State Directorships for Career and Technical Education and Adult Education and Family Literacy. Additional responsibilities include oversight and leadership for all curricular areas, instructional technology, and the development and implementation of the NYSED Virtual Learning System web portal.

MARK WHITNEY, Ph.D., is CORD's Manager of Publication Services. In that capacity he has provided editorial control and quality assurance on hundreds of CORD documents, including curriculum materials (both printed and online), reports, surveys, proposals, books, and articles.

Career Pathways: Education with a Purpose

Dan Hull

Public secondary education in the United States has lost sight of its *purpose*. It no longer serves the majority of American young people by helping them make long-range decisions, choose careers, become good citizens, and prepare for higher education. In short, public secondary education in the United States no longer helps the majority of its students prepare to become capable, successful, and personally fulfilled *adults*.

Evidence of this deterioration, particularly in urban schools, has been emerging for four or five decades, as our country has attempted to transfer to public education responsibilities that have been increasingly abandoned by homes, churches, social service agencies, community economic development organizations, the military, and apprenticeships (or employer job training). A declaration of crisis in our schools was issued by the 1983 report "A Nation at Risk," which warned that the academic achievement of U.S. high school students lagged significantly behind that of their counterparts in other developed countries. In reaction to this revelation, governors and state legislators called for the adoption of

1

rigorous academic standards for all students. Along with the new standards came high-stakes testing designed to hold schools and teachers more accountable for student academic achievement. Unfortunately, teachers and principals have reacted to this mandate by devoting an inordinate amount of class time to "teaching to the test," rather than exploring teaching strategies that can improve student learning more broadly. Teachers and principals are not to blame for this unfortunate and counterproductive state of affairs. They are under constant pressure to raise test scores. The fault lies with educational leaders and policymakers — who have lacked the vision and courage to reestablish and maintain an environment that nurtures effective teaching and learning.

The ineffectiveness of today's public school system negatively impacts some students more than others. In his 1984 landmark book *The Neglected Majority*, Dale Parnell lamented the dearth of educational alternatives available to the more than 60 percent of our young people who, by the ninth grade, performed below grade level in core academic areas such as math, science, and language arts. In the eyes of educational leaders, those students lacked "head skills" and consequently either were placed in a "general track" and socially promoted, or were provided "hand skills" through traditional vocational education. Parnell proposed the Tech Prep Associate Degree (TPAD) program, which empowered "neglected majority" students to improve their academic skills through contextual teaching and continue their education and training after high school in articulated technical programs in cooperating community and technical colleges. The TPAD concept was an important step in the right direction: It sought to reestablish a *purpose* for education — a purpose that students could understand and employers could respect.

In 2001 the federal government passed the No Child Left Behind (NCLB) law, which reemphasizes and heightens the states' efforts to make schools accountable to federal guidelines for evidence of school improvement. So far, most of NCLB's funding and accountability measures have focused on elementary schools. To date there is very little evidence that

2

high schools have improved. American high schools continue to fall short of their potential in at least four key areas:

- *High school dropout rates* — Dropout rates remain high, especially among poor and minority students. The National Center for Education Statistics, for example, reported that in the year 2000, 3.8 million young adults "were not enrolled in a high school program and had not completed high school."[1] Similarly, the National Commission on the High School Senior Year reported that in some cities as many as 40 percent of high school students drop out before graduation.[2]

- *Generally low academic expectations* — A 2001 report of the National Commission on the High School Senior Year stated that "in 1997, only 43 percent of high school seniors reported themselves to be in demanding 'academic' programs, compared with 45 percent in 'general education' and 12 percent in vocational education programs." The report went on to say that "among 1998 graduates, according to the U.S. Department of Education, just 44 percent earned the minimum number of academic credits recommended in 1983 by the National Commission on Excellence in Education in its seminal report, *A Nation at Risk*."[3] Similarly, a recent nationwide survey of teenagers conducted by the National Governors Association suggested that many students believe that their high school experience was too *easy*. Of the more than 10,000 teenagers

---

[1] National Center for Education Statistics, *Dropout Rates in the United States: 2000* (Washington, DC: U.S. Department of Education, Office of Educational Research, 2001, NCES 2002-114), v.

[2] *The Lost Opportunity of the Senior Year: Finding a Better Way. Preliminary Report of the National Commission on the High School Senior Year* (http://www.nps.k12.va.us/aaa/CIA/lostop/ Senior_Year_Report_Final.pdf, accessed July 2005), 15.

[3] National Commission on the High School Senior Year. (2001). *Raising Our Sights: No High School Senior Left Behind*. Princeton, New Jersey: Woodrow Wilson National Fellowship Foundation, 7 (citing information published by the National Center for Education Statistics).

surveyed, "fewer than two-thirds believe that their school had done a good job challenging them academically or preparing them for college. About the same number of students said their senior year would be more meaningful if they could take courses related to the jobs they wanted or if some of their courses could be counted toward college credit."[4]

- *Low secondary-to-postsecondary transition rates* — According to the National Center for Education Statistics, since 1998 the percentage of students who enter postsecondary education immediately following high school is around 64 (somewhat lower for minority students).[5] Given the importance of postsecondary education in today's job market, that number is far too low. One contributor to lackluster secondary-to-postsecondary transition rates is the phenomenon known as the "wasted senior year." For at least the last two decades, educators have recognized that the high school senior year (and often the junior year) tends to be poorly used. "The senior year . . . should be the embarkation point that launches the well-prepared student toward success in postsecondary education or the ever-more-complex workplaces of the new economy. The high school senior year and graduation . . . become not so much a finish line as a relay station. [Unfortunately, today] the handoff is fumbled and the baton too often dropped."[6]

- *College remediation* — The National Commission on the High School Senior Year calls today's remediation rates astounding. According to the commission, "remediation takes place in all community colleges, in four out of five public four-year universities, and in more than six out of ten private four-year institutions. Large numbers and

---

[4] Michael Janofsky, "Students Say High Schools Let Them Down," *New York Times*, July 16, 2005 (accessed via http://www.nytimes.com).

[5] National Center for Education Statistics, *The Condition of Education 2005* (http://nces.ed.gov/pubs2005/2005094.pdf), 58.

[6] National Commission on the High School Senior Year, 12.

proportions of students require remediation on these campuses. The proportion ranges from a low of 13 percent at private four-year colleges to a high of 41 percent at public two-year institutions. Well over one-quarter of all students (29 percent) require remediation in one or more subjects; 24 percent are required to take remedial mathematics courses, while 13 percent and 17 percent, respectively, are required to enroll in remedial reading and writing courses. The cost of remediation has been estimated to be between $260 million and $1 billion, annually."[7]

The effects of the inadequacy of today's high schools reach well beyond the educational sphere. Employers are well aware of — and increasingly dissatisfied with — the inabilities of secondary (and even postsecondary) graduates to meet the demands of the workplace. The results of a 2001 survey conducted by the National Association of Manufacturers (NAM) indicate that "manufacturers see a serious problem with the availability of future workers. Seventy-eight percent of respondents [to the NAM survey] believe public schools are failing to prepare students for the workplace . . . despite a decade of various education reform movements. Respondents said the biggest deficiency of public schools is not teaching basic academic and employability skills." The survey results also indicate that employers in manufacturing see the "top deficiency" as "a lack of basic employability skills."[8] This is consistent with the recommendations of the SCANS report (1991), which called for a three-part foundation of **basic skills** (reading, writing, arithmetic and mathematics, speaking, and listening), **thinking skills** (thinking creatively, making decisions, solving problems, seeing things in the mind's eye, knowing how to learn, and reasoning), and **personal qualities**

---

[7] *The Lost Opportunity of the Senior Year,* 14.

[8] National Association of Manufacturers, *The Skills Gap 2001: Manufacturers Face Persistent Skills Shortages in an Uncertain Economy* (http://www.nam.org/s_nam/doc1.asp?CID=200958&DID=224443; accessed July 2005).

(individual responsibility, self-esteem, sociability, self-management, and integrity).[9]

WE'RE TREATING THE SYMPTOMS — NOT THE INHERENT PROBLEMS

Accountability in public education is necessary and vital, but relying on the rewards and penalties of old-style standardized tests will not, and cannot, significantly improve our schools.[10] Traditional vocational education has been severely criticized in recent years for using secondary schools to "train" students in job tasks, or to run pieces of equipment. It seems to me that using academic class time to drill students on how to pass test questions is "test training." Neither of these examples represents good education.

Improving public high schools in the United States — for all students — calls for six systemic changes:

- Requiring each student to select an *interest area* that gives him or her a purpose for remaining in school and answers the question, "Why do I have to learn this?" For some students, the interest area may be athletics, music, or liberal arts. For most, it will be career pursuits.

---

[9] The Secretary's Commission on Achieving Necessary Skills, *What Work Requires of Schools: A SCANS Report for American 2000* (U.S. Department of Labor, 1991) (http://wdr.doleta.gov/SCANS/whatwork/whatwork.pdf; accessed July 2005).

[10] This statement is not intended to suggest that standardized testing is categorically detrimental to the quality of education. On the contrary, testing is necessary. Without it, states cannot know which students and schools are succeeding and which need help. Nevertheless, over the past several years education researchers have amassed considerable evidence that the increasing attention paid to standardized tests has tended to narrow the educational experience to low-level knowledge and skills. For more on growing recognition of the need for a "new generation of tests," see *Testing: Setting the Record Straight, Achieve Policy Brief, Issue Number One* (Summer 2000), published by Achieve, Inc., in collaboration with the National Governors Association (http://www.achieve.org).

- Requiring each student to formulate a thoughtful and achievable *plan* to prepare for the next step after high school graduation. The next step may be college, employment, an apprenticeship, or enlistment in the military service.

- Providing a *context* within which students learn required, rigorous academics. Usually, the context will be the interest area.

- A *restructured curriculum* that supports the interest area, the chosen plan, and the context. The curriculum must be designed on the basis of approved state and national academic, skill, and employability (soft skills) *standards*.

> Traditional vocational education has been severely criticized in recent years for using secondary schools to "train" students in job tasks, or to run pieces of equipment. It seems to me that using academic class time to drill students on how to pass test questions is "test training." Neither of these examples represents good education.

- A *secondary-to-postsecondary curriculum framework* that provides for and encourages smooth transition from high school to college and allows students in the eleventh and twelfth grades to begin taking (academic and career-oriented) college courses through dual enrollment. This will allow students to graduate from high school with substantial numbers of higher education credits.

- Restructuring large high schools (over 100 students per grade) into *small learning communities* organized around student interest areas.

Accomplishment of these systemic changes is, indeed, a tall order. In fact, it constitutes a task that public high schools should not take on alone. These changes must be designed and implemented with the cooperation, support, and participation of partners from higher education, employers, community leaders, and policymakers. Most of the changes can be modeled after successful practices found in Tech Prep and other innovative strategies. In a few cases, scientifically based evidence is available to prove the effectiveness of innovative strategies; more often than not, we must rely on *promising practices*, substantiated by useful, anecdotal evidence. But, in the process, each partnership must benchmark where it is and frequently measure the progress being made.

A VITAL U.S. ECONOMY DEPENDS ON A WELL-EDUCATED WORKFORCE

In 1998, the Center for the Development of Leadership Skills at Rider University surveyed 428 employers regarding the skills they would most highly value from their employees.[11] (The sample of small-to-very-large employers included most career fields.)

The top five skills identified (in all career fields) were these:

- Computer literacy
- Critical thinking
- Problem solving
- Teamwork
- Interpersonal relations

Academic achievement was also an attribute that most employers valued highly. (Computer literacy should be regarded as a foundational subject in middle schools, high schools, and colleges.) An examination of the entire Rider study showed that its results complemented the findings of the 1991 SCANS report. Of course employers want their workers to be familiar with, and trainable in, the specialties of their fields—but they want the foundations first. Career preparation in secondary education must focus on the foundations and the "technical core."

---

[11] *Who Is Most Likely to Succeed?* (Rider University, Center for the Development of Leadership Skills, 1998).

Employers who hire high school graduates want about the same thing that colleges want from their applicants: a solid foundation in useful academics (problem solving), a focus on the careers they want to pursue, employability (soft) skills, and completion of a core of technical subjects related to their chosen fields of study. The redesigned high school curriculum envisioned here could be structured so that all graduates would be prepared to enter some form of higher education. But if they needed or wanted to go to work right out of high school, they would be employable in their chosen fields.

> Employers who hire high school graduates want about the same thing that colleges want from their applicants: a solid foundation in useful academics (problem solving), a focus on the careers they want to pursue, employability (soft) skills, and completion of a core of technical subjects related to their chosen fields of study.

In South Carolina, employers are saying that, while 85 percent of their jobs require education and training beyond high school, only 20 percent require at least four-year college degrees. This means that 65 percent of the jobs require some education beyond high school, but not four-year degrees. (The preferred credential is the associate degree.)[12]

The institutions that are ideally positioned to provide this postsecondary education and training are the country's almost 1200 community and technical colleges. These institutions, which are plentiful in every region of the country, are one of our greatest assets. Indeed, given that their mission includes the preparation of well-qualified technicians for the 65 percent of today's jobs that require only associate degrees and/or postsecondary certificates, they are essential if the United States is to retain its position as the economic leader of the world. But community and technical colleges cannot do it

---

[12] South Carolina Governor's Workforce Education Task Force, *Pathways to Prosperity: Success for Every Student in the 21st-Century Workplace* (October 2001), 3, 7.

alone; they must partner with "feeder high schools" and universities.

The National Science Foundation (NSF), through its Advanced Technological Education (ATE) initiative, annually provides $45 million in grants to community and technical colleges to support the creation, improvement, and dissemination of associate degree programs in new and emerging technologies. Despite their excellent programs, many of the colleges that receive ATE funds struggle to recruit adequate numbers of students. That struggle points to the need for a *student pipeline* in which high school students choose technical fields early and lay a solid foundation that enables them to transition smoothly to articulated two-year postsecondary programs in those fields. In an attempt to create that pipeline for colleges with ATE programs, NSF and the National Tech Prep Network (NTPN) have jointly sponsored ATE/Tech Prep meetings (typically half-day sessions just prior to the annual NTPN conference) at which educators and business partners network and share ideas. NSF/ATE funds are being used by ATE recipient colleges to build partnerships with the high schools in their service areas.

It is absolutely essential that the student pipeline (from high schools to two-year technical programs) be enlarged and improved—and that partnering secondary schools and community and technical colleges align high school graduation requirements with college entrance requirements.

BUILDING ON THE TECH PREP MODEL

In 1990, during the reauthorization of the Carl D. Perkins Vocational and Applied Technology Education Act, the U.S. Congress recognized the need to make significant changes in career and technical education (CTE). To do this, Congress created a "Tech Prep set-aside" (i.e., a separate funding stream) to fund innovative secondary-postsecondary partnerships designed to improve the academic proficiency of technical students and facilitate student transition from secondary to postsecondary institutions through articulation agreements. The legislation also encouraged integration of academic and technical courses and funded materials and teaching strategies for applied, or contextual, approaches to academic learning.

Over 900 partnerships (Tech Prep consortia) of secondary and postsecondary institutions and employers and thousands of articulation agreements have been created. Because of Tech Prep's success as a catalyst for innovation, funding for Tech Prep was increased and the legislative set-aside has continued for 15 years. In 1992, the Tech Prep legislation was amended to permit 4+2 partnerships (along with the original 2+2), allowing students to begin Tech Prep in the ninth grade. In 1998, when the Perkins III legislation was reauthorized, the basic state grant placed greater emphasis on contextual teaching (a Tech Prep initiative) and the Tech Prep set-aside was modified to place greater emphasis on raising academic standards and stronger participation by the postsecondary institutions, including universities.[13]

Unfortunately, the language of the Perkins legislation has been interpreted to mean that Tech Prep success should be measured as a separate track within CTE (i.e., that students in Tech Prep programs should be identified and that their academic and career success and sustainability should be measured). This has been very difficult to accomplish given that Tech Prep funding (which represents about one-tenth of all Perkins funds) has been used primarily to sponsor *innovation*, which has benefited both Tech Prep and non-Tech Prep students.

As an innovative change agent, Tech Prep has been extremely successful.

- Cooperation is now widespread between secondary and postsecondary teachers as well as between academic and technical faculty members.

---

[13]Debra Bragg, *New Lessons about Tech Prep Implementation: Changes in Eight Selected Consortia Since Reauthorization of the Federal Tech Prep Legislation in 1998* (National Dissemination Center for Career and Technical Education, 2002) (https://www.nccte.org/publications/infosynthesis/r&dreport/NewLessons-Bragg-2.pdf; accessed July 2005).

- The technical curricula in high schools have moved away from narrow "job training" and more toward development of foundational and career skills. Consequently, students are not "tracked" — they have many options and plenty of opportunities to *change their career goals without being penalized.*

- Contextual teaching of academics has been demonstrated to be effective in improving the academic achievement of "neglected majority" students.[14]

> [In Tech Prep, and Career Pathways] students are not "tracked"—they have many options and plenty of opportunities to *change their career goals without being penalized.*

- More high school students are making decisions about their career pursuits.

- Larger percentages of secondary Tech Prep graduates are continuing their education and career pursuits in cooperating colleges.[15]

- Tech Prep students are entering colleges with advanced standing and/or substantial postsecondary credits already earned.

Tech Prep provides education with a *purpose!*

As a "change agent" Tech Prep has served — and continues to serve — a very important role in public education. As it has matured from 1990 to 2005, it has embraced and enhanced

---

[14] Elliott Medric, Sarah Calderon, and Gary Hoachlander, "Contextual Teaching and Learning Strategies in High Schools: Developing a Vision for Support and Evaluation," in *Essentials of High School Reform: New Forms of Assessment and Contextual Teaching and Learning,* edited by Betsy Brand (American Youth Policy Forum, September 2003), 35–71.

[15] Bettina L. Brown, "Promising Tech Prep Outcomes," *The Highlight Zone: Research @ Work,* no. 3 (National Dissemination Center for Career and Technical Education, 2001) (http://www.nccte.org/publications/infosynthesis/highlightzone/highlight03/highlight03-techprep.pdf; accessed July 2005).

other innovative strategies, such as worksite learning, dual enrollment, and career academies (small learning communities).

In 2003, the U.S. Department of Education's Office of Vocational and Adult Education (OVAE) sponsored

> **Tech Prep provides education with a *purpose!***

an initiative designed to identify working models of *technical programs of study* and post information about them on a web-based *National Clearinghouse for Career Pathways.* A definition and criteria for Career Pathways were established.[16] Over 50 Tech Prep partnerships applied for admission to the clearinghouse. Reports on twenty partnerships were posted; ten others submitted excellent, extensive information. In this yearlong exercise, CORD observed several things:

- Some Tech Prep partnerships are excellent and provide great opportunities for "neglected majority" students.

- Some partnerships are very strong in some aspects of Tech Prep, while other partnerships are very strong in others.

- There are no *ideal models.*

Out of this project (and others), a clearer definition has emerged as to what an ideal Career Pathway should be based upon:

- It has the basic characteristics of a 4+2 Tech Prep program of study, but it goes beyond what has been required of Tech Prep.

- It is for all students.

- It requires a new curriculum framework (structure) based on standards that are developed jointly by secondary and postsecondary partners (with assistance and guidance from employers).

---

[16] Dan M. Hull, "Career Pathways: The Next Generation of Tech Prep," *Connections,* vol. 14, no. 5 (http://www.cord.org/ uploadedfiles/Vol14No5.pdf; accessed July 2005; accessed July 2005).

- The curriculum keeps *options open;* students can build on this foundation to pursue advanced degrees in higher education.
- The curriculum is standards-based and technology-based — not equipment-based.
- It prepares students for careers — not just their first jobs.
- Completers must have the ability to acquire new information and skills as technical fields change.
- In the future, all careers will require high levels of *useful academics.*
- Most careers will require education beyond high school.
- World-class workers must be *problem solvers* who can tackle open-ended, multidisciplinary problems. (Reciting from rote learning and "teaching the task" should be minimized in Career Pathways.)

> World-class workers must be *problem solvers* who can tackle open-ended, multidisciplinary problems.

Coincidently, with the evolution of Tech Prep toward Career Pathways, the U.S. Congress is planning reauthorization of Perkins to align all CTE with good Tech Prep — or Career Pathways. Details of this legislative plan and its implication will be discussed in Chapter 4.

WHAT ARE CAREER PATHWAYS AND HOW DO WE GET THERE?

In early 2004, CORD's National Clearinghouse for Career Pathways personnel met with representatives of the College and Career Transitions Initiative (CCTI) to "hammer out" a succinct description of the term *Career Pathway.* The resulting definition is shown in Figure 1-1.

A **Career Pathway** is a coherent, articulated sequence of rigorous academic and career/technical courses, commencing in the ninth grade and leading to an associate degree, baccalaureate degree and beyond, an industry-recognized certificate, and/or licensure. The Career Pathway is developed, implemented, and maintained in partnership among secondary and postsecondary education, business, and employers. Career Pathways are available to all students, including adult learners, and lead to rewarding careers.

The essential characteristics of an ideal **Career Pathway** are the following:

1. The secondary pathway component:
   - Meets state academic standards and grade-level expectations.
   - Meets high school testing and exit requirements.
   - Meets postsecondary (college) entry/placement requirements.
   - Provides foundation knowledge and skills in chosen career clusters.
   - Provides opportunities for students to earn college credit through dual/concurrent enrollment or articulation agreements.

2. The postsecondary pathway component provides:
   - Opportunities for students to earn college credit through dual/concurrent enrollment or articulation agreements.
   - Alignment and articulation with baccalaureate programs.
   - Industry-recognized skills and knowledge in each cluster area.
   - Opportunities for placement in the chosen career clusters at multiple exit points.

3. Pathway partners ensure a culture of empirical evidence is maintained by:
   - Regularly collecting qualitative and quantitative data.
   - Using data for planning and decision-making for continuous pathway improvement.
   - Ongoing dialog among secondary, postsecondary, and business partners.

Figure 1-1. Definition of Career Pathway

At this point, it is appropriate to distinguish between Career *Pathways* and career *clusters,* and to define *curriculum frameworks.* As is the case in many innovative elements in education, new terms are sometimes used in different, even contradictory, ways. For the purpose of this book, the following definitions will be adopted:

Career cluster— A career cluster is a grouping of occupations according to common knowledge and skills for the purpose of organizing educational programs and curricula. In 1998 the U.S. Department of Education/OVAE defined sixteen career clusters (listed in Chapter 3). The State Directors of Career and Technical Education subsequently developed databanks of skills and required knowledge for each of the sixteen career clusters. (This work is described in Chapter 3.)

Career Pathway— A Career Pathway is a 4+2 program of study leading to employment in an occupational field and/or continued education and training. A Career Pathway is not a "track" that limits student choice. A cluster can encompass many Career Pathways. The high school portion of a Career Pathway is sufficiently broad to support postsecondary education and training for other occupations within the cluster.

Curriculum framework— A curriculum framework is the *plan* for a 4+2 program of study, or Career Pathway. Curriculum frameworks consist of two elements: (1) recommended grade-9–14 course sequences that satisfy requirements for high school graduation and transition to postsecondary education and training and (2) course descriptions, with prerequisites, recommended grade levels, credits, and standards to be achieved by students. Curriculum frameworks reflect academic, employability (SCANS) and technical (skill) standards *as well as entrance requirements for postsecondary curricula.*[17] Development of part 1, the course sequence (sometimes called an *egg crate*), begins with a blank chart such as the following.

---

[17] Dan M. Hull, "Redefining CTE: Seizing a Unique Opportunity to Help the 'Neglected Majority' Become World-Class Students, Workers and Citizens," *Techniques,* May 2003.

	Grade	English	Mathematics	Science	Technology	Technology	Other
Foundation	9						
	10						
Technical Core	11						
	12						
Technical Specialty	13 1st Semester						
	13 2nd Semester						
	14 1st Semester						
	14 2nd Semester						

When the egg crate has been filled in, each box holds the title of a course. (More information on curriculum frameworks is included in Chapter 3.)

Part 2 of the curriculum framework provides the beginning of a curriculum planning guide that will ultimately include course outlines, suggested textbooks and other reference materials, computer hardware and software requirements, example activities and projects, assessment strategies, and suggestions for worksite experiences.

HOW DO CAREER PATHWAYS DIFFER FROM TECH PREP?

In many ways, Career Pathways are an extension of good Tech Prep practices. The key element in a Career Pathway is the *articulated, secondary-postsecondary curriculum*. But Career Pathways require a different approach to curriculum.

In Tech Prep, the secondary institution usually has its own employer advisory committee and develops its curriculum separately. Likewise, the college has its own advisory committee and develops its own curriculum. Then a third party (the consortium) brings the technical teachers from the high school together with the technical faculty members from the college to *align* the curriculum, remove redundancies, and develop articulation agreements.

In a Career Pathway, academic and technical teachers from the high school meet with academic and technical faculty members from the college—and a single, joint employer advisory committee—to design a curriculum framework for grades 9–14. To the maximum extent possible, eleventh- and twelfth-grade students are allowed to take selected courses for dual credit. Also, to significantly reduce (if not eliminate) the need for remediation at the postsecondary level, academic requirements for high school graduation are aligned with the college's entrance requirements. (A few Tech Prep consortia are already moving in this direction.)

> In many ways, Career Pathways are an extension of good Tech Prep practices. The key element in a Career Pathway is the *articulated, secondary/ postsecondary curriculum.* But Career Pathways require a different approach to curriculum.

ISN'T THIS WHAT WE'RE ALREADY DOING IN TECH PREP?

Probably not, but Career Pathways can most easily be created from Tech Prep partnerships (or using Tech Prep practices) if we're willing to improve some areas that might have been neglected and *stretch a little farther* beyond what we planned. To assist a partnership (consortium) in identifying areas in which improvement—or *stretching*—is needed, we've created the Career Pathways Self-Study Instrument, presented as Figure 1-2.[18]

---

[18] For a printable version of the instrument, see Dan M. Hull, "Career Pathways: The Next Generation of Tech Prep," *Connections,* vol. 14, no. 5 (http://www.cord.org/uploadedfiles/Vol14No5.pdf; accessed July 2005).

The instrument was designed to help existing secondary-postsecondary partnerships measure their progress in Career Pathways against eighteen benchmarks. The benchmarks help partnerships see where they are and, even more important, where they should be going. The reliability of the instrument rests on several key points:

- The eighteen benchmarks were derived from the consensus definition of Career Pathways (see Figure 1-1).

- The benchmarks were validated by educational experts from across the country.

- The benchmarks have been rigorously tested against the findings of educational research.

- The rating criteria for the instrument (i.e., the significance of each item's choices, 1–5) represent the consensus of a panel of experts.

- The instrument has been presented and favorably reviewed at a number of well-attended events, including the 2004 national NTPN conference in Minneapolis (3000+ attendees) and several workshops hosted by the Career Pathways Strategic Improvement Coalition (CPSIC; see http://www.cord.org/cpsic). (Though CPSIC is still in only its first year, the CPSIC workshops have thus far attracted around 800 people representing 30 states and Washington, D.C. Attendees have included over 240 administrators and 44 officials of state departments of education.)

The details of the development and validation of the Career Pathways Self-Study Instrument are provided in Appendix 1.

At this point, the best way to understand Career Pathways is to stop reading and use the instrument to determine where your partnership is on each of the eighteen benchmarks. To see what each selection (1, 2, 3, 4, or 5) signifies, see Appendix 2. [*The reader should attempt to complete the instrument before going on to the next paragraph.*]

Scale: 1 = This is NOT being done. 5 = This is being done VERY WELL.	1	2	3	4	5
1. Career Pathways are guided by one or more 4+2 (+2) curriculum frameworks.					
2. Career Pathways include comprehensive student career guidance and counseling.					
Secondary component:					
3. Meets academic standards and grade level requirements.					
4. Meets high school standardized testing and exit requirements.					
5. Meets postsecondary (both 2-year and 4-year college) entry and placement requirements.					
6. Provides academic and technical foundation knowledge and skills in a chosen Career Pathway.					
7. Provides opportunities for students to earn college credit through dual/concurrent enrollment or articulation agreements.					
Postsecondary component:					
8. Provides opportunities for students to earn college credit through dual/concurrent enrollment or articulation agreements.					
9. Provides alignment and/or articulation with baccalaureate programs.					
10. Provides industry-recognized knowledge and skills.					
11. Provides employment opportunities for high-wage, high-demand careers in the chosen Pathway and provides multiple exit points.					
Business:					
12. Ensures that students are learning current, in-demand skills.					
13. Provides students work-based learning experiences after the 11th grade.					
14. Supports student recruitment and provides ongoing support for the Career Pathway program.					
Partnership ensures a culture focused on improvement by:					
15. Collecting qualitative and quantitative data on academic and career success, retention rates, dropouts, graduation, transitions, and remediation.					
16. Using data for planning and decision-making.					
17. Providing targeted professional development for faculty, administrators, and counselors to improve teaching/learning and integration of technical and academic instruction.					
18. Maintaining ongoing dialogue among secondary, postsecondary, and business partners.					

Figure 1-2. Career Pathways Self-Study Instrument

For more on the instrument and its use, visit www.cord.org.

The instrument is useful as a *planning tool* because it can help a partnership determine how it should improve in the coming year. After completing the instrument, the practitioner is able to identify benchmarks in which his or her partnership ranks relatively low and design strategies for improving in those areas.

The remaining chapters in this book provide understanding and insight into effective strategies for improvement in each area.

EDUCATION WITH A PURPOSE

Imagine an ideal partnership (or consortium), one that earned a 4 or a 5 for every criterion on the Career Pathways Self-Study Instrument. I believe the high school(s) in that consortium would have a clear sense of *purpose*. But the role of the high school(s) in that ideal consortium would be very different from the role that conventional high schools have filled for many years. In our perfect consortium, the **high school role** would be to:

- Provide context for academic achievement,
- Provide motivation (and desire) for students to remain in school,
- Provide a *level playing field* for students with different learning styles,
- Provide guidance for career selection and a foundation for career pursuit,
- Use career preparation to provide interdisciplinary problem-solving and critical thinking, and
- Provide a foundation for lifelong learning — and lifelong earning.

Likewise, the role of the college in the partnership would be different from the role of conventional colleges. In our perfect consortium, the **college role** would be to:

- Provide the leadership to convene the partnership,

21

- Provide curriculum assistance and professional development for secondary teachers,
- Participate in recruiting students into and helping them select appropriate Career Pathways,
- Share its employer advisory committee with the high schools,
- Share its labs and equipment with high schools,
- Provide the opportunities for dual enrollment and dual credit, and
- Be accountable for the quality of its graduates to employers — and to higher education.

That sounds like the *purpose-driven* educational experience I would want for my grandchildren.

Chapter 2 Preview

Postsecondary component:		
11. Provides employment opportunities for high-wage, high-demand careers in the chosen Pathway and provides multiple exit points.		
Business:		
12. Ensures that students are learning current, in-demand skills.		

Every Career Pathway partnership must determine which career preparation programs are appropriate for its community and state. These programs should be based on well-researched forecasts of future jobs and economic development goals. In this chapter, Meeder and Couch emphasize that we must look beyond this to national and global projections and demographic shifts. They also sound a sobering note of alarm: "Young Americans have been lulled into a sense of entitlement and don't realize that [apart from significant education reform] they may not have the skills to compete for jobs in a global environment." Finally, the authors provide a rationale for postsecondary education and training and for teaching soft skills, creativity, innovation, and entrepreneurship. As you read the chapter, think about how these elements can be embedded in Career Pathways to ensure that our future workers are equipped for the high-wage jobs that Americans have long enjoyed as a result of hard work, superior education, and good governance.

D.H.

2

WHERE ARE THE GOOD JOBS?

Hans Meeder and James R. Couch

INTRODUCTION

Every leader in education, business, and government is asking, "Where are the good jobs going to be?" "Just tell me what the jobs are, what skills they require, and we'll design our education system around that set of knowledge and skills."

If only it were that simple. A large part of the 20th century was spent trying to create a model for the comprehensive American high school that would prepare students for gainful employment in the Industrial Age. And that effort largely succeeded. But the world has kept changing, and the pace of change has continued to accelerate with the emergence of a tightly integrated global economy.

In this chapter we will discuss the economic imperatives driving change in our schools, and why innovative, high-quality strategies like Career Pathways are critical for the economic success of today's young people and our communities, states, and nation.

ECONOMIC IMPERATIVE 1: THE SHIFTING GLOBAL LANDSCAPE

In his recent book *The World Is Flat*, Thomas Friedman discusses the rapid integration and connection of national economies brought about by multiple "flattening forces" such as the fall of the Berlin Wall, the rise of the Internet, new workflow software, outsourcing, and offshoring. Since the early 1990s, dozens of new market-based economies have entered the world economy, while transportation and communication costs have rapidly fallen, making it easier to move products from place to place. Information technologies have further transformed the workplace.

But even since the year 2000, global integration has further accelerated, in response to the "flattening forces" that are leveling the world economic playing field.

Friedman refers to three eras of globalization and explains the characteristics of each. We would encourage the reader not to skim over this as arcane economic trivia. This has a direct bearing on the world in which we live today, and the future world our students will inherit and for which they will one day take responsibility. The better we understand these dynamics, the better preparation we can provide. According to Friedman,

> the first [era of globalization] lasted from 1492—when Columbus set sail, opening trade between the Old World and the New World—until around 1800. I would call this Globalization 1.0. . . . The key agent of change, the dynamic force driving the process of global integration, was how much brawn—how much muscle, how much horsepower, wind power, or later steam power—your country had. In this era, countries and governments . . . led the way in breaking down walls and knitting the world together, driving global integration. . . .
>
> The second great era, Globalization 2.0, lasted roughly from 1800 to 2000, interrupted by the Great Depression and World Wars I and II. . . . In Globalization 2.0, the key agent of change, the dynamic force driving global integration, was multinational companies. . . . In the first half of this era,

global integration was powered by falling transportation costs, thanks to the steam engine and the railroad, and in the second half by falling telecommunication costs—thanks to the diffusion of the telegraph, telephones, the PC, satellites, fiber-optic cable, and the early versions of the World Wide Web. . . .

Globalization 3.0 is shrinking the world from a size small to a size tiny and flattening the playing field at the same time. . . . The dynamic force in Globalization 3.0—the thing that gives it its unique character—is the newfound power for *individuals* to collaborate and compete globally. And the lever that is enabling individuals and groups to go global is . . . software—all sorts of new applications—in conjunction with the creation of a global fiber-optic network that has made us all next-door neighbors. . . .

Globalization 3.0 is going to be more and more driven not only by individuals but also by a much more diverse—non-Western, non-white—group of individuals. Individuals, from every corner of the flat world are being empowered. (Friedman, pp. 9–11)

We already know that low-cost manufacturing such as textiles, toys, and electronics assembly has moved to China and other low-cost countries. This is called "offshoring." In South Carolina and North Carolina, communities built around textile manufacturing and furniture manufacturing have experienced significant job disruptions. When the Pillotex Corporation announced the closure of facilities in North Carolina in July 2003, several thousand employees lost their jobs. Even though the plant had been struggling for years and job cuts seemed imminent, almost half of the workers who lost their jobs lacked even high school diplomas.

But during this period, we've become aware of another emerging phenomenon—outsourcing. Outsourcing is the disassembling of a work process and sending part of that work process to another location, either domestic or foreign, where it can be done by a lower-cost provider.

The 10 Great Flatteners

1. **Fall of the Berlin Wall**—The events of November 9, 1989, tilted the worldwide balance of power toward democracies and free markets.

2. **Netscape IPO**—The August 9, 1995, offering sparked massive investment in fiber-optic cables.

3. **Workflow software**—The rise of applications from PayPal to VPNs enabled faster, closer coordination among far-flung employees.

4. **Open-sourcing**—Self-organizing communities, à la Linux, launched a collaborative revolution.

5. **Outsourcing**—Migrating business functions to India saved money *and* a third world economy.

6. **Offshoring**—Contract manufacturing elevated China to economic prominence.

7. **Supply-chaining**—Robust networks of suppliers, retailers, and customers increased business efficiency. See Wal-Mart.

8. **Insourcing**—Logistics giants took control of customer supply chains, helping mom-and-pop shops go global. See UPS and FedEx.

9. **In-forming**—Power searching allowed everyone to use the Internet as a "personal supply chain of knowledge." See Google.

10. **Wireless**—Like "steroids," wireless technologies pumped up collaboration, making it mobile and personal.

Source: *The World is Flat* by Thomas Friedman, summarized in *Wired Magazine*, May 2005

In today's world, an Indian accountant can pull up scanned-in data from a W-2, enter the data into a U.S. tax return, and send back the nearly complete return in time for a U.S. accountant to finish it when he or she goes online the next morning. Special workflow software called Virtual Tax Room allows the Indian accountant to view tax information but prevents confidential information from being viewed, downloaded, or printed.

Many rural and small hospitals have outsourced radiology. Digitized X rays are sent to remote radiologists (in the United

States, India, or Australia) who review them and make recommendations to the attending physicians.

Call center operations that are considered low-wage and low-prestige here in the United States are considered high-wage and high-prestige in India, which for decades has invested in regional technology universities that rival MIT and Stanford University in their science and engineering prowess.

Some examples of outsourcing surprise and amuse us. A hotel concierge in Santa Clara, California, operates from a spare bedroom with a camera and microphone. The people he supervises receive his instructions via a flat-screen video monitor in the hotel lobby about 40 miles away. In Washington, D.C., a Pakistani firm demonstrates how a virtual receptionist can answer phones, greet visitors, and let the FedEx man into the office — from 7500 miles away. And in several McDonald's restaurants in the mid-West, drive-through customers actually talk to call center operators in Colorado. The operators take orders, match them with photos of customers to ensure that the right customers get the right orders, and then in an instant send the orders to window operators. Overall profits are up because of greater order accuracy, faster serve time, and higher volume in the drive-through lanes.

As Friedman says "Any job that can be digitized can be outsourced."

ECONOMIC IMPERATIVE 2: THE DEMOGRAPHIC CHALLENGE

The forces of globalization are creating pressure on U.S. workers because it is becoming easier and easier to move work around the globe. Moreover, as the need for American workers to upgrade their skills and competitiveness increases, we will be losing a large cohort of well-educated, highly productive baby boomers from the U.S. workforce — a loss that current college-going rates are not sufficient to replace. Although by 2000 the percentage of American workers with postsecondary education was 59, compared to 28 percent in 1973 (see

Figure 2-1), the rising trend thus indicated will still not satisfy the need of the coming years.

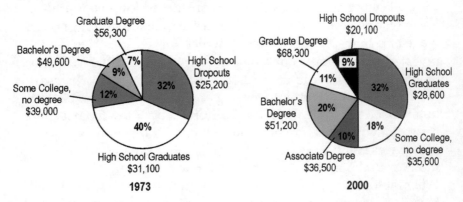

Figure 2-1. Distribution of Education Levels and Salary Averages, 1973 and 2000. Percent of prime-age (30–59) employment. Earnings in 2000 dollars. *Source:* Authors' analysis of current population survey (March 1974 and 2001)

Carnevale and Desrochers explain the dynamics between baby boomer retirement and the educational trends of subsequent generations of American workers in this way:

By 2020 there will be about 46 million baby boomers with at least some college who will be over 55 years of age. These boomers are working today, but they will age beyond 55 years from here on out. Over the same period, if we maintain current attainment rates in postsecondary education, there will likely be about 49 million new adults with at least some college—a net gain of about 3 million. If the Bureau of Labor Statistics projections of a 22 percent increase in jobs that will require at least some college by 2010 continue through 2020, **roughly 15 million new jobs that require college-educated workers will be created.**

This far exceeds the small net increase expected in the college-educated population (emphasis added).[1]

Carnevale and Desrochers conclude that there will be a resulting shortage of about **12 million college-educated workers in the U.S. Workforce by 2020.**

ECONOMIC IMPERATIVE 3: INDICATORS OF AN OUTDATED PREPARATION SYSTEM

In a speech before the nation's governors in February 2005, Microsoft founder Bill Gates made a provocative statement about American high schools.

American high schools are obsolete. By obsolete, I mean that our high schools, even when they are working exactly as designed, cannot teach our kids what they need to know today. Training the workforce of tomorrow with high schools of today is like trying to teach kids about today's computers on a 50-year-old mainframe. It's the wrong tool for the times.

Coming from Gates, statements like these are tough medicine. But viewed in historical context, his observations are right on the mark.

During the 20th century, decision makers worked hard to design an education system that was aligned to their aspirations for a healthy society in which individuals from differing social classes were satisfied with their standing and were doing work that was appropriate to their abilities and interests. Vocational programs were designed for students who had strong aptitudes in technology, installation and repair of machinery, and entry into the skilled trades. College preparatory programs were designed for the management cadre that would direct the production of the workforce, and to prepare other professionals such as accountants, lawyers, physicians, political leaders, and the clergy. A general

---

[1] Anthony P. Carnevale and Donna M. Desrochers, *The Missing Middle: Aligning Education and the Knowledge Economy* (Washington, D.C.: Educational Testing Services, April 2002).

education that taught reading, writing, some math, and life adjustment was enough to prepare any industrious young person to enter the middle class.

In some ways, that approach seems to have been well grounded. But racism and ethnic bias were lurking just beneath the surface. While America generally embodied greater openness and opportunity than other nations at the time, we still promoted legal separation of the races, and the belief that ability is determined by race and ethnicity was still widespread.

The high school of the 20th century was also designed to keep young people in school for longer and longer periods, to protect older workers so they could find and keep work. This was particularly important during the Great Depression and with the return of veterans following World War II.

For several decades following World War II, the United States dominated the world economy and was the undisputed leader in manufacturing and agricultural exports.

But this top-down experiment in workforce engineering had a fatal flaw. It did not anticipate the pressures that the emerging world economy would place on U.S. workers as new technologies changed the nature of the workplace, and how global competition and integration would transform the economic landscape.

During the late 1970s and the 1980s, the United States experienced serious international competition in manufacturing for the first time in many decades, causing massive layoffs of production workers and middle management. At the same time, new technologies converged to change the American workplace permanently. Those changes, which pushed critical analysis and decision-making to lower-level workers, were further accelerated in the 1990s with the emergence of the personal computer, embedded technologies in manufacturing and manufactured goods, and new management structures that focused on quality improvement at all levels of operation.

These trends, along with more recent developments, have increased the need for high-wage "knowledge workers" in the U.S. economy.

At the same time, we can clearly see serious problems emerging in the educational outcomes of young Americans — relatively high dropout rates, inadequate math skills (especially among minorities), high postsecondary remediation rates, and the failure of high schools to challenge students to rise to their potential. Those performance indicators suggest a major problem with today's American high school, from a systems perspective. Many of America's young people are not seriously preparing for the demands of college and the workplace, and public high schools are not adequately meeting the needs of *all* our young people. Consider these facts:

- Far too many students earn high school diplomas without having the knowledge and skills necessary for success in postsecondary education and the workplace. This indicates that the high school experience lacks focus and rigor.

- Far too many young people leave high school before earning diplomas. This indicates that many students are not engaged in the high school experience, that they don't consider the curriculum valuable, and that academic programs too often fail to help struggling students catch up.

- Far too many students fail to make successful transitions to postsecondary education and training or employment. This is especially true of disabled youngsters; for them the high school experience often lacks effective transition planning activities.

FORECASTING CAREER OPPORTUNITIES

As already noted, it is next to impossible to forecast where America's job mix is headed. Jaithirth "Jerry" Rao, president of an Indian accounting firm that specializes in outsourcing U.S. tax returns, puts it this way:

It's easy to predict for someone living in India. In ten years we are going to be doing a lot of the stuff that is being done in America today. We can predict our future. But we are

33

behind you. You [Americans] are defining the future. America is always on the edge of the next creative wave.[2]

If education decision makers too narrowly define the job mix, and rigidly align our education and job training system to these forecasts, we could repeat the mistakes of the 20th century social engineers. It would be analogous to the negative effects of "teaching to the test."

Many educators recognize the folly of devoting inordinate amounts of time and attention to drilling students for high-stakes tests. They know that "teaching to the test" is not conducive to real understanding and analysis. In the same way, "training to the job" — that is, drilling students on narrow, task-specific job skills — does not prepare students to become continuous learners who can adapt to changing job requirements. Today's students need career preparation that is both broad enough to enable them to learn and adapt quickly, and specific enough to be valuable to employers, particularly small businesses.

It is also important that we focus on preparation for postsecondary education, though without trying too hard to control which postsecondary routes students take, whether certification programs or two-year colleges or four-year colleges and universities. As Figure 2-2 shows, the percentages of unskilled, skilled, and professional jobs in 1997 were 15, 65, and 20, respectively. This does not mean that today (only a few years later), we should attempt to put in place a rigid system that channels 20 percent of students into four-year colleges, 65 percent into two-year colleges, and 15 percent into no postsecondary education at all.

> Today's students need career preparation that is both broad enough to enable them to learn and adapt quickly, and specific enough to be valuable to employers, particularly small businesses.

---

[2] Friedman, *The Earth Is Flat*, 15.

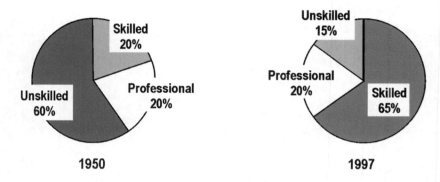

Figure 2-2. Percentage of Unskilled, Skilled, and Professional Jobs in 1950 and 1997
(*Source:* National Summit on 21st Century Skills for 21st Century Jobs)

It may be wiser to establish an objective of having all, or almost all, students college-ready, and to significantly increase the number of students who not only enter college but *persist* in college and succeed in earning skill certificates and/or degrees.

HIGH GROWTH JOB TRAINING INITIATIVE

A very helpful resource in thinking about career opportunities and Career Pathways for U.S. students is the U.S. Department of Labor's High Growth Job Training Initiative.[3]

The High Growth Job Training Initiative identified 13 sectors that meet the following criteria: (1) they are projected to add substantial numbers of new jobs to the economy or affect the growth of other industries, or (2) they are existing or emerging businesses that are being transformed by technology and innovation that require new skill sets for workers.[4] The 13 sectors are the following:

---

[3] For more on this initiative, see http://www.doleta.gov/BRG/JobTrainInitiative/ (accessed July 2005).

[4] These high-growth industries do not represent all sectors of the U.S. economy and, therefore, do not duplicate the career clusters framework identified by the States' Career Clusters Initiative. See http://www.careerclusters.org/ (accessed July 2005).

Advanced manufacturing
Aerospace
Automotive
Biotechnology
Construction
Energy
Financial services
Geospatial technology
Health care
Hospitality
Information technology
Retail
Transportation

The following bulleted items give a "snapshot" of each of the industries. More extensive information on each, including a description of the range of skills and education associated with jobs within the industry cluster, can be found at the Department of Labor's website.

Advanced Manufacturing

- The manufacturing sector continues to account for 14 percent of U.S. gross domestic product (GDP) and 11 percent of total U.S. employment. Moreover, manufacturing firms fund 60 percent of the $193 billion that the U.S. private sector invests annually in research and development. (U.S. Department of Commerce)

- Manufacturing salaries and benefits average $54,000, higher than the average for the total private sector. Two factors in particular attract workers to manufacturing: higher pay and benefits, and opportunities for advanced education and training. (National Association of Manufacturers)

- A 2003 survey of U.S. manufacturing employers found that 80 percent of respondents said that they had a serious problem finding qualified candidates for the highly technical world of modern manufacturing. (National Association of Manufacturers)

Aerospace

- The aerospace industry comprises companies producing aircraft, guided missiles, space vehicles, aircraft engines, propulsion units, and related parts. Aircraft overhaul, rebuilding, and parts are also included. (U.S. Bureau of Labor Statistics)

- Other sectors of the economy depend on aerospace businesses and related disciplines for technical skills and technologies that are critical elements of our security infrastructure and improve America's position in the global marketplace. (President's Commission on the Future of the United States Aerospace Industry)

- Aerospace Industries Association President and CEO John Douglass stated that with $161 billion in sales, U.S. aerospace is a strategic industry in the nation's economy, homeland security, and national defense.

Automotive

- The GDP in 2001 for motor vehicles and equipment was $111.4 billion, a 1 percent share of the national total. The GDP in 2001 for auto repair, services, and parking was $99.5 billion, a 1 percent share of the national total. More than 3.7 percent of America's total GDP is generated by the sale and production of new light vehicles. (U.S. Bureau of Economic Analysis and Alliance of Automobile Manufacturers)

- The automotive industry is one of the largest industries in the United States. It creates 6.6 million direct and spin-off jobs and produces $243 billion in payroll compensation, or 5.6 percent of private sector compensation. For every worker directly employed by an automaker, nearly seven spin-off jobs are created. (Alliance of Automobile Manufacturers)

- One out of every 10 jobs in the United States is dependent on the automotive industry. No other industry is linked to so much manufacturing or generates more retail business and employment. (Alliance of Automobile Manufacturers)

- Total automobile dealership dollar sales reached $679 billion in 2002. Total dealership employment was 1,129,600 workers and payroll was nearly $49 billion in 2002. (National Automobile Dealers Association)
- Dealership sales in 2002 as a percentage of total retail trade in the United States were 21.7 percent. (National Automobile Dealers Association)

Biotechnology

- Jobs for biological technicians, a key biotechnology occupation, are expected to grow by 19.4 percent between 2002 and 2012, while the need for biological scientists is projected to grow by 19 percent. (U.S. Bureau of Labor Statistics, National Employment Data)
- The biotechnology industry employed 713,000 workers in 2002 and is expected to employ 814,900 workers in 2007. (Economy.com, Industry Workstation, Biotech industry forecast)
- The population of companies engaged in biotechnology is dynamic; growth in the biotechnology-related workforce has been vigorous, averaging 12.3 percent annually for companies that provided data for 2000–2002. Companies with 50 to 499 employees experienced the fastest growth, with an annual increase of 17.3 percent, while growth among larger firms was 6.2 percent. (U.S. Department of Commerce, *A Survey of the Use of Biotechnology in U.S. Industry,* Executive Summary for the Report to Congress)

Construction

- The construction industry is predicted to add approximately 1 million new jobs between 2002 and 2012, an increase of 15 percent. (U.S. Bureau of Labor Statistics)
- With total employment expected to reach 7.8 million by 2012, the construction industry is predicted to be among the economy's top 10 sources of job growth. (U.S. Bureau of Labor Statistics)

- Construction has a very large number of self-employed workers. Opportunities for workers to form their own firms are better in construction than in many other industries. (U.S. Bureau of Labor Statistics)

- Projected employment growth between 2002 and 2012 is substantial for a wide range of construction-related occupations, such as electricians (154,000 new jobs), carpenters (122,000 new jobs), and construction managers (47,000 new jobs). (U.S. Bureau of Labor Statistics)

Energy

- The energy industry incorporates a broad range of sectors including petroleum and natural gas extraction, refining, and distribution; electric power generation and distribution; and mining.

- Public utilities employed about 600,000 workers in 2002. Electric power generation, transmission, and distribution provided almost three in four jobs (436,000), while natural gas distribution (116,000) and other systems (48,000) provided the remainder. (U.S Bureau of Labor Statistics)

- The GDP for the energy industry, including electric and gas utilities, nuclear power generation, mining (including coal and minerals), and oil and gas extraction, in 2003 was $352 billion, a 3.2 percent share of the national total. (U.S. Bureau of Economic Analysis)

Financial Services

- The financial services industry is composed of three primary sectors: banking, securities and commodities, and insurance. (U.S. Bureau of Labor Statistics)

- The financial industry's annual rate of growth (1.2 percent annually between 2002 and 2012) represents 964,000 new jobs created by 2012. (Jay Berman, *Monthly Labor Review,* February 2004)

- The 2003 gross domestic product generated by the financial industry was over $2.5 trillion in current dollars, a

20.4 percent share of the total GDP. (U.S. Bureau of Economic Analysis)

- The following financial services occupations are expected to increase in employment by over 18 percent from 2002 to 2012: personal financial advisors (34.6 percent), financial analysts (18.7 percent), and credit analysts (18.7 percent). (U.S. Bureau of Labor Statistics)

- Employment growth is expected in management and professional jobs in banking, customer service, and securities and financial services sales. (U.S. Bureau of Labor Statistics)

- Growing areas of the insurance industry are medical services and health insurance, in addition to the industry's expansion into the broader financial services field. (U.S. Bureau of Labor Statistics)

Geospatial Technology

- The market for geospatial technologies in 2002 was estimated at $5 billion. This market is projected to have annual revenues of $30 billion by 2005, consisting of $20 billion in the remote sensing market and $10 billion in the geographical information systems (GIS) market. (Gaudet, Annulis, and Carr, *Building the Geospatial Workforce,* Urban and Regional Informational Systems Association Special Education Issue, 2002)

- Geospatial products and specialists are expected to play a large role in homeland security activities. The need for information-gathering to protect critical infrastructure has resulted in an enormous increase in the demand for such skills and jobs. (Lorraine Castro, NIMA Human Resources Department, 2003)

- Increasing demand for readily available, consistent, accurate, complete, and current geographic information and the widespread availability and use of advanced technologies offer great job opportunities for people with many different talents and educational backgrounds. (U.S. Geological Survey and U.S. Bureau of Labor Statistics)

Health Care

- The health care industry is predicted to add nearly 3.5 million new jobs between 2002 and 2012, an increase of 30 percent. (U.S. Bureau of Labor Statistics)

- From 2002 to 2012, 10 of the 20 fastest-growing occupations are concentrated in health services. These positions include medical assistants (59 percent growth), physician assistants (49 percent growth), home health aides (48 percent growth), and medical records and health information technicians (47 percent growth). (U.S. Bureau of Labor Statistics)

- Projected rates of employment growth for the various segments of the industry range from 12.8 percent in hospitals, the largest and slowest-growing industry segment, to 55.8 percent in the much smaller home health care services. (U.S. Bureau of Labor Statistics)

Hospitality

- Accommodation and food services make up about 8.1 percent of all employment. (U.S. Bureau of Labor Statistics)

- Employment in the accommodation and food services industries is predicted to grow 18 percent between 2002 and 2012, adding more than 1.6 million new jobs. (U.S. Bureau of Labor Statistics)

- Of the 8,740,000 total workers employed in the accommodation and food services industries in 2003, 5,343,000 work full-time (61 percent), while 3,397,000 work part-time (39 percent). (Annual average for 2003, according to the Current Population Survey, a joint project of the U.S. Bureau of Labor Statistics and Census Bureau)

Information Technology

- Information technology (IT) is the fastest-growing sector in the economy with a 68 percent increase in output growth rate projected between 2002 and 2012. (U.S. Bureau of Labor Statistics)

- Employment opportunities are expected to be good in the IT industry as demand for computer-related occupations increases due to rapid advances in computer technology, continuing development of new computer applications, and the growing significance of information security. (U.S. Bureau of Labor Statistics)

- Ninety-two percent of all IT workers are in non-IT companies, 80 percent of which are small. (Information Technology Association of America)

Retail

- The GDP for retail trade in 2002 was $947.9 billion in current dollars, a 9 percent share of the national total. (U.S. Department of Commerce, Bureau of Economic Analysis)

- The retail trade industry is predicted to add 2.1 million new jobs between 2002 and 2012, an increase of 14 percent. (U.S. Bureau of Labor Statistics)

- The retail industry offers a substantial number of employment opportunities because part-time and temporary work is plentiful in a wide variety of formats ranging from small, independent retailers to national and multinational retail chains. Solid store experience can lead to an array of retail management and store support career ladders. A college degree can afford direct entry into management training programs and regional- and/or corporate-level career paths. (U.S. Bureau of Labor Statistics and National Retail Federation Foundation)

Transportation

- The transportation industry is very global; its growth has been spurred by the increased adoption of new technologies that allow time-specific delivery and electronic tracking of cargo. (Hoover's Online)

- Employment in the transportation industry is expected to increase from 4,205,000 jobs in 2002 to 5,120,000 jobs in 2012, an increase of 914,000 jobs. (U.S. Bureau of Labor Statistics)

- Between 2002 and 2012 there will be substantial employment opportunities in a wide range of transportation-related occupations, such as:
  - Truck drivers, heavy and tractor-trailer: 337,000 new jobs
  - Bus and truck mechanics and diesel engine specialists: 38,000 new jobs
  - Railroad conductors and yardmasters: 10,000 job openings (U.S. Bureau of Labor Statistics)

Source: Department of Labor Employment Administration, http://www.doleta.gov/BRG/JobTrainInitiative/

DO JOBS REALLY REQUIRE COLLEGE DEGREES?

For the last several years (at least since 1990), education leaders have acknowledged that a broad set of competencies is necessary for people to become economically self-sufficient in the modern U.S. economy. These competencies are not academic skills and knowledge per se, but they are *related* to academic skills and knowledge. They are the "SCANS" competencies (Secretary's Commission on Achieving Necessary Skills). The SCANS report delineated "enabling skills" and "functional skills." **Enabling skills** "underlie the performance of functional skills. They include reading and writing, mathematics and computer skills, listening and speaking, and other areas. . . . Enabling skills relate to the basic knowledge a person must have to develop functional skills, such as a core vocabulary required for discourse in many contexts or the basic arithmetical procedures required to compute at different levels." **Functional skills** "reflect what people in a wide range of jobs actually do at work. These skills are exhibited at many different levels and in different proportions, depending on the job, but with enough common aspects of content and cognitive and behavioral performance to constitute a 'skill.'"[5]

We also know that demand for workers with college degrees has been growing. Among all jobs in the U.S. economy, those requiring associate degrees are projected to increase the fastest, by 32 percent through 2010. Jobs that require bachelor's degrees are expected to grow by 24 percent.[6] Those projections are based on assumptions about the knowledge and skills gained via different levels of educational programs. They are not fixed in concrete. They reflect the *perception* among employers that high schools programs are not very rigorous, that two-year postsecondary programs are more rigorous than high school programs, and that four-year postsecondary programs (and beyond) are more rigorous still.

> Among all jobs in the U.S. economy, those requiring associate degrees are projected to increase the fastest, by 32 percent through 2010.

An interesting question presents itself: Do all workers really need college degrees for economic success, or is the demand for college degrees related to other factors?

As far back as 1996, Richard Murnane and Frank Levy postulated that the demand for workers with college degrees is driven not by the content embedded in particular college programs but by the fact that the degrees serve as a proxy for the knowledge, skills, and aptitudes that employers want but cannot get from students with only high school diplomas. Murnane and Levy further indicate that these "new basic

---

[5] The Secretary's Commission on Achieving Necessary Skills, *Identifying and Describing the Skills Required by Work* (Washington, D.C.: U. S. Department of Labor, 1990, http://wdr.doleta.gov/SCANS/idsrw/scansrep.pdf; accessed July 2005).

[6] D. E. Hecker, *Employment Outlook 2000–10: Occupational Employment Projections to 2010. Monthly Labor Review November 2001* (Washington, D.C.: U. S. Department of Labor, Office of Occupational Statistics and Employment Projections, Bureau of Labor Statistics, 2001).

skills" are "hard skills" that include (1) basic mathematics and problem-solving abilities at levels much higher than many high school graduates now attain, (2) "soft skills" that include the ability to work in groups and make effective oral and written presentations, and (3) the ability to use personal computers to carry out basic tasks such as word processing.[7]

In 2004, **The American Diploma Project (ADP)**, led by Achieve Inc. in cooperation with EdTrust and the Fordham Foundation, released the results of a study that benchmarked the knowledge and skills needed by America's young people. By benchmarking the demands placed on college freshmen and entering employees (i.e., those who enter the workforce directly out of high school), the ADP found a very strong convergence between the mathematical reasoning and oral and written communication skills needed for both college-level work and direct entry into workplace. In short, "the ADP research found that there is a common core of knowledge and skills, particularly in English and math, which students must master to be prepared for both postsecondary education and well-paying jobs."[8]

If education reformers succeed in ratcheting up the quality of a high school education and compressing more learning into grades 1–12 (even moving some postsecondary content down into the eleventh and twelfth grades), over time this could change employer perceptions about the value of the high school diploma and the income premium that is placed on associate degrees and bachelor's degrees.

Of course, our international competitors are seeking higher education in record numbers. China increased its postsecondary participation by 258 percent between 1990 and 2000, with 13.7 million participants, compared to 15.7 million postsecondary participants in the United States. India has

---

[7] Richard R. Murnane and Frank Levy, *Teaching the New Basic Skills: Principles for Educating Children to Thrive in a Changing Economy* (New York: The Free Press, Simon and Schuster, Inc., 1996).

[8] Retrieved from Achieve website (http://www.achieve.org/achieve.nsf/ADP-Network?OpenForm), July 2005.

increased its college-going rates by 92 percent during the same period and has 9.4 million college participants.

It is not enough simply to ask for America's young people to go to college and for taxpayers to support expansion of college facilities and programs. We must ensure that students are getting a more rigorous preparation through the current universal K–12 system. Only then can we expand our postsecondary investments in ways that yield the best possible results in the international marketplace.

CLOSING THE "AMBITION GAP"

From an international perspective, Friedman worries about two things when it comes to the preparation of American students. One concern, of course, is the skills gap that seems to be emerging as fewer and fewer young Americans choose careers that place emphasis on science and technology.

But on a deeper level, Friedman is also concerned about an "ambition gap": Young Americans have been lulled into a sense of entitlement and don't realize that they may not have the skills to compete for jobs in a global environment.

The Ambition Gap: Young Americans have been lulled into a sense of entitlement and don't realize that they may not have the skills to compete for jobs in a global environment.

Surrounded by technology and living in relative affluence, many young Americans are succumbing to a culture of entertainment and consumerism. We concur with Friedman's concern and would like to offer strategies for reclaiming America's legacy of hard work and risk-taking.

One instructive example comes from High Tech High School, the first of a network of small high schools that originated in San Diego, California. In a guided tour of the school in 2003, founder and CEO Larry Rosenstock noted, "We insist that our students become producers, not just consumers. That's why we don't allow them to play any video games on the computers here." The only video games students can play on campus are the ones they develop and program themselves!

High Tech High, of course, is not alone. In hundreds of high-quality career- and arts-oriented academies, regional vocational and technical centers, and Tech Prep partnerships, young adults are using their acquired knowledge and skills to create, produce, and innovate. They are learning to be knowledge **workers**, not just knowledge **learners**.

To motivate and prepare young Americans to participate in this global economy, we would like to suggest **additional competencies** that our students will need.

First (and this relates to the academic subjects of world history and geography), Americans should have a **deep understanding of world history and the global economic system**, particularly in Asia. With over 2.2 billion people residing in India and China alone, we cannot afford for our citizens to be ignorant of their traditions and ambitions. It is very likely that our young people will someday collaborate in business with people from either or both of those countries, so they must be ready to make cross-cultural collaboration work.

Another key area of focus is **personal characteristics such as hard work, ambition, teamwork, leadership, and honesty**. The new South Carolina Education and Economic Development Act goes so far as to list 25 of those virtues and requires that every local school board create an explicit plan for instilling them. Of course, the best way to acquire those character traits is to participate in the real-world learning experiences that Career Pathways programs offer. Career Pathways practitioners should have clear strategies for teaching specific academic and technical competencies and instilling character qualities and virtues deemed essential by states and districts. Those character traits are critical to the future competitiveness and independence of our young people, both as economic producers and as participating community members.

It is also vital that we instill entrepreneurial concepts in our students early. **Creativity, innovation, and entrepreneurship** are the hallmarks of the American economy, but much of what is offered in schools is based on the assumption that most students will eventually become employees—working for someone else. Economic growth and financial independence stem from the ability to start, manage, and grow businesses. Experience has shown that, in most cases, small businesses do not fail because of lack of skills but because of poor business management practices. Especially in inner-city areas, we must instill the spirit of entrepreneurship through our CTE programs. This will require the development of teaching materials that are designed for use across a wide array of Career Pathways.

CONNECTING PREPARATION TO YIELD COLLEGE- AND WORK-READINESS

What can local education leaders do? At state and local levels, leaders must develop strategies that address economic realities. Development of a broad consensus around the need for change is essential before specific reform options are put on the table.

South Carolina's experience in this regard is instructive. Since 2000, South Carolina has undertaken a thorough review of its education system to ensure that its high school graduates are ready to create and fill the jobs of the 21st century. The governor's office convened a task force that issued a detailed report titled *Pathways to Prosperity* in fall 2001. The report offers a "roadmap for building systemic solutions to . . . broad societal issues" such as global competition, technological change, the proliferation of information, and the increasing complexities of the workplace. The report issues nine specific recommendations dealing with career preparation, educational standards and testing, student retention, character education, business involvement in the educational process, and communication between educational stakeholders, among other issues that will continue to affect American education far into the 21st century.[9]

---

[9] South Carolina Governor's Workforce Education Task Force, *Pathways to Prosperity: Success for Every Student in the 21st-Century Workplace* (October 2001).

The South Carolina Department of Education followed up the report by developing detailed guides based on career development opportunities in the following clusters:[10]

Architecture and construction
Arts, A/V technology, and communication
Business, management, and administration
Education and training
Health science
Hospitality and tourism
Information technology
Science, technology, engineering, and mathematics
Transportation, distribution, and logistics

In spring 2005 the state legislature capped off a two-year legislative process with passage of the South Carolina Education and Economic Development Act. Under this landmark legislation, the previous college-prep and Tech Prep tracks will be eliminated, and rigorous academic preparation based on the state's academic standards will be delivered in the context of student-selected career clusters. Every student will study "college prep" academics. Every student—with parent and counselor input—will develop an individual graduation plan (IGP) that will map out a course sequence for all four years of high school. The purpose of the IGP is to ensure that the student completes his or her academic core courses as well as a sequence of career-oriented courses in one of the career clusters offered through the local school system. Each of the career clusters will offer significant opportunity for dual enrollment and advanced credits, so the typical student can obtain nine or more college-level credits in the process of completing high school. While most students will probably wait the customary four years to receive their high school diplomas, in reality they will have compressed their high school experience into three years and used their senior year for further career exploration and college-level work. Students who start ninth grade far behind their peers use ninth grade as

[10] South Carolina has identified 16 career clusters for organization of its career education programs.

49

a catch-up year and complete their high school requirements in grades 10–12.

South Carolina appears to be the first state that, through legislation, has fully integrated the concepts of rigorous academics, career counseling, and career-oriented curriculum for all students, finally eliminating the old three-track system— college prep, voc-ed, and general track.

CONCLUSION

So where will the good jobs be? If America plays its cards right, the good jobs will be right here! Jobs held by Americans will be interesting and challenging and, in most cases, will pay livable wages. Lower-skilled jobs will be outsourced and offshored to countries where workers are glad to be paid a few thousand dollars a year. Of course, some low-skilled jobs, anchored by geography in the United States, will be filled by young people working their way through school, by part-time retirees, and (especially) by recent immigrants. Because jobs in the United States will involve higher-level skills, innovation, and creative uses of technology, they will offer livable wages.

But we must drive home to ourselves and our children that Americans are not *entitled* to high-wage jobs. The ones we have were earned by hard work and good governance. To maintain high standards of living in this new era, the first thing we have to do is get rid of our sense of entitlement.

There is no way around this. This will require a significant, continual upgrading of the skills and aptitudes of all American workers, every day of their schooling and careers. And for more and more workers, schooling and career will be interspersed and concurrent, rather than sequential.

Our schools must change. Expectations for all students must be increased. Our educators must learn to partner with business and political leaders to build consensus about the kind of skills our students need. We must design, test, and refine approaches that, like Career Pathways, integrate high-level academic skills with skills and knowledge in high-growth, high-demand careers and that create seamless connections between secondary and postsecondary schools.

The connections between secondary and postsecondary must be systematized through legislation and policy. And we must dramatically improve the way our teachers instill academic and career skills in our students.

America's commitment to education has been the hallmark of its enduring economic success and upward social mobility. Today, thousands of committed teachers, school and college leaders, parents, community organizations, and elected officials at the local, state, and federal levels are working hard to modernize and reenergize our education systems so that they will meet the demands of the 21st century. We are more than confident that we will succeed, and we will all benefit from the success of today's young people as they emerge and compete on a worldwide playing field.

Chapter 3 Preview

1. Career Pathways are guided by one or more 4+2 (+2) curriculum frameworks.	
Secondary component:	
3. Meets academic standards and grade level requirements.	
6. Provides academic and technical foundation knowledge and skills in a chosen Career Pathway.	
Postsecondary component:	
10. Provides industry-recognized knowledge and skills.	
11. Provides employment opportunities for high-wage, high-demand careers in the chosen Pathway and provides multiple exit points.	

As an engineer, I have always enjoyed planning, designing, and creating things. Since I've been in education, I've been particularly interested in curriculum design and development. Whether one is creating a laser, a computer, a building, or a curriculum, the principles and processes are very much the same.

This chapter deals with the structure, resources, and process pertaining to the creation of curriculum frameworks for Career Pathways. It is a tedious, meticulous process, but it is vitally important that every partnership begin to create curriculum frameworks very early in the development, or redesign, of its programs.

Many Tech Prep consortia will feel that they have already accomplished this; in my opinion, they haven't. Secondary-postsecondary articulation was a great accomplishment, but it falls short of the standards for secondary-postsecondary curriculum frameworks set forth in this chapter.

Traditionally, curriculum changes in CTE have been brought about by giving teachers lists of job competencies and asking them to make the changes accordingly. The structural changes called for in curriculum frameworks for Career Pathways require more time and expertise than most teachers can provide. Teachers are more interested in, and more able to create, the courses and lesson plans after the frameworks have been completed.

The new curriculum frameworks will define the uniqueness of Career Pathways. *And they will drive all the other elements of the programs: career guidance, course content, teaching strategies, assessments, and dual credit, to name a few.*   D.H.

3

Curriculum Frameworks: What, How, and When We Teach

Dan Hull and Kim Green

Any architect or building contractor will tell you that certain elements are required in house building, and that the sequence in which they occur is essential. Those elements, and the order in which they are to be carried out, are specified in a *building plan*. Creating Career Pathways is similar in that it requires certain elements in a certain sequence. Career Pathway elements, and the order in which they are to be carried out, are specified in a *curriculum framework*.

The following table illustrates the analogy between house building and Career Pathway building. Curriculum frameworks are the *building plans* of Career Pathways; they specify the *what, how,* and *when* of teaching.

Elements of House Construction	Elements of Career Pathways
Specifications	Career area, standards
Site selection	Grade level coverage (9–14)
Restrictions	State course requirements, higher education entrance requirements, apprenticeship requirements
Style (two-story, ranch, etc.)	School/college organization (tech center, career academy, magnet school)
Building Plan	**Curriculum Framework (= Career Pathway Plan)**
Foundation	Academics, soft skills
Rooms	Courses
Plumbing, walls, electrical, HVAC, etc.	Student experiences (discussions, problems, labs, internships, etc.)
Windows, doors	Guidance, counseling

The first four items listed in the second column of the table are fundamental to the creation of a curriculum framework. They must be clearly articulated to and understood by all who participate in the creation of the plan. The details of the educational process for any given Career Pathway (i.e., what actually goes on in the classroom from one day to the next) flow *from* the curriculum framework for that pathway. Just as we cannot begin laying the foundation of a house or constructing its rooms, windows, or plumbing until we have a building plan, we cannot fill in the details of a Career Pathway until its curriculum framework — its building plan — has been completed and approved.

In the early days of Tech Prep, secondary schools had their curriculum frameworks (plans) and colleges had theirs. After each level (secondary and postsecondary) had constructed its own program, the two levels attempted to join the programs through articulation agreements. But in most cases, they had different "foundations" (academic and technical expectations), and the "rooms" (courses) were difficult to align. This is why so many high school graduates begin postsecondary education only to discover that they still need remedial courses. It is also one of the reasons dual enrollment plans are so difficult to formulate and implement.

THE *STRUCTURE* OF CURRICULUM FRAMEWORKS

Designers of curriculum frameworks should keep in mind three general guidelines (all of which derive from the definitions of the terms *Career Pathways* and *career clusters* provided in Chapter 1).

Every career cluster contains multiple Career Pathways.

- The secondary portion of every Career Pathway should be broad enough to allow students to transition to other Career Pathways within the same cluster. (Students should also be able to transition easily to pathways in other clusters.) In most instances, the secondary portion of a pathway is not occupation-specific instruction.

- At the completion of the secondary portion of their Career Pathways, high school graduates should be prepared to continue their studies at colleges or universities *and* be qualified for employment within their chosen fields.

In effect, the first two guidelines stipulate that high school students concentrate on *fundamentals* (both academic and technical) and that academic and technical courses support and complement each other.

For the high school portion of the Career Pathways experience to work smoothly, three conditions must be met:

- At the end of the eighth grade, students are well prepared academically and have chosen Career Pathways in which they have interest and aptitude.

- Students begin high school "on grade" in their English, mathematics, and science studies, and remain on grade throughout high school.

- The Career Pathway curriculum begins not later than the ninth grade.

55

This does not mean that Career Pathway students are "tracked" early in high school. During the ninth and tenth grades, the chosen Career Pathway provides a *context* in which students learn how academic concepts are used outside the classroom, explore career opportunities in their chosen fields of interest, and acquire employability (soft) skills—which everyone needs. One healthy outcome of the ninth- and tenth-grade portion of the Career Pathway experience is that some students decide that the Career Pathways they initially chose are *not* what they want to continue to pursue. In the eleventh grade they can easily change pathways (or even clusters) without losing credits or getting behind.

In the eleventh and twelfth grades, Career Pathway students continue their academic studies and begin taking courses in the *technical core* of their chosen pathways. To the extent possible, these technical courses should be common to all Career Pathways within the career clusters to which the students' chosen pathways belong. Where schedules allow for elective courses (particularly in the twelfth grade), students should be allowed to take *dual credit* technical core and specialty courses that earn postsecondary credit.

The first two years of postsecondary study in Career Pathways entail additional academic coursework, along with technical specialty courses pertaining to the students' chosen careers. Students who complete those two years qualify for associate degrees or comparable certifications, are well prepared to enter the workforce in their chosen fields, and are qualified to continue their studies at four-year colleges and universities.

Figure 3-1 shows the basic outline of the curriculum framework structure.

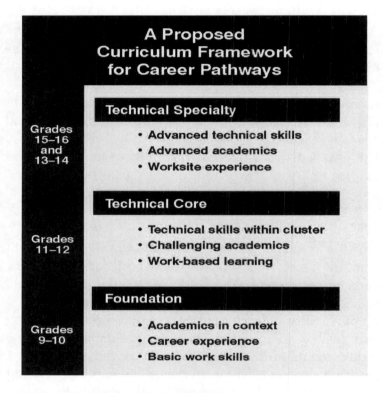

Figure 3-1. Structural Design for Curriculum Frameworks

The overall effect of this design at the secondary level is that curriculum frameworks support state academic standards, provide career context and focus, and keep student options open. The effect at the postsecondary level is that high school graduates who apply to college are focused and well prepared academically and technically and probably have already earned postsecondary credits.

THE *RESULT* OF CURRICULUM FRAMEWORKS

The distinctive *structure* of curriculum frameworks produces a distinctive *result*. Recall the definition of *curriculum framework* from Chapter 1.

A curriculum framework is the *plan* for a 4+2 program of study, or Career Pathway. Curriculum frameworks consist of two elements: (1) recommended grade-9–14 course sequences that satisfy requirements for graduation and entrance into postsecondary education and training and (2) course descriptions, with prerequisites, recommended grade levels, credits, and standards to be achieved by students. Curriculum frameworks reflect academic, employability (SCANS) and technical (skill) standards *as well as entrance requirements for postsecondary curricula.*[1]

This is another way of saying that curriculum frameworks determine both the *content* and *delivery* of instruction.

- **Content** (i.e., *what* is taught). The overall course content of a curriculum framework should satisfy three sets of requirements: (1) the technical, academic, and employability skill requirements of *employers*, (2) state-mandated academic standards and graduation requirements, and (3) the entrance requirements of *partnering postsecondary institutions*. The requirements in items 2 and 3 are easily ascertained through state departments of education and higher education institutions. The requirements in item 1 are much more difficult to pinpoint. They are determined by finding the commonalities among skill standards aggregated by career cluster. And the commonalities definitely exist. All related career fields require common sets of knowledge components and skills. Consequently, all the Career Pathways within a given career cluster should teach the knowledge components and skills that are common to that cluster. (See the discussion of the States' Career Clusters Initiative in the following section.)

- **Delivery** (i.e., *when* and *how* the content is taught). Curriculum frameworks provide guidelines for the scope

---

[1] Dan M. Hull, "Redefining CTE: Seizing a Unique Opportunity to Help the 'Neglected Majority' Become World-Class Students, Workers, and Citizens," *Techniques,* May 2003.

and sequence — i.e., the *when* — of courses taken. Curriculum frameworks also provide guidelines on pedagogy — the *how*. The Career Pathways experience calls for a new teaching paradigm that combines contextual teaching; integration of academic and career content; hands-on laboratories, simulations, and demonstrations; and employer-provided work-based learning experiences (including internships).

MORE ABOUT CAREER CLUSTERS

Traditional vocational education meant preparing people for specific jobs. While this was sufficient for the economy of the 20th century, the new marketplace, the influence and rapidity of advances in technology, and the globalization of business and industry have signaled significant workplace changes and trends that make this traditional preparation insufficient. (See Chapter 2.)

> Career clusters represent broad groupings of occupations and industries organized around common elements.

Career clusters respond to this new workplace dynamic and provide a broader, more rigorous academic and technical preparation leading to a clear pathway into postsecondary education and the modern workplace. "Career clusters identify pathways from secondary schools to two- and four-year colleges, graduate school, and the workplace, so students can learn in school what they will need to be able to do in the future. This connection to future goals motivates students to work harder and enroll in more rigorous courses" (www.careerclusters.org).

The career clusters concept can be traced to the vision and hard work of the state CTE directors, who, both collectively and individually, have supported initiatives to move CTE into the mainstream of high school reform. In December 1984, members of the National Association of State Directors of Career Technical Education Consortium (NASDCTEc) met with representatives of CORD and the Agency for Instructional

Technology (AIT) in Anaheim, California, to discuss strategies for overcoming the widespread problem of poor math, science, and communication skills among students in vocational education. That meeting ultimately led to the creation of applied-academics curricula that have benefited many tens of thousands of American students over the last two decades. The state CTE directors have made a substantial financial contribution to the development of applied-academics curricula and funded the creation of the *Curriculum Integrator* system (1997), which enables educators to customize their curricula by integrating what they teach with the standards that employers expect in the workplace.

> **The career clusters concept can be traced to the vision and hard work of the state CTE directors, who, both collectively and individually, have supported initiatives to move CTE into the mainstream of high school reform.**

Beginning June 1, 2001, with federal seed funding, the state CTE directors undertook leadership of the States' Career Clusters Initiative, whose purpose was to craft a new framework for instruction in which students understand the portability of their skills and the inter-relatedness of professions in a broad spectrum of current industries. The project sought specifically to increase academic rigor, give students more current and durable technical skills, improve alignment between secondary and postsecondary education, and improve career guidance and planning. The project focused on a comprehensive range of career specialties within the sixteen broad career fields, or *clusters*, recognized by the U.S. Department of Education's Office of Adult and Vocational Education (OVAE).

Agriculture, Food, and Natural Resources
Architecture and Construction
Arts, Audio-Video Technology, and Communication
Business, Management, and Administration
Education and Training
Finance

Government and Public Administration
Health Science
Hospitality and Tourism
Human Services
Information Technology
Law, Public Safety, Corrections, and Security
Manufacturing
Marketing, Sales, and Service
Science, Technology, Engineering, and Mathematics
Transportation, Distribution, and Logistics

Sixteen states volunteered to develop the databases for the clusters, using committees comprising national representation of educators (secondary and postsecondary), employers, labor, and others. Each committee spent hundreds of hours sorting career specialties and their associated standards into Career Pathways within this sixteen-cluster framework. Though these advisory committees worked independently, they agreed that Career Pathways would not be occupation-specific but would represent broad syntheses of common knowledge and skills within the clusters. This represents a dramatic shift from current career preparation and articulation. The committees' work vastly improves the ability of states and localities to develop and adapt curricula that equip students for the real demands of the workplace.

Career clusters represent a significant departure from conventional vocational education in that they promote (and demand) academic rigor and give students versatile skills that equip them for ranges of related occupations, rather than for narrow, task-specific jobs. For example, in conventional vocational training in health care a student might enroll in a program titled Certified Nursing Assistant. The student would acquire narrowly focused skills that lead to a single certification, nothing more. In the career clusters approach, on the other hand, that same student would enroll in a *Career Pathway* titled Therapeutic Services within the Health Science cluster. The student would acquire a broad range of knowledge and skills that are common to the numerous career specialties within that pathway. As a result, the student would have many options (both educational and professional), possess portable skills, and understand the commonality among occupations within the Therapeutic Services pathway. The standards for the Therapeutic Services pathway specify that a person in that field *must understand the treatment plan and collaborate in planning procedures that support the goals of the patient according to facility protocol and regulatory guidelines and within their scope of practice.*

> **Career clusters represent a significant departure from conventional vocational education in that they promote (and demand) academic rigor and give students versatile skills that equip them for ranges of related occupations, rather than for narrow, task-specific jobs.**

Obviously, this is a much more rigorous expectation than a traditional vocational program's duty-and-task check list.

The States' Career Clusters Initiative developed a *pathway model* for each of the sixteen clusters. Figure 3-2 is an abbreviated version of the pathway model for the Health Science cluster. The figure shows the five Career Pathways that are available to students within that cluster: Therapeutic Services, Diagnostic Services, Health Informatics, Support Services, and Biotechnology Research and Development. The figure also provides a sampling of the numerous career specialties that are open to students within each pathway.[2]

---

[2] For more complete lists of career options, see www.careerclusters.org.

HEALTH SCIENCE CAREER CLUSTER

Planning, managing, and providing therapeutic services, diagnostic services, health informatics, support services, and biotechnology research and development

Pathways	Therapeutic Services	Diagnostic Services	Health Informatics	Support Services	Biotechnology R&D
Sample Career Specialties	• Acupuncturist • Anesthesiologist Assistant • Art/Music/Dance Therapist • Athletic Trainer • Audiologist • Certified Nursing Assistant • Chiropractor *30 others; see* *www.careerclusters.org*	• Cardiovascular Technologist • Clinical Lab Technician • Computer Tomography (CT) Technologist • Cytogenetic Technologist • Cytotechnologist *18 others; see* *www.careerclusters.org*	• Admitting Clerk • Applied Researcher • Community Services Specialists • Data Analyst • Epidemiologist • Ethicist • Health Educator • Health Information Coder *14 others; see* *www.careerclusters.org*	• Biomedical/Clinical Engineer • Biomedical/Clinical Technician • Central Services • Environmental Health and Safety • Environmental Svcs • Facilities Manager • Industrial Hygienist *4 others; see* *www.careerclusters.org*	• Biochemist • Bioinformatics Associate • Bioinformatics Scientist • Bioinformatics Specialist • Biomedical Chemist • Biostatistician • Cell Biologist *15 others; see* *www.careerclusters.org*
Cluster K & S	**Cluster Knowledge and Skills** Academic Foundation • Communication • Systems • Employability Skills • Legal Responsibilities • Ethics • Safety Practices • Teamwork • Health Maintenance Practices • Technical Skills • Information Technology Applications				

Figure 3-2. Pathway Model for the Health Science Cluster
(*Source:* http://www.careerclusters.org/ClusterDocuments/hldocuments/HLFinal.pdf)

Under the heading "cluster knowledge and skills" the figure shows the broad areas in which students should become proficient before working in career specialties in the Health Science cluster: Academic Foundation, Communication, Systems, Employability Skills, Legal Responsibilities, Ethics, Safety Practices, Teamwork, Health Maintenance Practices, Technical Skills, and Information Technology Applications.

The States' Career Clusters Initiative produced, and continues to maintain, a database of knowledge and skills *statements* that define what students in each of the sixteen career clusters should know and be able to do.[1] For each broad area of knowledge and skills (Academic Foundation, Communication, Systems, Employability Skills, etc.) within each cluster, the database provides a "foundation standard" (not shown in the previous figure; see www.careerclusters.org). For example, the foundation standard for Systems (the third of the areas listed above) is as follows.

> Health care workers will understand how their role fits into their departments, their organizations, and the overall health care environment. They will identify how key systems affect services they perform and quality of care.
> (*Source:* http://www.careerclusters.org/ ClusterDocuments/hldocuments/HLFinal.pdf)

At the **cluster** level, the database provides *performance elements* and *measurement criteria* (not shown in the previous figure; see www.careerclusters.org). The following figure shows the performance elements and measurement criteria for Systems in the Health Science cluster.

---

[1] For more on the VTECS Direct® database, visit http://www.vtecs.org/.

HEALTH SCIENCE:
CLUSTER-LEVEL KNOWLEDGE AND SKILLS

SYSTEMS

Foundation standard: Health care workers will understand how their role fits into their departments, their organizations, and the overall health care environment. They will identify how key systems affect services they perform and quality of care.

Performance Element: Understand Systems Theory

    Measurement criterion: Describe systems theory and its components

    Measurement criterion: Construct a general systems model using inputs, throughputs, and feedback loop

Performance Element: Understand the Health Care Delivery System

    Measurement criterion: Construct a healthcare delivery system model

    Measurement criterion: Predict where and how factors such as cost, managed care, technology, an aging population, access to care, alternative therapies, and lifestyle/behavior changes may affect various health care delivery system models

    Measurement criterion: Project outcomes as interconnected components of a modified health care system

    Measurement criterion: Calculate the cost effectiveness of two separate health care delivery systems using the same client procedure

Performance Element: Describe Health Care Delivery System Results

    Measurement criterion: Diagram the interdependence of health care professions within a given health care delivery system and pertaining to the delivery of quality health care

    Measurement criterion: Design a system analysis process that evaluates the following outcomes: client satisfaction, productivity, cost effectiveness, and efficiency

    Measurement criterion: Evaluate the impact of enhanced technology on the health care delivery system

Performance Element: Understand System Change

    Measurement criterion: Analyze the cause and effect on health care system change based on the influence of: technology, epidemiology, bio-ethics, socioeconomics, and various forms of complimentary (nontraditional) medicine

Figure 3-3. Cluster-Level Knowledge and Skills for Systems Within the Health Science cluster
(*Source:* http://www.careerclusters.org/ClusterDocuments/hldocuments/HLFinal.pdf)

At the **pathway** level, the database identifies several *pathway topics* for each pathway. For example, the pathway topics for the Therapeutic Services pathway in the Health Science cluster are as follow.

Client Interaction • Employ Intra Team Communication • Collect Information • Treatment Planning and Implementation • Monitor Client Status • Evaluate Patient Status

Each pathway topic is associated with a *pathway KS [knowledge and skills] statement*. Each of those statements is associated with one or more *performance elements,* each of which is associated with one or more *measurement criteria.*

The following figure provides the pathway knowledge and skill statement, performance elements, and measurement criteria for the pathway topic "Client Interaction" within the Therapeutic Services pathway within the Health Science cluster.

CLUSTER: HEALTH SCIENCE

PATHWAY: THERAPEUTIC SERVICES

Pathway Topic: Client Interaction

Pathway KS Statement: Therapeutic services professionals will be able to explain planned procedures to patients and health professionals including goals, side effects, and coping strategies. They will use various strategies to respond to questions and concerns of patients.

Performance Element: Use Oral Communication

    Measurement criterion: Assess patients' understanding of the information provided

    Measurement criterion: Demonstrate empathy for patients

    Measurement criterion: Modify communication to the needs of the patients and appropriate to the situation

Performance Element: Use Written Communication

    Measurement criterion: Develop clear written patient information and instructions

    Measurement criterion: Keep written records as appropriate

---

Figure 3-4. Pathway-Level Knowledge and Skills for the Therapeutic Services Pathway Within the Health Science Cluster (Source: http://www.careerclusters.org/ClusterDocuments/ hldocuments/HLFinal.pdf)

As the reader can see, the performance expectations in the Career Clusters approach to CTE are both thorough and broad. As a result, regardless of the cluster or pathway a student pursues, he or she is well prepared for a broad range of technical specialties and/or further education.

STEPS TO DESIGNING A CURRICULUM FRAMEWORK

Curriculum frameworks can be designed at the state level (resulting in models for local adoption and/or adaptation), the regional level (involving one college and multiple high schools), or the local level (involving one college and one high school). We strongly encourage coordination of development efforts at the state level. Not only will this coordination diminish duplication of effort, but having common curriculum frameworks within states can serve as a backbone for statewide articulation agreements.

To begin the process, the leadership will need to select a person or organization to facilitate, coordinate, and conduct the design process. Consider having cochairs—one secondary and one postsecondary—who would promote shared ownership and buy-in. Prior to commencement of the design process, a Career Pathways Advisory Committee consisting of representatives of all partnering institutions and relevant employers should be selected. (Details on the relationships within and goals for Career Pathways partnerships are discussed in Chapter 7.)

Although high school teachers and college faculty members may be able to contribute to the design of the framework, their greatest contribution will be in the development of courses after the framework has been completed.

Step 1: Outline the format for an "egg crate"
Recall from Chapter 1 that one of the components of a curriculum framework is a grade-9–14 course sequence, sometimes called an "egg crate." The following figure shows an empty egg crate, ready to be filled in.[2]

---

[2] While this egg crate reflects the beginning of a Career Pathway in the ninth grade, we recognize that there are many state, regional, and

	Grade	English	Mathematics	Science	Technology	Technology	Other
Foundation	9						
	10						
Technical Core	11						
	12						
Technical Specialty	13 1st Semester						
	13 2nd Semester						
	14 1st Semester						
	14 2nd Semester						

For the secondary level, determine the number of classes scheduled per day (or credits per year), then provide the same number of empty boxes per row in the egg crate. In the preceding example there are six boxes (class periods) per row (day). If the secondary schedule allows for *seven* credits per year, add another row in the egg crate.

At the postsecondary level, leave the number of boxes per row the same as the number per row at the secondary level. (This will probably accommodate more courses than would actually be offered, in which case some boxes will remain blank.)

Step 2: Insert the required courses in the egg crate
At the secondary level, identify the mathematics, science, English, social studies, and other courses required by the state for graduation. In mathematics and science, these may vary

---

local governance and school types that might require or allow for instruction to have a "starting point" other than the ninth grade. For the purposes of this chapter we have used the 9–14 model as a reference. We encourage you to adapt the model to your schedule, governance, and school type.

according to the field of study. For instance, a field of study such as engineering or health may require that additional or more advanced mathematics or science courses be included. The egg crate also provides space for you to note other courses that may be required for graduation. For example, CPR certification may be required for health careers or OSHA certification for the trades.

Examine the partner college's admission requirements in English, mathematics, and science. If the requirements exceed what students learn in feeder high school courses, adjust the high school courses accordingly or provide for whatever alternate high school courses are necessary to align secondary course content to postsecondary entrance requirements.

Insert the appropriate mathematics, science, social studies, and other general education courses (as required) into the appropriate boxes at the secondary level.

In the postsecondary portion of the egg crate, place the English (communication), mathematics, science, humanities, and other courses required to complete an associate degree.

Verify course selection with the appropriate departments and/or faculty members in the secondary and postsecondary institutions.

Step 3: Design and/or select ninth- and tenth-grade career-related courses

The purpose of the ninth- and tenth-grade portion of a Career Pathway is to provide the *foundation* for pursuing a career and to help the student confirm or reject his or her initial decision about a career field. The purpose is *not* to begin narrowing coursework to a particular career field. Ideally, the curriculum framework should identify a two-semester course in the ninth grade and a two-semester course in the tenth grade. In addition, in academic courses the chosen Career Pathway should be used as a context for teaching and learning.

The ninth and tenth grades are a critical time to engage students in their learning. Too often this is when students begin to lose focus and the highest rates of dropping out of school occur. Career Pathway instruction gives much-needed context and relevance to the student's academic coursework. It also provides opportunities to explore career options within the student's area of interest and to learn soft (employability) skills, job-seeking/job-keeping skills, and study skills. Following is a description of a typical ninth-grade course. (The course would be different for each career cluster.)

Personal Management for Career Success

This ninth-grade course helps students plan and prepare for careers. The course assumes that students have selected career fields prior to entering the ninth grade. Personal Management for Career Success provides a context for the program of study the students are beginning. It can be configured to cover one semester or one year. Through a variety of **activities**, **projects**, and **research**, students will

- Learn about **career resources** available to them at their local schools and in their communities.
- Research possible **career options** within the chosen career fields and confirm that these are the career areas they want to pursue.
- Identify **personal strengths and weaknesses**, learning styles, and career interests.
- Create **personalized education plans** that will map out the courses, certifications, and degrees needed to attain the careers of their choice.
- Learn **study skills** to help them throughout their studies.
- Learn and apply **soft skills** such as goal-setting, teamwork, and communication.
- Learn **job-seeking skills** such as interviewing and resume and job application preparation.
- Begin electronic or hardcopy **portfolios** on which they can build throughout their lifetimes to use in demonstrating their capabilities to potential employers.
- Learn **career-specific vocabulary**.
- Learn **job-keeping skills** such as time management, work ethics, standard operating procedures, and protocols.
- Research and prepare oral, written, and multimedia **presentations** using a variety of software applications.
- Participate in a variety of **worksite activities** such as field trips, case studies, simulations, presentations by invited speakers, and industry mentoring programs.

Technology is pervasive in all career fields. Therefore, it is recommended that the tenth-grade course enable students to effectively use computer software and Internet applications relevant to their career areas of interest. Specifically, the course should focus on applications such as the following:

- Advanced word processing
- PowerPoint presentations
- Spreadsheets
- Project management/scheduling
- Financial management
- Research using the Internet
- Computer data acquisition
- Use of platforms (course software) for e-learning

Although the *context* of a selected Career Pathway is used in these two (ninth- and tenth-grade) courses, the courses' content is broad enough to serve as a foundation for all clusters. If students change pathways after the tenth grade, they will still be prepared to begin the technical core of any pathway in the eleventh grade.

Step 4: Sort the required career courses into the technical core *and the* technical specialty *courses*

Technical core courses are those that are common to all Career Pathways within a given career cluster. To the extent possible, all secondary career courses offered in the eleventh and twelfth grades should be within the technical core.

In the Science, Technology, Engineering, and Mathematics Cluster, this can be accomplished relatively easily.[3] The technical core for the Engineering and Technology pathway will contain courses in topics such as electronics, digital systems, mechanical/fluid systems, and engineering graphics.

---

[3]For the pathway model for this cluster, see http://www.careerclusters.org/ClusterDocuments/scdocuments/ 1SCModel.pdf.

In the Transportation, Distribution, and Logistics cluster, the technical core is not as large or well defined (partly because the cluster comprises seven pathways).[4] For example, the Facility and Mobile Equipment Maintenance pathway (which encompasses career specialties in automotive service and bus and truck maintenance) would likely involve secondary specialty courses in topics such as electrical systems and front end/brakes, while the Sales and Service pathway would involve more business-oriented courses.

At least two one-semester courses from the technical core should be provided in each of the eleventh and twelfth grades.

Step 5: Complete the egg crate (provide course titles for the curriculum framework)
First, complete the grade-9–12 portion of the framework. Ensure that all required courses, the ninth- and tenth-grade career-related courses, and the technical core courses have been placed in the framework. Label the available vacancies (blank boxes) as "electives." Some electives may be required by the high school for fine arts courses, athletics, clubs, and so on. Others could be labeled "career electives."

Complete the postsecondary portion of the framework, using the required and technical courses necessary for completion of an associate degree. When completing both the secondary and the postsecondary portions of the framework, it is important to ensure seamless instruction across the two levels and to create opportunities for dual and concurrent enrollment and credit.

Step 6: Identify and develop appropriate standards
There are three major types of standards: academic standards, employability (or soft) skill standards, and business and industry skill standards. Standards have been published by numerous entities. States publish standards for courses offered in their public high schools, and national education

---

[4]For the pathway model for this cluster, see http://www.careerclusters.org/ClusterDocuments/trdocuments/ 1TRModel.pdf.

organizations have developed academic standards. The National Council of Teachers of Mathematics, for example, has developed math standards for K–12 while the American Mathematical Association of Two-Year Colleges (AMATYC) has created math standards for the postsecondary level. Employability standards include SCANS and the National Career Development Guidelines. Numerous business and industry standards developed at the national, state, and local levels reflect the technical and professional skills and knowledge required for employment in given fields. The database of the States' Career Clusters Initiative is a valuable source in which standards have been grouped and interpreted according to the U.S. Department of Education's sixteen career clusters.

Once all of the relevant standards have been identified and assembled, they should be reviewed, revised (as needed), and adapted to local conditions by an advisory committee comprising business and industry representatives and secondary and postsecondary educators. This might include aligning state standards to national standards, narrowing broad national skill standards to local industry needs, and similar processes.

Dealing with multiple sets of standards can be unwieldy; it might involve examining hundreds or even thousands of individual statements as to what people in various academic pursuits and occupations should know and be able to do. One way to manage large numbers of standards is to use *integrated curriculum standards* (ICS). [5]

[5]In 1998, 27 state CTE departments funded the development of a standards-integration system called the Integrated System for Workforce Education Curricula (ISWEC). This led to CORD's development of *Curriculum Integrator* (CI), a computer-based tool designed to facilitate the process of creating ICSs. CI is a database of national academic, employability, and business and industry standards that can be searched by key words to identify related standards. State and local standards can be added as needed. CI was funded by a consortium of the following states: Alabama, Alaska, Arkansas, Connecticut, Hawaii, Idaho, Kansas, Louisiana, Maine,

> **Integrated curriculum standard (ICS):** A standard of expectation for performance that reflects a synthesis of business/industry standards, academic standards, and employability standards around a specified topic. When taken collectively, ICSs provide the building blocks for curriculum development, assessment design, and evaluation.

An ICS is developed by identifying commonalities across all of the standard sets that are applicable to the curriculum. For each topic or activity, all standards that describe what a person should know and be able to do with respect to that topic or activity are integrated into a single statement of expectation. Those statements are then gathered by theme into *rubrics*, assessment instruments that show students what is expected of them and enable them to monitor their progress. Sample rubric themes include teamwork, communication, basic mathematics, technical writing, using reference materials, and safety. An example of an ICS can be found in Appendix 3.

As ICSs are completed, recommended assessment strategies for each should be developed. Assessment can take any of several forms: examination of notes taken during class and through outside research; student analysis of case studies, scenarios, and simulations; student-developed charts and graphs; student-teacher conferences; extended paper-and-pencil tests; journal entries; narrative writing; on-demand demonstrations; portfolios; student projects; rubrics; structured observations; and videotaping and photography.

An example rubric for the teamwork ICS can be also found in Appendix 3.

Step 7. Map standards to courses
Once a complete list of standards has been developed, whether they are ICSs or standards taken directly from their original

---

Michigan, Minnesota, Montana, Nebraska, New Mexico, North Carolina, Ohio, Oklahoma, Pennsylvania, South Carolina, South Dakota, Tennessee, Texas, Utah, Vermont, Washington, West Virginia, and Wyoming.

sources, it must be determined where they are best addressed within the curriculum framework. Some standards might be addressed in only one course. Standards introduced in a given course might be reinforced in one or more subsequent courses as students build proficiency. It should not be assumed that only academic courses will address academic standards and that only CTE courses will address employability or business and industry standards. Indeed, one of the benefits of ICSs is that they break down preconceived barriers between disciplines (Figure 3-5).

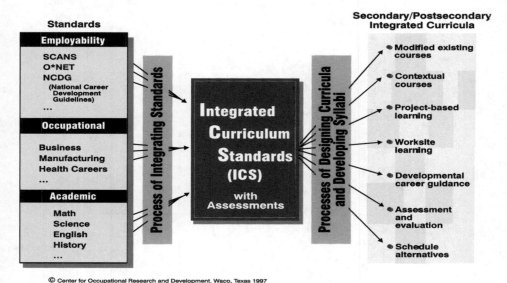

© Center for Occupational Research and Development, Waco, Texas 1997

Figure 3-5. *Curriculum Integrator: Processes for Building Integrated Curricula*

WHAT A COMPLETED EGG CRATE LOOKS LIKE

Following is a sample course sequence for a program in International Marketing.

Figure 3-6. Associate in Arts Degree Articulating to a Bachelor of Business Administration Degree

This curriculum framework is based on articulated programs from Indian River Community College and Florida's State University System to partner with local high schools in IRCC service area.#

		Language Arts	Mathematics	Science	Social Sciences/ Humanities	Health/PE and Cluster	Cluster and Career Major
Postsecondary—BBA	16th Grade 2nd Sem		Business Specialty	Business Specialty	Business Specialty	Global Strategy and Policy	Marketing Management
	16th Grade 1st Sem		Business Elective	Business Specialty	Operations Management	Quantitative Methods in Admin	Principles of Financial Mgt
	15th Grade 2nd Sem	Business Communication	Foreign Language or Free Elective		Business Specialty	Business Law	Intro to Mgt and Org Behavior
	15th Grade 1st Sem	Writing for Management	Foreign Language or Free Elective		Business Elective	Money & Banking or Urban Regional Econ	Management Info Systems
Postsecondary—AA	14th Grade Summer						Managerial Accounting
	14th Grade 2nd Sem		Elementary Statistics	Microeconomics	History	Humanities Elective	Financial Accounting II
	14th Grade 1st Sem		Business Calculus	Macroeconomics	History	Humanities Elective	Financial Accounting I
	13th Grade 2nd Sem	English Comp II	College Algebra	Natural Science		Principles of Management[2]	Computer Apps for Business[2]
	13th Grade 1st Sem	English Comp I[2]	Intermediate College Algebra	Natural Science		Business Elective	Introduction to Business[2]

		Language Arts	Mathematics	Science	Social Sciences/ Humanities	Health/PE and Cluster	Cluster and Career Major
Secondary	12th Grade	Business English or English IV[1]	Algebra II[1]	Free Elective[1]	Elective—For. Language or Humanities or Social Science[1]	Computer Applications for Business[1]	Principles of Management[1]
	11th Grade	English III	Geometry/ Contextual Math	Contextual Lab Science	Elective—For. Lang. or Social Sci or Humanities	IT Applications for Business[1]	Introduction to Business[1]
	10th Grade	English II	Algebra/ Contextual Math	Physics/Chem/ Contextual Sci	World History/ Government	Health/PE	Business Elective
	9th Grade	English I/ Contextual Communication	Prealgebra/ Contextual Math	Bio./Contextual Bio./ Chemistry	U.S. History	Basic Computer Usage	Personal Mgt. for Career Success

#The BBA in business management is but one of several specialties from which students can choose. Others include Accounting, Finance, and other Business/Management degrees.

[1]All courses have the potential to be dual-credit in the eleventh- and twelfth-grade years.

[2]If these courses were taken as dual-credit, a course from the next semester may be substituted.

FROM CURRICULUM FRAMEWORKS TO CURRICULA: COURSE DEVELOPMENT

Once the curriculum framework has been completed, the standards to be covered in each course identified, and the assessment strategy formulated, curriculum development can proceed.

If a course that the framework calls for already exists, determine whether all of the standards that have been mapped to the course are in fact taught or reinforced in the course. If not, look for places where the appropriate content can be added. Conversely, check to see whether the course includes content that is not supported by the standards. If so, try to determine why the content is being taught. If the only answer seems to be, "It's always been taught that way," consider deleting the content.

In situations in which new standards are to be introduced into existing courses, the new standards often address soft skills such as teamwork. In many cases, these are most effectively addressed not by *what* is taught but by *how* it is taught. While simply telling students to form collaborative groups will not make them proficient in teamwork skills, activities can be structured in such a way that students will learn to work well in teams.

To develop new courses, organize the standards in a logical sequence and develop teaching and learning experiences that will lead students to achieve the standards. Then create a content outline that encompasses the standards and the knowledge or skills they require. Finally, break the content into units.

For each unit, determine specific learning objectives. List activities and/or experiences that address the objectives (the more the better). Keep in mind differences in student learning styles and the availability of resources. The curriculum should equip teachers to explore topics in different contexts (personal, societal, or occupational). For example, a chemistry teacher should be able to discuss pH with respect to nutrient availability in soils (agriculture), digestion (health), acid rain (natural resources), and other contexts. Try to list multiple activities and contexts so that activities can be switched out if necessary. For instance, a guest speaker might be available to cover a given topic one year but not the next. The teacher should be able to present the same topic by showing a video, having the students conduct online research and prepare their own presentations, or some other means.

Finally, prepare individual lesson plans. (This is the work of the teachers.) Include assessment strategies for each lesson. These assessments should align with the assessments identified for the standards.

Course planning should be a *team process* involving teachers from all curriculum areas. As teachers work out the details of their individual syllabi, they should be encouraged to interact with teachers of other subjects and look for opportunities to integrate subject matter. (Additional information on teaching to standards, integration of subject matter, and assessments is presented in Chapter 5.)

CURRICULUM FRAMEWORKS DRIVE ALL ELEMENTS OF CAREER PATHWAYS

Designing and developing curricula for Career Pathways is hard, tedious work that requires expertise and cooperation from curriculum specialists, content specialists, employers, and secondary and postsecondary administrators and teachers. But the effort is worth it, because new curriculum frameworks are the vital *plans* that determine how all the other elements of the teaching and learning process come together. Curriculum frameworks determine:

- Structure—how we engage students early in career planning *without tracking*
- Engagement—how we keep students interested in school
- Expectations and achievement—how we ensure that students are effectively taught what they need to learn, and are taught to a sufficiently high level
- Guidance—how and when students and parents can understand and knowledgably consider career options

- Assessment — how we measure student progress and the effectiveness of the educational process

- Workforce competitiveness — how we ensure that employers are equipped with the workers they need and that communities have workers (at all levels) who can drive economic development

- Articulation/dual credit — an efficient, encouraging, student transition from secondary to postsecondary education

MOVING FROM NATIONAL STANDARDS AND CAREER PATHWAY STRUCTURES TO STATE CURRICULUM MODELS AND LOCAL ADAPTATION/ADOPTION

In this chapter we have attempted to show the importance and structure of Career Pathway curriculum frameworks as well as how they are created. Our hope is that this information can be used for creating state Career Pathway models that can be adapted for use by local and regional partnerships within states. The following recommended procedures could save state and local curriculum designers and developers hundreds of hours and ensure some degree of uniformity across the states and the nation, while preserving local autonomy and customization.

At the state level

1. Select the Career Pathways within a career cluster and identify career specialties that will be contained within each pathway.
The States' Career Clusters Initiative, working with national representation of employers and labor, has maintained this work at the national level for all sixteen clusters. Refer again to Figure 3-2, an abbreviated version of the pathway model for

the Health Science cluster.[1] The model identifies five Career Pathways (Therapeutic Services, Diagnostic Services, Health Informatics, Support Services, and Biotechnology Research and Development). For each pathway the model lists a broad range of career specialties for which education and training in that pathway prepare the student. (The remarks that follow use the Health Science cluster merely as an example. The process described is applicable to any cluster.)

Employers serving on a statewide Health Science Advisory Committee would examine the pathway model excerpted in Figure 3-2, along with the corresponding database. They would then confirm that the five pathways identified in the model (along with their associated career specialties) are appropriate for their state, or they would develop a revised pathway model that is better suited to their state's workforce development needs.

2. Select the knowledge and skills appropriate for each Career Pathway. The employers on the statewide Health Science Advisory Committee (or a subcommittee for a particular pathway) would examine the knowledge and skill statements (i.e., the foundation standards, performance elements, pathway knowledge and skill statements, and measurement criteria; see Figures 3-3 and 3-4) and either accept them as is or develop new statements that are better suited to their situation. This process would be duplicated for each Career Pathway within the cluster.

Throughout this process, the committee's work would be greatly facilitated by beginning with the database from the States' Career Clusters Initiative. Furthermore, the statewide committee will begin its work from an up-to-date, nationally validated list. Accurate and reliable nationally validated skill standards as well as up-to-date knowledge and skill statements are the backbone of quality curriculum and instruction.

---

[1] For the complete pathway model, see http://www.careerclusters.org/ClusterDocuments/hldocuments/HLFinal.pdf.

3. Follow the seven steps to designing a Career Pathways curriculum framework as described earlier in this chapter. The result will be the State Model for the Career Pathway.

At the local level

1. Using a pathway committee (see Chapter 7), review the Career Pathways specialties listed. Determine which specialties will be served within the service area of the partnership.

2. The committee will also review the knowledge and skill listing provided in the state model. Should gaps be identified, the committee will customize the knowledge and skill statements for the pathway and seek state approval.

3. The committee will review and modify the curriculum framework provided in the state model, considering changes in the required knowledge and skills and special requirements of the partnering schools and colleges. State approval for changes will likely be required.

This recommended practice of (1) establishing a national database of clusters, pathways, and validated knowledge and skills; (2) adapting the States' Career Clusters Initiative database to state standards and employment needs; (3) creating statewide models of Career Pathways; and (4) adapting the state models to local needs can result in Career Pathway partnerships that are responsive to workforce needs while providing *purposeful education programs* with transportable credentials.

The authors wish to express their gratitude to Bonnie Rinard, Research Associate, CORD; Kristin Zastoupil, Public Relations and Marketing Associate, CORD; and Frank Jennings, Chief Operating Officer, CORD, for their assistance in the writing of this chapter.

Chapter 4 Preview

Tech Prep funding at the federal level was no accident. It appeared in the 1990 Perkins reauthorization as part of a deliberate effort to provide equal educational opportunities for all students. In addition to the Tech Prep Act, the 1990 Perkins Act initiated standards-based school reform in federal policy by integrating CTE and academic education, moving CTE away from narrow job training, and placing more emphasis on postsecondary transitions. Tech Prep was the vehicle for demonstrating the positive impact of the reform through innovative models. Federal funding to create Career Pathways in this year's anticipated reauthorization of Perkins is a deliberate effort to extend the work of Tech Prep.

This chapter briefly traces the history of CTE in federal policy, highlighting the milestones that have led to the current effort to create equal educational opportunities for all students — an effort that is culminating in Career Pathways.

States also have the opportunity to participate in and reinforce this effort. New York's new CTE initiative provides an excellent model.

But, as the authors point out, the changes that really matter are those that are enacted at the local level, as schools, colleges, and employers across the country partner to improve education and career opportunities for America's young people. An understanding of the trends outlined in this chapter will greatly benefit Career Pathway partnerships as they move forward in meeting the benchmarks for excellence.

D.H.

ALIGNING CAREER PATHWAYS WITH FEDERAL AND STATE POLICIES AND STANDARDS

Hans Meeder and Jean C. Stevens

INTRODUCTION

In thinking about the future of career and technical education (CTE), Tech Prep, and Career Pathways, we must carefully consider the complex interaction among federal policy, state policy, and local practice. Federal policy can either drive change or protect the status quo. State leaders can take federal policy further than the letter of the law requires, or they can take a minimalist approach. But regardless of what happens at the national and state levels, it is ultimately up to *local* leaders to build high-quality programs. And to do that, they must be thoroughly familiar with federal and state policy.

In this chapter, we discuss the issue of alignment of Career Pathways with federal and state policies and standards. We approach the topic from five perspectives, each covered in a separate section. First, we look at certain flawed assumptions that strongly impacted the American high school experience during the 20th century. Next, we provide an overview of the "modern" era of school reform that commenced with the *Nation at Risk* report (1983). That period, which continues to the present, witnessed significant reforms of the Perkins Act during the 1990s and the passing of the No Child Left Behind Act in 2001. Third, we review how state-level policy in New York is providing a highly promising model for integrating academic and CTE content, and in so doing is raising academic expectations for all students and ratcheting up the quality of CTE programs. Fourth, we discuss the significance of the current status of the reauthorization of the Perkins Act. And finally, we describe the implications of the current CTE environment for practitioners who will implement Career Pathways at the state and local levels.

CTE AND THE FLAWED ASSUMPTIONS OF 20TH-CENTURY EDUCATIONAL PHILOSOPHY

The Flawed Assumption of Fixed Ability

CTE (called "manual education" and "vocational education" in its previous forms) has been shaped and supported by federal policy longer than any other program in American public schools. "Manual education" was introduced in the 1880s with the opening of the Baltimore School for the Manual Arts. A few years later proponents of the Progressive Education movement "argued that bookish curriculum blocked social progress and that it was unfitted to the hordes of immigrant children crowding into the urban schools."[1] Many reformers suggested that it was unrealistic and possibly socially dangerous to offer an academic curriculum to all students, since only a small number would need it for college. In 1914, a national commission on vocational education was established, and,

---

[1] Ravitch, Diane, *Left Back: A Century of Battles Over School Reform* (New York: Touchstone Books, Simon and Schuster, 2000).

three years later, the Smith-Hughes Act of 1917 codified the growing interest in vocational training. Smith-Hughes directly supported the expansion of vocational education within the states by providing direct subsidies for hiring and paying teachers and for training vocational teachers.

In 1918, the Commission on the Reorganization of Secondary Education released the seven Cardinal Principles of Secondary Education. The commission stated that high school had many social purposes, of which acquisition of academic skills was only one. The core idea was that high schools should provide different curricula for different groups of students, depending on differences in goals, attitudes, and abilities.

The years following World War I saw the emergence of the Intelligence Testing movement, which was based on the flawed belief that intelligence is fixed, innate, and strongly correlated to race and ethnicity. The Prosser Resolution of 1945 took a similar view. It stated that schools should prepare 20 percent of young people for college and 20 percent for skilled occupations; the remaining 60 percent should receive "life adjustment education" to prepare them for low-skilled work or homemaking responsibilities.

The launch of the Sputnik satellite in 1958 caused great concern about the need for mathematicians and scientists, but did not cause people to question the prevailing belief that one of the main purposes of high schools is to *sort* students by intelligence and aptitude. In a widely hailed report titled "The American High School Today" (1959), James B. Conant claimed that only 15 percent of high school students had the mental ability to take rigorous courses in mathematics, science, and foreign language. He felt that perhaps another 10 to 20 percent might stretch to take academic programs as well. But the remaining 65 to 75 percent of students should learn job skills.

The Progressive Education movement was also based on the presumption that intelligence and ability are innate and fixed. It assumed that many (if not most) students — especially African Americans, Asians, Hispanics, and eastern and southern Europeans — should take vocational or nonacademic "life adjustment" classes rather than pursue college. In the name of social order and democracy, the philosophy of

Progressive Education stated that young people should prepare for their destined station in life. It largely abandoned the ideal of education as a means of moving up the social ladder. This philosophy was not universally adopted among educators, administrators, and parents, but it had a significant impact on the culture of American education and on the structure of American high schools.

The Flawed Assumption of Social Stability and Slow Change

A second flawed assumption of 20th-century educational philosophy was that the society and economy for which we are preparing our young people are stable and that change is relatively slow. Neither is true. Since the 1970s, the U.S. economy and workplace have changed significantly and rapidly, calling for much higher levels of skills and knowledge than anticipated during the heyday of America's global industrial dominance. In a very short time, America has evolved from an industrial economy to a knowledge economy, even in the manufacturing sector. The globalization of business and industry requires workers to acquire transferable skills that can be applied — and quickly adapted — in a wide and rapidly changing variety of work settings. The impact of the changing complexion of the workplace is not limited to business and industry. It calls for sweeping changes in the way we educate our young people.

Implications of the Flawed Assumptions

Both of these assumptions negatively impact the lives of our young people. In effect, the first tells them that the purpose of school is to prepare one for his or her predetermined station in life. This assumption implicitly denies the power of education and shifts the focus of the educational enterprise from teaching and learning to social guidance and control. During the last thirty years, we have seen aggressive educational policies lift entire nations out of abject poverty. We also have accumulated massive evidence here in the United States that schools can profoundly improve the life trajectories of students. Further, rapid advances in our knowledge of human genetics have debunked racial and ethnic stereotypes of innate intelligence. Federal legislation, as we shall see, is now built on the presumption that all students *can* learn and that schools *can* make a difference.

The negative impact of the second flawed assumption is that students go through school oblivious to the fierce competitiveness of the adult world they are about to enter. And when the time comes for them to compete in the global marketplace, they are not ready.

Both of these assumptions largely prevailed until dismay with educational outcomes was given voice by the National Commission on Excellence in Education through the *Nation at Risk* report in 1983. Federal legislation since the 1980s has been built upon the premise that all students need transferable academic skills, and that all students need a broad introduction to careers rather than basic job preparation.

STANDARDS-BASED SCHOOL REFORM AND FEDERAL POLICY FOR CTE

In this section we discuss some of the "nuts and bolts" of federal legislation during the last fifteen years. To be effective proponents and developers of Career Pathways partnerships, educators need an accurate overall sense of what has taken place at the federal level since around 1990.

The 1990 reauthorization bill (Carl D. Perkins Vocational and Applied Technology Education Act of 1990) embraced the recommendation of *A Nation at Risk* that all American youths gain a strong foundation in academic skills. The 1990 Perkins Act also responded to significant changes in American corporate life, namely, that, during the 1980s layers of middle management were removed from American business and front-line workers were given increased responsibility and decision-making authority in the areas of quality control and productivity. These new responsibilities demanded a broader mix of knowledge and skills than those possessed by workers

89

narrowly trained to carry out repetitive, job-specific tasks. The 1990 Perkins Act called for (1) integrating CTE and academic education so that each student would gain strong basic and advanced academic skills in a career setting and (2) moving CTE away from narrow job preparation to broad exposure to "all aspects of the industry."

Another important innovation of the 1990 Perkins Act was the creation of the Tech Prep Act, which authorized $125 million nationwide to fund academically and technically rigorous courses offered through agreements between secondary schools and community colleges. The Tech Prep Title provided planning and demonstration grants intended to help consortia of local educational agencies and postsecondary education institutions develop and operate four-year (2+2) Tech Prep programs leading to associate degrees and/or certificates. Further, Tech Prep was designed to help create strong systemwide links between schools, colleges, and employers.

An important next phase in education reform began when, in 1989, President George H.W. Bush convened the nation's governors in Charlottesville, Virginia, to adopt nine ambitious national education goals. In 1994, President Bill Clinton (who, as governor of Arkansas, had led the development of the national education goals) signed into law the Goals 2000: Educate America Act (P.L. 103-227). The act was designed to help states establish academic standards and assessments as well as broad school improvement plans. The act also provided funding to continue the development of model academic standards by an array of national organizations representing core academic disciplines.

Another key piece of legislation from 1994 was the School-to-Work Opportunities Act. Administered jointly by the U.S. Department of Education and the U.S. Department of Labor, that program was designed to help states create school- and employer-based internships and work-based learning opportunities in which students could see the close connection between their school experience and future career opportunities.

The Improving America's Schools Act (IASA, also 1994) added to the impetus for building school systems around agreed-to education standards. IASA required states to develop challenging content and performance standards in at least mathematics and language arts and establish high-quality assessments that measure student performance on the standards. The standards and assessments were required once for grades 3–5, once for grades 6–8, and once for grades 10–12. While the standards and assessments applied to all students, specific provisions for accountability, public reporting, and school restructuring applied only to high-poverty schools that received federal Title I funds.

In 1998, Congress reauthorized the Perkins Vocational and Technical Education Act. The 1998 law emphasized the importance of academics and strong connections between secondary and postsecondary education, driving more money to the classroom. Most notably, a new accountability system was established to measure outcomes in academic and technical skill acquisition, program completion, advancement to further education and training and the workplace, and success in serving students from nontraditional backgrounds. Under the plan, each state has the authority to devise performance indicators for each performance measure. Each state negotiates performance targets with the U.S. Department of Education and is accountable for meeting the targets.

In implementing the 1998 act, each state worked in consultation with the U.S. Department of Education to create an accountability system for assessing progress in improving CTE student outcomes. However, the measures of student achievement and graduation rates for CTE are not necessarily aligned with the general school performance accountability system used within each state, nor are the performance measures comparable across the states. Thus, since each state has broad authority to develop its own performance measures, and federal authority is quite limited, it is difficult to measure how much impact the federal accountability requirements have really had on the performance of state CTE systems.

President George W. Bush called for a major reform of the Elementary and Secondary Education Act through No Child

Left Behind (NCLB, 2001). That bill calls for each state to create an accountability system to report on student performance, not just as a whole, but disaggregated by race, socioeconomic level, English proficiency, and disability. Further, every school, regardless of whether it receives federal funds, must report on student performance and set annual targets for student progress in each school. The envisioned end result is that, by the school year 2013–2014, every student will reach a specified level of proficiency in reading and language arts and mathematics. NCLB requires that schools administer at least one assessment in reading and language arts and one in mathematics to students during grades 10–12, and that schools set targets for moving all students to proficiency in those subject areas. While this requirement does not create an intensive accountability environment in high schools, it promotes academic rigor in high schools. NCLB already appears to have spurred efforts to ensure that all students reach minimum levels of academic proficiency. Many states are imposing additional requirements, such as end-of-course exams, high-stakes exams, and increases in numbers and kinds of courses required for high school graduation.

The general concern expressed by some CTE leaders is that, on the whole, NCLB's emphasis on academics might divert attention and resources away from CTE. Educators in fine arts and the social sciences have expressed parallel concerns.

As 2005 draws to a close, our nation faces important decisions about the future direction of our education policy. What can we do to ensure that our students — *all* of our students — graduate high school; are well prepared for college, work, and citizenship; and can make near-seamless transitions to the next levels of education and/or training? The debate is far from settled. Whether we can find the right answers will depend to a large extent on the willingness of proponents of Career Pathways and Tech Prep to step forward and make their voices heard.

A PROMISING NEW STATE-LEVEL INITIATIVE IN NEW YORK

As the preceding historical overview shows, federal policy has had a great influence on state policy. Still, states' have considerable autonomy in crafting their education policy. In this section we show how a new CTE initiative in New York is providing a model for ensuring that CTE continues to be a strong force in the educational enterprise far into the future. As the reader will see, one reason for the new program's success is that it aligns well with federal policy and has in place mechanisms for ensuring that it can meet the stringent accountability requirements of future legislation.

New York's Tradition of High Standards

The state's new CTE initiative builds on a long tradition of emphasis on high educational standards. Especially in the last two decades, New York has undertaken several initiatives designed specifically to raise standards in the education of its young people.

- The 1983 *A Nation at Risk* report prompted the state's board of regents (BOR) and then Commissioner of Education Gordon Ambach to take a serious look at education standards, policies, and graduation requirements. During the 1980s, the BOR undertook the Regents Action Plan, a statewide initiative in which regional forums of key stakeholders focused on increasing academic and assessment requirements for all students.

- In March 1991 the BOR approved an initiative called *A New Compact for Learning.* Led by a state curriculum and assessment council, seven curriculum and assessment committees developed 28 learning standards and performance indicators in seven content areas and provided recommendation on resource guides and core curriculum and assessment.

- The year 1995 saw the initiation of the Schools Under Registration Review process (SURR). Under SURR, the

New York State Education Department (NYSED) identified substandard schools. Those that failed after three years were given the opportunity to be redesigned or were closed by the state. This process continues today and is clearly well aligned to the NCLB.

- In 1996, the BOR approved the New York State Learning Standards and passed regulations that would phase-in the Regents examination requirements for all students, thus eliminating the general track. In December 1997, the BOR approved a proposal to raise graduation requirements to 22 credits and require the eventual passage of five Regents examinations. The proposal also established a safety net for students with disabilities.

- In 1998, the Regents Task Force on Closing the Performance Gap was formed to develop strategies for raising the performance of historically low-performing students, thereby "closing the gap" between high and low achievers.

Integration of CTE and Core Academics Through the State's New CTE Initiative

The Proposal of the National Advisory Panel on CTE

During much of the 20th century, CTE programs and academic programs coexisted peacefully within the comprehensive American high school. But education reforms of the past 20 years, particularly advanced reforms like those in New York, have led to difficult questions about the role of CTE in academic reform. As academic and graduation requirements increase, students are able to devote less time to courses other than core academics. Where, then, does CTE fit into the big picture of education reform today?

To meet this question head-on, in fall 1999 the BOR formed the National Advisory Panel on Career and Technical Education, which comprised experts (both researchers and teachers) in integrating academic and technical instruction; experts in assessment; representatives of business and labor; representatives of higher education; and other interested persons such as administrators and counselors. A series of Focus Forums was also held across the state. The National Advisory Panel and the Focus Forums were charged with developing recommendations on integration of academic and CTE content, assessment, and diploma options for CTE students. The deliberations of the National Advisory Panel and Focus Forums (1999–2000) culminated in a proposal for the certification and recertification of CTE programs in New York. Following were the key elements of the proposal:

- Certification and recertification of CTE programs would be based on criteria established by NYSED.

- Schools would be given flexibility in the delivery of core academic courses.

- Each program would include a technical assessment component based on industry standards.

- Each program graduate would receive a technical endorsement on a Regents diploma or on a Regents diploma with advanced designation.

The New York Office of Workforce Preparation and Continuing Education conducted seven regional CTE conferences throughout the state in October and November 2000. Each conference featured a keynote overview of the CTE proposal. Researchers from the Evaluation Consortium at the University of Albany attended the conferences and documented and analyzed over 500 written evaluations of the proposal. According to the evaluations, 90 percent of participants supported the proposal's recommendation for increased flexibility, 77 percent supported the proposed program approval process, 97 percent agreed with the proposal's recommendation for close collaboration between educators and business and industry representatives, and 82 percent wanted to implement the proposed work skills and employability profile.

Alternative proposals and/or suggestions for modifying the proposal were solicited from a wide range of stakeholders. In general, there was strong support for developing and maintaining high-quality CTE programs and allowing flexibility in content and delivery. The revised proposal included modifications that, in some cases, allow integrated and specialized courses to fulfill both academic core credit requirements and CTE sequence requirements. (Example: integrated science [3rd unit of credit] in Practical Nursing)

In February 2001, the final version of the proposal was submitted for approval by the BOR. Under the plan outlined in the final proposal, CTE students must meet the following requirements:

- Pass five required Regents examinations or approved alternatives

- Complete a minimum of 22 units of credit to graduate

- Complete a minimum of 14.5 units of credit to meet academic core course requirements

- Complete 3.5 units of credit through a sequence/electives

- Complete a maximum of one unit of credit in English, mathematics, science and economics and government through either a fully integrated program with documentation of academic core requirements, specialized CTE courses, or a combination of the two approaches

School districts and BOCES (Board of Cooperative Educational Services, i.e., regional CTE centers) began submitting program approval applications in July 2001. As of August 8, 2005, 26 local education agencies and 38 BOCES have submitted certification forms to NYSED requesting approval for CTE programs (Table 4-1).

Table 4-1. CTE Program Approvals in New York, 2001–2005

Career Area	Received	Approved
Arts/Humanities	70	60
Business/Information Systems	129	93
Health Services	96	81
Engineering/Technologies	352	322
Human and Public Services	176	163
Natural and Agricultural Sciences	58	58
Totals	**881**	**777**

Career and Technical Education Resource Center (CTERC)

Beginning in 2005, New York established a Career and Technical Education Resource Center (CTERC) to provide additional state-level support for CTE. The goal of the CTERC is to help CTE programs meet, exceed, and/or continually improve upon the performance standards set forth in Perkins and NCLB. The CTERC program focuses on two strategies: professional development and technical assistance (as required by both Perkins and NCLB). Activities carried out in conjunction with those strategies concentrate on the following:

- Educator awareness and use of the K–12 New York State CDOS Learning Standards
- Integration of academic and CTE content
- Awareness and implementation of the CTE Program Approval Process, the Career Plan, and High Schools That Work initiatives
- Collaboration with postsecondary institutions to create a smooth transition process
- Collaboration with teacher preparation programs to help future teachers understand curriculum integration and improve the overall quality of instruction
- Meeting, exceeding, and/or continually improving performance related to Perkins and NCLB standards
- Inclusion and performance of special populations (as defined under Perkins)
- Enrollment in gender nontraditional CTE programs

Evaluation of the New CTE Initiative

When New York's BOR adopted the state's new CTE program approval process, it asked for a multiyear evaluation to monitor the impact of the newly adopted policy. The first report was provided in December 2004. Following are some of the most positive findings of the evaluation:

- The new policy was favorably viewed as an opportunity to raise the quality of CTE programs.

- CTE programs were supervised and taught by experienced educators.
- Business and industry representatives figured prominently on CTE external review boards and took proactive roles in CTE programs.
- Well over half the respondents claimed that their professional staffs were New York State-certified in their program areas.
- The most sought-after professional development topics were on integrated course development, technology integration, and teaching diverse learners.
- CTE courses reflected research-based methods and commencement-level learning standards in both academic and technical content.
- Work-based partners were predominantly used to provide applied learning experiences for CTE students.
- Most CTE programs used national technical competency tests.
- Articulation agreements were clearly communicated to students.
- According to CTE teachers, students and their parents saw improvement in students' skills and were satisfied with the quality of CTE programs.
- Teachers claimed that CTE programs had met the needs of student population groups.
- Increases in CTE enrollment, particularly in the technology and healthcare fields, were similar to projected job trends for New York State.
- The majority of CTE program completers achieved technical skill proficiency, passed technical assessments, and were successfully placed.

The evaluation also pointed out areas that represented special challenges or in which improvement was needed. For example, many CTE programs had difficulty finding suitable industry-based technical assessments. The weakest component of many programs was work-based learning; this is an area in which program quality is largely dependent on local economies.

Findings from the evaluation suggest several directions in which to expand the state's CTE initiative, strengthen existing programs, and build local capacity.

1. Conduct follow-up studies of CTE graduates

2. Study enrollment and outcome patterns for additional CTE program cohort years

3. Perform in-depth analysis of nonparticipating school districts

4. Design and pilot the use of a quality CTE indicator system for local self-assessment and program improvement

Judging from first-year evaluation data, the state's new CTE initiative enjoyed several positive outcomes, as indicated by enrollment increases, academic and technical skills attainment, and stakeholder perception. The evaluation data also encourage the exploration of additional areas of inquiry, areas that will lead to better understanding of the impact of the CTE initiative at the local level.

The results of the second-year evaluation should position New York for a smooth transition to the new legislation, whatever its accountability requirements. Many of the provisions in both the House and Senate versions of the reauthorized legislation are already covered in the state's CTE program approval process.

It is anticipated that the new Perkins legislation will position New York to continue to strengthen the quality of its CTE programs, use data in an even more targeted fashion, make transitions from secondary to postsecondary education more seamless, and ensure that program graduates are well prepared for further education and/or entry into high-skill employment. The New York experience is showing that today's growing demand for talented, motivated, and well-educated people can be met with strong federal legislation, well implemented and supported by strong state policy.

THINKING THROUGH CHANGES TO THE PERKINS ACT

Performance Among CTE Students: The Good News and the Bad

Before reviewing changes to the Perkins Vocational and Technical Education Act, it would be useful to review some key indicators of the performance of CTE students.

While nearly every public school student takes at least one CTE course in high school, federal policy has focused on those 44 percent of students who concentrate their studies in CTE and complete the equivalent of three or more yearlong courses in specific occupational areas such as health, automotive technology, and business services. About 25 percent of public high school students earn three or more credits in a single occupational area, while the remaining 19 percent complete courses in multiple occupational areas.

For more than a decade, the United States has made improving the *academic* achievement of CTE concentrators and easing their access to postsecondary education national priorities.

> For more than a decade, the United States has made improving the *academic* achievement of CTE concentrators and easing their access to postsecondary education national priorities.

As mentioned earlier, the *Nation at Risk* report recommended that every high school student complete a core academic curriculum of four years of English and three years each of math, science, and social studies. These "new basics" were recommended not just for students who wanted to pursue postsecondary education after high school, but also for students who planned to enter the workforce. Between 1990 and 2000, the proportion of CTE students who completed the "new basics" more than doubled. In 1990, only 18 percent of CTE students completed the "new basics" core curriculum. By 2000, the percentage had jumped to 51. That is great news. Yet, two decades after *A Nation at Risk,* and one decade after we made improving the academic achievement of CTE students a priority, we find ourselves only halfway toward the goal of a meaningful high school curriculum for every student.

Another positive sign is that over the last decade, the performance of CTE students on the National Assessment of Educational Progress (NAEP) reading and math tests has improved. The average NAEP composite math score for twelfth-grade CTE students was 11 scale points higher in 2000 than in 1990, and their composite reading score was 8 scale points higher in 1998 than in 1994. These increases are noteworthy. Yet CTE students still lag behind their peers on the NAEP assessments. Only 9.5 percent demonstrated proficiency or advanced skills in math in 2000, and only 29 percent were proficient or advanced in reading in 1998. Two-thirds of our CTE students are still leaving high school without the math and reading skills they need.

Thanks to the work of members of the National Tech Prep Network and other CTE leaders, we are also offering students more CTE programs that provide clear pathways into postsecondary education. The Department of Education asked MPR Associates to examine the features of high school CTE course offerings and how they changed over the decade. To do this, MPR used high school course catalogs that were collected as part of the NAEP high school transcript studies in 1994 and 2000.

MPR found that, between the options offered at their home high schools and at area vocational centers, the average high school student had about 17 different CTE programs from which to choose in both 1994 and 2000.

In 1994, on average, only one of those programs provided opportunities for students to earn postsecondary credit. By 2000, students could select from an average of four programs that offered opportunities to earn postsecondary credit while still in high school.

About 60 percent of students in 2000 attended high schools that had articulation agreements with postsecondary institutions for at least one academic, CTE, or other elective course, up from 37 percent of students in 1994.

This is progress, but, as a nation, America remains far from offering young people the diverse array of choices they deserve. In 2000, 40 percent of high schools did not have even one articulation agreement with a postsecondary institution, and only about a quarter of CTE programs gave students an opportunity to earn college credit.

Federal policies that further promote academic preparation and smooth secondary-to-postsecondary transitions are certainly in order.

The U.S. Department of Education's Recommendations Regarding the Perkins Act

During 2003 and 2004, the Bush administration announced several proposals to replace Perkins with a new Secondary and Technical Education Act. The proposal announced in early 2005 — to eliminate Perkins and replace it with a broad block grant for high school improvement — was soundly rejected by Congress. Still, some elements of the earlier Bush administration proposals have been included in legislation under consideration by Congress. Key concepts thus far put forth by the Administration include the following:

- Widespread implementation of Career Pathways that include rigorous academic coursework offered in career contexts with tight linkages between secondary and postsecondary education

- Emphasis on rigorous academic coursework integrated with CTE

- More stringent accountability for local program providers

- Tighter linkages between state assessment measures and measures specified by NCLB

- Encouragement of programs that lead to baccalaureate degrees, not just associate degrees and certifications

- Programs offered on the basis of their relevance to the labor market and economic development

Congressional Action on the Perkins Act

During 2004, the House and Senate both introduced and took action on legislation to reauthorize Perkins. Both bills adopted some concepts from the Administration's recommendations, but neither fundamentally restructured the basic state grant program, as the Administration had recommended. The House and Senate bills were numbered H.R. 4496 and S. 2686, respectively. The legislation advanced only as far as the respective House and Senate education committees in 2004. Legislation introduced in 2005 was substantially similar to the 2004 bills; it is discussed in the following pages.

Highlights of the Anticipated Legislation
- Career Pathways
- Rigorous technical coursework
- Strategic accountability
- Tech Prep continued
- Common academic core

In 2005, in response to the administration's proposal to eliminate Perkins, Congress reintroduced H.R. 366 and S. 250 to reauthorize it. Although technically each bill is new legislation, lawmakers from each chamber began where they left off in the previous session of Congress. Both House and Senate bills were substantially similar to those acted upon during 2004.

At the time of this writing (late summer 2005), the fate of the final legislation is uncertain. On March 10, 2005, the Senate passed S. 250, the "Carl D. Perkins Career and Technical Education Improvement Act of 2005," by a unanimous vote of 99-0. And on May 4, 2005, the full House voted 416-9 to approve its Perkins reauthorization bill, H.R. 366, the "Vocational and Technical Education for the Future Act."

While there are significant differences between the House and Senate versions, there is also an emerging consensus about what the new law will look like. In some form, the forthcoming Perkins legislation will include the following components.

Career Pathways (model sequences of courses). Career Pathways are career-focused programs that include rigorous academic courses (in reading, language arts, mathematics, and

103

science). A well-crafted Career Pathway model that begins early in ninth grade can offer a full complement of academic courses and introduction to a broad career cluster. By the eleventh and twelfth grades, a student who is ready academically can begin taking dual enrollment courses or advanced-credit AP-style courses in both academic and technical areas.

Under both the House and Senate versions of the legislation, every local grantee, whether a high school or a postsecondary provider, will be required to offer at least one Career Pathway to its students. And the state will have an oversight responsibility, ensuring consistency, transferability, and portability from one Career Pathway to another.

More rigorous technical coursework. Both the House and Senate bills make reference to industry-recognized credentials and jobs that are in demand in the marketplace. Every state will develop mechanisms, in coordination with the U.S. Department of Education, to ensure that programs are up to date and offer the most rigorous technical skills possible.

Stronger accountability for results at the state and local levels. Every local program will set performance targets using the performance measures identified by the state. Local programs will be held accountable for how well they meet their performance targets. Our students don't just need access to CTE programs, they deserve access to *high-quality* CTE programs.

Tech Prep continuation. Under both the House and Senate bills, Tech Prep funding will be maintained in some form. Tech Prep will exist as either a protected funding stream within the larger state grant program or a separate section in title I of Perkins.

Common academic core. Congress is unlikely to specify any number or type of academic courses in which CTE students must participate, but the legislation may include subtle markers that give greater definition to terms such as "rigorous and challenging academics," which is found through the proposed reauthorizations. Several states, including those that are part of Achieve Inc.'s American Diploma Project Network, are taking action to create a recommended set of core academic courses that includes what was once considered a "college prep" curriculum: algebra I, geometry, algebra II, physics, chemistry, biology, two credits of foreign language, and three and a half credits of the social sciences. In many of these states, students are still given the opportunity (or required) to earn four full years of credit in career-oriented classes.

IMPLICATIONS FOR STATE AND LOCAL EDUCATORS

While far from perfect, the United States' commitment to education contributed to its competitiveness throughout the 20th century. The United States led the world in expanding access to education, beginning first by providing a secondary education to all young people, and then by opening the doors of postsecondary education to virtually everyone, not just the elite. But other nations have been emulating our example and are closing the gap. We may have the best-educated 55-to-64-year-olds in the world, but our education edge has eroded or disappeared among younger generations. We rank number one in the world in the percentage of 55-to-64-year-olds who have completed secondary and postsecondary education. Among 25-to-34-year-olds, however, we rank number eight in secondary completion and are tied with Japan at number three in postsecondary completion. The performance of our middle and high school students on international academic assessments is mediocre.

Clearly, we need a jumpstart to accelerate our progress and help us regain our competitive edge. Let us hope that Congress and CTE leaders (along with the Bush administration) will work closely together to reauthorize Perkins.

We have made progress in meeting the goals we set out to achieve more than a decade ago. CTE administrators and teachers have taken this work seriously. Programs in many communities look very different today than they did in 1990. CTE students are better prepared than they were ten years ago.

Unfortunately, however, we are still far from attaining our goals. After ten years of reform, most CTE students are still leaving high school without the solid academic preparation they need, and we are still not offering young people a diversity of quality CTE options that lead to further learning and good, high-demand jobs.

In 2005, as education leaders continue to reform high schools, CTE programs, and programs linking secondary and postsecondary education through Career Pathways, it is vitally important that we check our underlying assumptions about student capacity and the rate of change in the workplace. Are we giving our students transferable learning skills, or just training them for jobs that seem valuable at the moment but may be gone tomorrow?

> After ten years of reform, most CTE students are still leaving high school without the solid academic preparation they need, and we are still not offering young people a diversity of quality CTE options that lead to further learning and good, high-demand jobs.

In the context of raising academic expectations, developers and advocates of Career Pathways and Tech Prep should ask themselves two very important questions:

- Do policymakers clearly understand that high-quality Career Pathways adopt and endorse very rigorous academic content—the same content required for entrance into postsecondary education?

- Do policymakers understand that Career Pathways are a promising strategy to bring relevance to the school setting and help students succeed in more challenging academic content than they would be willing to undertake without the Career Pathway connection?

With the introduction of the Career Pathways concept, it is clear that Congress is seeking to transform all of CTE to provide rigorous academics in career contexts with programmatic connections to learning beyond high school. All of CTE will be transformed into something that looks like what Tech Prep was originally meant to be. Tech Prep has led the way and continues to do so.

But Tech Prep should not be, cannot be, isolated from the broader reforms of CTE. Tech Prep funding and implementation, in whatever form the new legislation requires, will have to be integrally connected to new requirements relating to Career Pathways and local accountability.

At the same time, states and local school districts are giving serious consideration to their concept of the American high school, considering how to ensure that *all* students graduate with a strong academic foundation, career awareness, and an understanding of their postsecondary options. As leaders review the purpose and mission of high schools, it is imperative that CTE leaders be involved in discussions about core curriculum and support a common core for all students. CTE leaders must insist on quality and rigor from all CTE programs. They must work hard to imbed state academic standards for reading and language arts into all CTE programs and, where possible, imbed mathematics and/or science standards. They should also develop model lesson plans for how teaching to the academic standards can be carried out.

We suggest that states also develop policies that require collaborative relationships between academic and CTE teachers. Only when everyone in the school is accountable for the performance of every student will teaching and learning begin to change substantially. And it will take stronger teacher-to-teacher collaboration to help make this happen.

Of course, success in implementing Career Pathways and the related transformation of American high schools and connections to postsecondary won't happen just through funding streams and federal regulations. Ultimately, education is about what happens in the classroom. Educators must create professional development networks—communities of learning.

This is an exciting, challenging time. Again, we are asking something of ourselves that no other nation has ever attempted, to prepare *every* child for success. Of course it's going to be difficult, but Americans can do it. We must do it, not only for the sake of our children and their personal success in this challenging, interconnected global economy, but for our shared success as a nation.

Chapter 5 Preview

It's no secret; the way to spell success in today's educational environment is to "improve student performance" in the academic areas of English, mathematics, and science. I prefer to add the phrase, "in useful academics."

In Chapter 1, I was particularly critical of the widespread practice of "teaching to the test." So, what are the alternatives?

In this chapter, a leading educational research scientist and a highly experienced state educational superintendent show how to identify state standards and offer four proven, research-based keys for improvement of student achievement:

1. *Communicate the standards.*

2. *Use research-based strategies to teach the standards.*

3. *Align curriculum horizontally and vertically.*

4. *Align curriculum and assessment.*

The chapter concludes with important strategies for effective, targeted teacher professional development in contextual teaching.

D.H.

IMPROVING STUDENT PERFORMANCE

Sandra H. Harwell and June St. Clair Atkinson

INTRODUCTION

Under No Child Left Behind (NCLB), states are required to develop rigorous academic standards for all students. States, districts, and schools must report on the extent to which their students meet those standards as demonstrated by performance on standardized assessments. The standards-based movement has caused a shift in the way educators reflect on student performance. Understanding that shift is essential to improving student performance. Career Pathways provide an excellent model for providing seamless education for all students and improving student performance in meeting rigorous academic standards.

Standards are broad statements of what students should know and be able to do by the time they complete public schooling. Typically, standards are the same for K–12, but some states have their own grade- and/or course-specific standards. Student performance indicators or benchmarks further define what constitutes success at each developmental level. Tables 5-1 and 5-2 present examples from the Florida Sunshine State Standards.

Table 5-1. Mathematics Standard A1 for Elementary Grades

Standard A1: The student understands the different ways numbers are represented and used in the real world.
Benchmark MA.A.1.2.1: The student names whole numbers combining 3-digit numeration (hundreds, tens, ones) and the use of number periods, such as ones, thousands, and millions and associates verbal names, written word names, and standard numerals with whole numbers, commonly used fractions, decimals, and percents.
Benchmark MA.A.1.2.2: The student understands the relative size of whole numbers, commonly used fractions, decimals, and percents.
Benchmark MA.A.1.2.3: The student understands concrete and symbolic representations of whole numbers, fractions, decimals, and percents in real-world situations.
Benchmark MA.A.1.2.4: The student understands that numbers can be represented in a variety of equivalent forms using whole numbers, decimals, fractions, and percents. (Also assesses A.1.2.1 and A.1.2.3)

Table 5-2. Mathematics Standard A1 for Middle School

Standard A1: The student understands the different ways numbers are represented and used in the real world.
Benchmark MA.A.1.3.1: The student associates verbal names, written word names, and standard numerals with integers, fractions, and decimals; numbers expressed as percents; numbers with exponents; numbers in scientific notation; radicals; absolute value; and ratios.
Benchmark MA.A.1.3.2: The student understands the relative size of integers, fractions, and decimals; numbers expressed as percents; numbers with exponents; numbers in scientific notation; radicals; absolute value; and ratios.
Benchmark MA.A.1.3.3: The student understands concrete and symbolic representations of rational numbers and irrational numbers in real-world situations. (Also assesses A.1.2.4 and D.2.3.1)
Benchmark MA.A.1.3.4: The student understands that numbers can be represented in a variety of equivalent forms, including integers, fractions, decimals, percents, scientific notation, exponents, radicals, and absolute value. (Also assesses A.1.3.1 and A.1.3.3)

The Standard A1 is the same for all levels; the benchmarks indicate the building blocks taught at each level for the same standard.

110

The major purposes of performance standards are to clarify for teachers, parents, and students what students are expected to learn and to determine how that learning is to be evaluated. Performance standards form a foundation for student evaluation, assessment, and instruction. They should reflect the skills necessary for student success at each new level of learning and help students navigate the complex problems they will face. Increasingly, standards must also require students to analyze information, solve problems, and make decisions.

> Career Pathways provide an excellent model for providing seamless education for all students and improving student performance in meeting rigorous academic standards.

In the past, many schools focused on raising student achievement to minimum levels of performance. Students were expected only to meet a preset minimum performance level in each course or content area. Students who performed at or above that preset level were considered "functionally literate." Today we have to think beyond that level. Given the challenges facing our nation's economy, we can no longer afford to be satisfied with minimum levels of performance. Educators must shift their focus from *minimal* standards to *rigorous* standards.

Minimal performance levels are assessed using *norm-referenced* assessments, which indicate how well students perform in comparison to their *peers*. But in today's high-stakes testing environment, *criterion-referenced* assessments are used to indicate how well students perform in meeting rigorous *standards*. To understand the difference between norm-referenced assessment and criterion-referenced assessment, think of a marathon. Each runner's time could be reported two ways:

- *Norm-referenced assessment*—Runners' times are reported based on where they placed in comparison with their peers: Runner A, with a time of 1 hour and 45 minutes, placed in the 99th percentile of the runners in the race. The average time of completion of the race for this group of runners was 2 hours and 10 minutes.

- *Criterion-referenced assessment* — Runners' times are reported based on how well they met the standard, which could be the current record for this particular race: Runner A completed the race in 1 hour and 45 minutes, 15 seconds slower than the current record for this race set in 2004. Now we know not only how fast the runner completed the race, but we also know how closely he or she approximated the standard for this race.

Criterion-referenced assessment has created a tremendous challenge for educators. Many need assistance in helping all students meet rigorous academic standards and in measuring student performance. For many educators, the shift from documenting that all students are functionally literate to measuring each student's success in mastering rigorous standards creates a high level of cognitive dissonance.

Once educators have begun to focus their attention on *level of mastery*, rather than minimal performance, we can begin a serious discussion of how to improve student performance in a standards-based, accountability culture.

Along with the requirement that student performance be measured against rigorous academic standards, states are required to document adequate yearly progress for each subgroup within their student populations. In other words, states must be able to demonstrate that *all* their students have met the standards. For teachers who believe that achievement stems from *ability* alone, and that only *some* students can be high achievers, this requirement only adds "fuel to the fire." But those teachers should consider the findings of empirical research. The belief that achievement is based entirely on ability is not

> Once educators have begun to focus their attention on *level of mastery*, rather than minimal performance, we can begin a serious discussion of how to improve student performance in a standards-based, accountability culture.

merely outdated; it has been largely disproved. Research has shown that, to a large extent, achievement results from *individual effort.*

To appreciate the remainder of this chapter, the reader must accept two premises: (1) Every educator is charged with the task of helping all students meet rigorous academic standards. (2) The most important factor in high-level student achievement is individual effort. Now that we've laid the groundwork, let's discuss the four keys to improving student performance.

> **Research has shown that, to a large extent, achievement results from individual effort.**

THE FOUR KEYS TO IMPROVING STUDENT PERFORMANCE

Key 1: Communicate the Standards

The first key to improving student performance is to make sure all educators in the system understand student performance expectations and know how to use the available assessment tools. Many states and national groups post their standards on the web. While doing so does not guarantee that teachers will get all the information they need, online access is a critical part of the communication process. Figure 5-1 is a sample page from the Florida DOE website. The page provides links to tools that can help teachers improve student performance on the Florida Comprehensive Assessment Test (FCAT).

> **The first key to improving student performance is to make sure all educators in the system understand student performance expectations and know how to use the available assessment tools.**

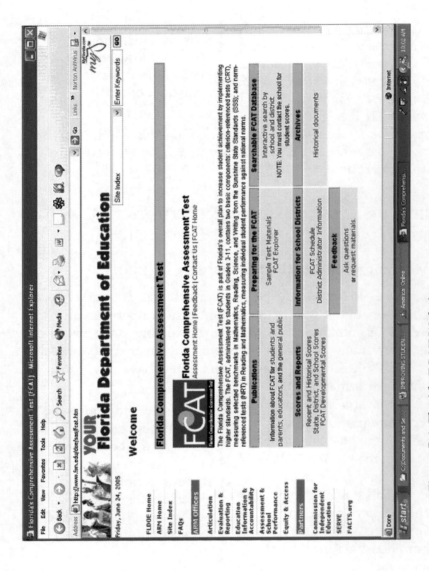

Figure 5-1. Florida FCAT Website
(Florida Department of Education, http://fcat.fldoe.org/)

States, districts, and schools must give classroom teachers opportunities to access tools that can help improve student performance.

Not only must teachers be able to access web-based tools and resources, they must know how to use them effectively. Classroom teachers, regardless of their fields, must develop an understanding of the performance standards that apply to all students. State standards are usually developed according to academic content, not by courses. Academic content areas are not the same as courses or classes. Not all standards are tested on high-stakes assessments. Teachers often misunderstand their role in teaching all standards. Geometry standards are taught in classes other than geometry including classes outside of mathematics. All teachers should teach writing standards, not just English teachers. Additionally, teachers are not always aware of the particular standards that are tested. A major key in helping educators understand and use standards is a sustained system of professional development. Later in this chapter the importance of professional development will be covered.

> Not only must teachers be able to access web-based tools and resources, they must know how to use them effectively.

Many states, districts, and schools are requiring all teachers to teach reading and writing across the curriculum. Many sites have required periods of sustained reading involving the entire school population. In spite of this, teachers continue to look at state standards as course-specific rather than content-specific. Teachers must begin to look at state standards with new eyes. If a teachable moment presents itself, it must be captured. If, for example, a student in an agriculture class is required to write a letter to a potential buyer of a steer, the agriculture teacher should use that teachable moment to teach the essentials of persuasive writing. In essence, the student's letter is a persuasive essay. The letter-

> A major key in helping educators understand and use standards is a sustained system of professional development.

writing assignment is a valuable opportunity for the student to learn that persuasive writing is *useful.*

Educators must understand that no single assessment can measure mastery of all the skills students will need in the future. A variety of assessments must be employed, and teachers must understand both the uses and limitations of assessment tools. Some assessment tools help identify areas in which students require intervention; others help to measure an educational system's effectiveness. Knowing which assessment to use is a critical factor in measuring student performance against academic standards. While meeting the requirements of federal legislation is important, we must also make sure that we know how to assess students on skills that are not effectively assessed by standardized tests. Again, professional development on the use of assessment tools is essential to improving student achievement.

Performance standards should be communicated not only to teachers but to students. There should be no secrets about what students are expected to learn or about how they will be assessed. Students' understanding of what is expected of them is fundamental to helping them achieve at higher levels. Students should be shown examples of high-quality work. They should also be given opportunities to practice articulating the standards they are expected to meet. That's a sure test of whether they really comprehend the standards.

> **Educators must understand that no single assessment can measure mastery of all the skills students will need in the future.**

Key 2: Use Research-Based Strategies to Teach the Standards

Marzano, Pickering, and Pollock's nine strategies — If educators really want *all* students to master rigorous academic standards, they must use instructional strategies that have been empirically documented to be effective. Marzano, Pickering, and Pollock describe empirical evidence for the effectiveness of nine teaching strategies, listed here in order of effectiveness:

- Identifying similarities and differences
- Summarizing and note-taking
- Reinforcing effort and providing recognition
- Homework and practice
- Nonlinguistic representations
- Cooperative learning
- Setting objectives and providing feedback
- Generating and testing hypotheses
- Questions, cues, and advance organizers[1]

These strategies are familiar to effective teachers. Effective teachers have long known intuitively that student learning improves when these strategies are used; now those teachers' intuition has been backed up by research.

Contextual teaching — Contextual teaching involves all nine of Marzano, Pickering, and Pollock's strategies but gives additional emphasis to building on prior knowledge and experience. CORD developed an acronym, REACT, for describing the five elements of contextual teaching.

- Relating (Learning in the context of life experiences)
- Experiencing (Learning in the context of exploration, discovery, and invention)
- Applying (Learning in the context of how the knowledge and information can be used)
- Cooperating (Learning in the context of sharing, responding, and communicating with other learners)
- Transferring (Using knowledge in a new context or novel situation — one that has not been covered in class)[2]

---

[1] R. Marzano, D. Pickering, and J. Pollock, *Classroom Instruction That Works: Research-Based Strategies for Increasing Student Achievement* (Alexandria, Virginia: Association for Supervision and Curriculum Development, 2001).

The more REACT elements included in a student activity, the more contextual the activity is. Contextual teaching allows students to create pathways for recall within the brain. More important, it allows them to move from learning through rote-memory to learning through understanding. With the current emphasis on standards and accountability, this is critical for student success. Students must learn through understanding of concepts rather than entirely through memorization of facts. For most of today's educators, this requires a shift in thinking. Figure 5-2 presents classroom strategies for ensuring that each REACT element is included.

> Contextual teaching allows students to create pathways for recall within the brain. More important, it allows them to move from learning through rote-memory to learning through understanding.

Element	Classroom Strategy
Relate	Teacher questions, first-person summaries, brainstorming, simulation/role-playing
Experience	Student demonstrations, guided practice, instructional technology, problem-based learning, project design, research, work-based learning, note-taking
Apply	Presentations, exhibits, student demonstrations, work-based learning, project-based learning
Cooperate	Project-based learning, exhibits, presentations, student demonstrations, problem-based learning, brainstorming
Transfer	Work-based learning, presentations, student demonstrations, problem-based learning, project-based learning, simulation/role-playing

Figure 5-2. Classroom Strategies for the REACT Elements (Contextual Teaching)

---

[2] D. Hull, *Opening Minds, Opening Doors: The Rebirth of American Education* (Waco, Texas: CORD Communications, 1993).

Key 3: Align Curriculum Horizontally and Vertically

Career Pathways provide the best possible means of aligning curriculum horizontally and vertically. The rigorous standards developed by many states provide a developmentally appropriate model for aligning benchmarks. State-level leaders must encourage districts and schools to use the model to align what is taught in each course, class, grade level, and integrated setting. By helping students recognize the importance of building on prior learning, teachers can "scaffold," or support, them through increasingly difficult applications, enabling students to transfer classroom learning to real-world problems, communicate effectively, and make decisions.

> By helping students recognize the importance of building on prior learning, teachers can "scaffold," or support, them through increasingly difficult applications, enabling students to transfer classroom learning to real-world problems, communicate effectively, and make decisions.

A good example of curriculum alignment is Tennessee's curriculum framework for manufacturing technology (Figure 5-3). The goal of the Tennessee State Department of Education in creating this pathway was to align secondary education, postsecondary education, and workforce requirements in a seamless, coherent pathway.

The College and Career Transitions Initiative (CCTI), through the League for Innovation in Community Colleges, used a similar framework to design the Career Pathways for partnerships selected as CCTI sites (Figure 5-4).

Grade	English	Mathematics	Science	Social Studies	Health, Computer and Elective	Cluster	
9	English I	Algebra I	Biology		Health/PE/Wellness	2 Career Management Success	Foundation
10	English II	Geometry		U.S. History	2 Programming Logic or other Computer Science	1 Engineering Design and CAD	Foundation
11	English III	Algebra II	Chemistry	World History		3 Principles of Machining and Manufacturing	Technical Core
12	English IV or Applied Communication	Optional: 4th Year of Mathematics	Applied Physics	½ unit each U.S. Gov. and Economics		Manufacturing Applications	Technical Core
13 1st Semester	English Composition	College Algebra and Trig.	1 Engineering Design	Orientation	2 Computer Applications in Manufacturing	3 Principles of Machining I	Technical Specialty
13 2nd Semester	Humanities Elective		Advanced CAD	Communication Elective	Technical Elective	Materials and Manufacturing Processes	Technical Specialty
14 1st Semester		Statistical Process and Quality Control	General Physics I	Principles of Economics	Electromechanical Devices	Technical Elective	Technical Specialty
14 2nd Semester		Metrology and Quality Control	Technical Elective	Tool Design	Technical Elective	Technical Elective	Technical Specialty

1, 2, 3: Secondary courses eligible for postsecondary (dual) credit, allowing early graduation or allowing opportunities for advanced technical electives

Figure 5-3. Course Sequence for Tennessee's Manufacturing Technology Curriculum Framework (developed by CORD for the Tennessee State Department of Education)

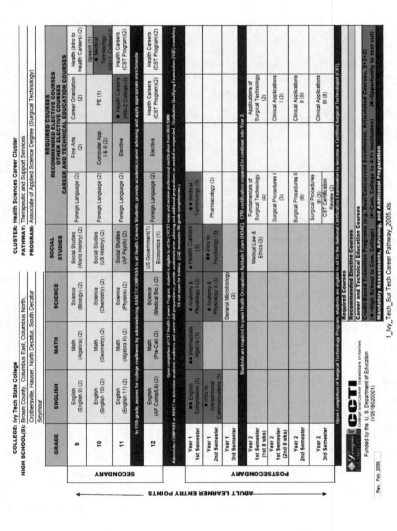

Figure 5-4. CCTI Ivy Tech State College Career Pathway

(College and Career Transitions Initiative, Ivy Tech State College Career Pathway;

http://www.league.org/league/projects/ccti/projects/files/ITSC_Career_Pathway_2005.pdf)

It is important to understand that these pathways are not simply sequences of courses. In both examples, the student performance standards for each named course have been aligned in a developmentally appropriate way by grade level and by course to create a seamless 4+2 program. These 4+2 programs of study are the essence of effective Tech Prep programs. Career Pathways, however, aim for alignment of standards beyond the first two years of postsecondary education. The resulting 4+2+2 programs (see the example in Chapter 3) provide seamless curriculum that give students maximum access to high-wage occupations with the flexibility to move from entry-level to management positions in any company.

Key 4: Align Curriculum and Assessment

To align "what is tested" with "what is taught," educators must have a clear understanding of student performance levels on different types of assessments. They must make sure they understand the overarching performance standards that all students are expected to meet and must reinforce those standards wherever appropriate. For example, at the high school level, it is important for ninth-grade teachers to know the high school graduation requirements as well as the content tested on high school graduation exams. Similarly, if end-of-course exams are given, all teachers should take an active role in helping prepare students for those exams.

Florida provides a good example: Florida students take the FCAT during the spring semester of the tenth grade as an exit test for high school. Students must score 2.5 or higher in mathematics and reading. Ninth-grade teachers need to understand what is tested so that students have sufficient opportunity to master the content tested on the tenth-grade FCAT. The tenth-grade FCAT results for one Florida district are presented in Table 5-3.

Table 5-3. FCAT Scores for One County in Florida

Test	Students Tested	Level 1	Level 2	Level 3	Level 4	Level 5	Level 3 and above
Reading	5137	46%	27%	14%	6%	8%	27%
Math	5124	21%	24%	26%	24%	6%	55%
		Mean Combined					
Writing	5195	3.7					

Source: (Florida Department of Education, http://fcat.fldoe.org/)

The students in this Florida county are functioning at lower levels in reading than in mathematics. If the goal is for students to perform at level 3 or above, even in mathematics, only 55 percent of the students are meeting the goal. Students functioning below level 3 will have difficulty at the next level after high school.

For teachers in this county, the implications are that more emphasis should be placed on reading and mathematics, especially reading. Keep in mind that these scores are for tenth graders. It might be safe to say that the ninth- and tenth-grade teachers should work to help students succeed at higher levels in reading. But what about eleventh- and twelfth-grade teachers? To put this into a context that demonstrates the need to align curriculum and instruction with assessment, see the Florida College Readiness Report for the same county. We are still looking at mathematics, reading, and writing, but we will see a shift in the picture when students leave high school and take the placement test for college-level coursework (Table 5-4).

**Table 5-4. College Readiness Report for
One District in Florida**

District	A
# Degree-seeking	817
# Tested in math	812
# Ready in math	334
% Ready in math	41.1%
# Tested in reading	809
# Ready in reading	465
% Ready in reading	57.5%
# Tested in writing	809
# Ready in writing	574
% Ready in writing	71.0%

Source: Florida State Department of Education,
http://www.firn.edu/doe/postsecondary/
reports02/COMMCOLLSUMMBYDIST/

Notice that 41.1 percent of the students tested college-ready in mathematics while 57.5 percent of the students tested college-ready in reading. What happened? While some educators will argue that these tests do not really predict college readiness, students still have to take them. So, what should public schools do?

Think about the kinds of things students are required to do during their eleventh- and twelfth-grade years. Most students will complete research papers during at least one of those years, and for most students the junior and senior years place heavy emphasis on reading.

What about mathematics? Many students do not take mathematics courses during the senior year, and for those on block schedule, the last mathematics class could be 1½ years before the college readiness test. For many students, how well they do on the test has nothing to do with ability; rather, it has a lot to do with the length of time between instruction and testing.

Career Pathways should help correct this problem by helping students focus on testing requirements at all levels and helping them take courses in sequences that promote success. It is essential that all educators working with students in Career Pathways use data such as those in the preceding tables for planning student instruction and interventions. Similar reports are available in most states.

In addition to standardized tests, educators must remember that it takes multiple assessment tools to determine whether students can apply what they have learned in multiple settings and in real-world contexts. Implementation of Career Pathways depends on recognition of the need for multiple assessment tools.

PLANNING FOR SUCCESS THROUGH PROFESSIONAL DEVELOPMENT

In our current accountability-driven culture, improving student performance is a must. Helping teachers shift their pedagogical models from the 20th century to the 21st will involve extensive professional development. What is more, we need to change the way we think about professional development. Conventional professional development — isolated events in which teachers put in a predetermined amount of seat time — has never produced very good results. We must begin to think of professional development as a *process* in which teachers meet performance objectives over time. To be effective, professional development must give participants ample opportunities for reflection, feedback, and attention to areas in which improvement in student achievement is being sought.

Planning professional development requires painstaking analysis of student performance data to determine which teachers should be involved and what types of professional development should be offered. For example, in the above-described school district in Florida, the professional development provider should reflect on the phenomenon of the low reading scores on the tenth-grade FCAT and the low mathematics scores on the college-readiness test. Considering

125

the differences between high school exit exam requirements and college placement test requirements, the professional development provider may want to offer different professional development plans for each subgroup, grades 9–10 teachers and grades 11–12 teachers. Clearly, each subgroup has unique needs. The professional development provider should also disaggregate student data by gender and race. That process will probably yield a much different picture of professional development needs than would analysis of aggregate data alone. The bottom line for professional development is this: *Base the plan on clearly defined gaps in student performance.*

Professional development should follow the National Staff Development Council standards for professional development.[1] The NSDC standards recognize three broad factors that affect the quality of professional development: context, process, and content. The quality of professional development is always affected by whether it is provided in an environment that is conducive to learning (context), whether it is based on research-documented practices (process), and whether it presents strong material (content). According to Joyce and Showers, "student achievement is the product of formal study by educators."[2] In other words, without thoughtful consideration of the relationship between teacher behaviors and student learning, student achievement will not be positively impacted. Remember also that the purpose of professional development is to change behaviors, first that of teachers, then that of students. Therefore, it is essential that the design of professional development begin with the desired behaviors in mind — student achievement that meets the expectations of higher education and the workplace.

---

[1] National Staff Development Council, *Standards for Staff Development* (Revised Ed), (Oxford, Ohio: Author, 2001).

[2] B. Joyce and B. Showers, *Student Achievement Through Staff Development.* (Alexandria, Virginia: Association for Supervision and Curriculum Development, 2002), 3.

Joyce and Showers identified four conditions that must exist if professional development is to affect student learning:

- A community of professionals comes together to study, put into practice what they are learning, and share results.

- The content of staff development aligns with instructional strategies that have a high probability of improving student learning and—just as important—student ability to learn.

> The purpose of professional development is to change behaviors, first that of teachers, then that of students. Therefore, it is essential that the design of professional development begin with the desired behaviors in mind—student achievement that meets the expectations of higher education and the workplace.

- The magnitude of change generated is sufficient that the students' gain in knowledge and skill is palpable. What is taught, how it is taught, and the social climate of the school change to such a degree that the increase in student ability to learn is manifest.

- The processes of staff development enable educators to develop the skill to implement what they are learning.[3]

Sparks and Hirsch recommend the following national professional development model for teachers:

- Create learning schools in which all staff members are involved in continuous learning in the areas in which they focus their teaching;

- Provide time for teacher professional development equaling 25 percent of each day, during which time teachers work together in planning lessons and sharing information; and

- Base professional development on the collaboration model—teachers learning from each other.[4]

---

[3] Joyce and Showers, *Student Achievement*, 4.

Online professional development — Providing effective professional development is expensive and difficult to fit into a school calendar. But the effort must be made. While it is important for the teacher to be in the classroom, it is just as important for the teacher to be given the tools necessary to unlearn ineffective teaching methods and replace them with effective teaching methods. To do this, teachers need time to reflect on their teaching practices and discuss with their peers what works and doesn't work in the classroom. Is there a way to accomplish this without huge commitments of time and money? The answer is yes. CORD has developed a highly effective series of online professional development programs that combine face-to-face and online interaction. Following an initial face-to-face session, participants interface with one another and with the course facilitator asynchronously via the Internet, which means that they can work almost entirely at home and at their convenience. The programs offer many advantages over more conventional approaches. In conventional, exclusively face-to-face professional development activities, there is usually little opportunity for *reflection*. The relatively short timeframe precludes it. But online courses can span several *weeks*, giving participants ample time to practice what they are learning and reflect on its effectiveness. The courses also give participants ample opportunity to discuss results via discussion boards administered by trained facilitators.

The courses have received high praise from participants. Following are sample comments.

- *It was great being able to get on the computer when I could fit it into my schedule and not have to drive to a location at a specified time to meet with other students. The convenience of an online course is a tremendous help for busy teachers everywhere. I would definitely do this again if given the opportunity.*

---

[4] D. Sparks and S. Hirsh, *A New Vision for Staff Development* (Alexandria, Virginia: Association for Supervision and Curriculum Development and National Staff Development Council, 1997).

- *What's different about an online course is: I feel that it is easier to make comments and express opinions. There is not a time limit to giving a response to some question or comment. I can think about my comments for minutes, hours, or days before I decide what I want to say. It is also easier because of the convenience. I always feel like I am rushing around to get everything done, and this course is a welcome change of pace.*

CONCLUSION

The need to document student performance in achieving rigorous academic standards has created a need for teachers to shift from sorting and selecting students on the basis of perceived "ability" to rigorous academic achievement for all students. By focusing on the four keys described in this chapter, educators can close the achievement gap. Career Pathways both depend on and support an approach to professional development in which teachers have opportunities to learn effective strategies that will affect learning for *all* students through data-driven professional development plans. Career Pathways are the best model for redesigning secondary and postsecondary education in ways that will lead to improved student achievement across the board, but their implementation will depend on a dynamic overarching strategy for professional development. Career Pathways— supported by strategic professional development—have the potential to make student achievement of rigorous academic standards a reality. Our pursuit of that reality is no longer a choice; it is a necessity if this country is to continue to boast a world-class workforce.

Chapter 6 Preview

Partnership ensures a culture focused on improvement by:		
15. Collecting qualitative and quantitative data on academic and career success, retention rates, dropouts, graduation, transitions, and remediation.		
16. Using data for planning and decision-making.		

Collecting useful data in education is important, but it isn't fun. To do it correctly and effectively requires a lot of hard, painstaking work. To avoid doing it means that you don't have a sound basis for reporting and improving. In today's environment, it could also result in loss of funding and the potential for "sunsetting" CTE.

The data-collection process must be well designed; engage the support of teachers and administrators; and ensure timeliness, efficiency, and meaningful analysis.

The authors of this chapter are an experienced educational psychologist and a statewide administrator and practitioner. They list three purposes of educational data:

- *Accountability*

- *Research*

- *Program improvement*

Most of the chapter is concerned with how data collection can and should be used for program improvement; successful examples are showcased for six states. The last section of the chapter is particularly important, because it presents a practical process for collecting and using data for program improvement. Don't stop reading this chapter until you have digested this last section.

D.H.

6

COLLECTING DATA FOR CAREER PATHWAYS

David Bond and Robert Franks

I. WHY DO WE HAVE TO COLLECT THIS?

If career and technical education (CTE) programs are to thrive, CTE partnerships must collect data that proves the value of their programs to policymakers at the federal level. Those policymakers have distinct perspectives on the *what, why,* and *how* of collecting data related to the Carl D. Perkins Vocational and Technical Education Act of 1998 (Perkins III) and its proposed reauthorization — perspectives that must be taken into consideration at the partnership level.

In 2001, the U.S. Department of Education's Office of Vocational and Adult Education (OVAE) and the states embarked on the Data Quality Initiative, whose purpose is to improve the quality and consistency of the performance data collected by states. This initiative led to the Peer Collaborative Resource Network (PCRN), an online forum (http://www.edcountability.net) that supports state-to-state communication, peer review, and resource sharing for improving state Perkins III accountability systems.[1] OVAE works with states to improve data quality by improving the selection and implementation of measurement approaches and the improvement of data-collection systems.

In spite of OVAE's emphasis on improving CTE data quality and accountability, the Administration's 2006 budget did not request renewed funding for the Perkins Basic State Grant or Tech Prep programs. Due to poor ratings of Perkins programs in the National Assessment of Vocational Education (NAVE) and the Program Assessment Rating Tool (PART), the U.S. Department of Education proposed that CTE programs be supported instead through the President's High School Initiative.

The goals of the U.S. Congress are seen in the requirements of Perkins III and its proposed reauthorization. According to a 2000 OVAE summary, Perkins III required a continued federal and state commitment to performance measurement and accountability. The law gave states, school districts, and postsecondary institutions greater flexibility in designing services and activities that meet the needs of their students and communities. In return for that flexibility, Perkins III established a rigorous state performance accountability system designed "to assess the effectiveness of the state in achieving statewide progress in vocational and technical education to optimize the return of investment of federal funds in vocational and technical education activities." There was also a shift from measuring student *gains* to measuring student *attainment.* States must report annually to the Department of Education on their progress in achieving agreed-upon levels of performance.[2]

Senate and House versions of Perkins reauthorization bills put more emphasis on accountability than Perkins III. A 2005

---

[1] Peer Collaborative Resource Network (http://www.edcountability.net/, accessed July 2005).

[2] U.S. Department of Education, Office of Vocational and Adult Education, *OVAE Core Indicator Framework for State Performance Accountability Systems* (January 2000).

summary provided by the Association for Career and Technical Education (ACTE) states:

The Senate bill proposes that the purpose of the accountability section is to support and determine the effectiveness of state and local programs, and adds a specific section on local accountability that did not exist in the 1998 law. Eligible recipients must now agree to accept the state levels of performance as their own or negotiate performance measures with the state the same way that states negotiate with the federal government, and report progress in achieving these performance levels on an annual basis. Through the accountability system, states and locals must make continuous and significant improvement in the career and technical achievement of CTE students, including special populations. Performance indicators in the bill are separated into secondary and postsecondary level measures. At the secondary level, the bill strengthens the ties of the technical skill attainment measure to industry standards and relates the academic skill attainment measure to NCLB. It also requires the development and implementation of Career Pathways.

The House bill proposes that the purpose of the accountability section be modified to support and determine the effectiveness of state and local programs, and adds a specific section on local accountability that did not exist in the 1998 law. Eligible recipients must now negotiate performance measures with the state the same way that states negotiate with the federal government, and report student progress in achieving these performance levels on an annual basis. This data must be disaggregated . . . using NCLB subgroups and any disparities between a subgroup and all other students must be identified. The section also creates separate core performance indicators for secondary and postsecondary students. The House version also requires the development and implementation

133

of model sequences of courses (similar to the Senate's "Career Pathways").[3]

After both houses of Congress passed legislation continuing the Perkins Act, the U.S. Department of Education appeared to ease its opposition to Perkins reauthorization, but wants to make sure that there are adequate accountability measures. Regardless of which data elements are required by law or regulation, data can be used for accountability, for research, and for program improvement; however, these purposes often go hand-in-hand. The bottom line is this: Without adequate data, the results of educational programs, new courses, uses of technology, increased counseling, and improved pedagogy are, at best, anecdotal.

> **The bottom line is this: Without adequate data, the results of educational programs, new courses, uses of technology, increased counseling, and improved pedagogy are, at best, anecdotal.**

Accountability — *Did we use the funding for what it was intended and did it make a difference?*

Accountability in education is a top priority. The federal No Child Left Behind Act of 2001 (NCLB) is the highest-profile example of this. Those involved in CTE are acutely aware that accountability is very important to the President, the U.S. Department of Education, and Congress as they determine the future of CTE program funding. To prove the worth of their programs, Perkins recipients must collect specific student outcome data. At a minimum, student outcomes must be assessed for each of the Perkins III four core indicators: (a) student attainment, (b) credential attainment, (c) placement and retention, and (d) participation in and completion of

---

[3] Association for Career and Technical Education, *Carl D. Perkins Act Reauthorization Resources, 109th Congress* (www.acteonline.org/policy/legislative_issues/Perkins_resources_1 09.cfm, Alexandria, Virginia, June 2005).

nontraditional programs. But much more information is often needed or required.

According to Medrich and White, data collection for accountability purposes involves five "levels" of data gathering and reporting: classroom reports to school; school reports to district; district reports to partnerships; partnerships report to states; states review and transmit data to the federal government; and the federal government compiles and reports data from all participating states to the President, Congress, and the public. Most of this is mandatory and is a significant endeavor for those required to collect the data.[4]

Several organizations serve as advocates for members in the area of CTE. Each has taken a stand on accountability and the data-collection issues that go with it. Four of those organizations are mentioned below.

In a joint communication to Congressional education committee staff members, the Association for Career and Technical Education (ACTE) and the National Association of State Directors of Career Technical Education consortium (NASDCTEc) supported most of the accountability measures in the House and Senate versions of the Perkins reauthorization bills. Both organizations support achievement of high standards at the secondary and postsecondary levels for academic and technical skills attainment. Both recognize the need for documentation of program completion (diploma, degree, certification) and placement in further education or employment, and both support cross-program alignment of measures of curricula, assessments, and standards.

The National Tech Prep Network (NTPN) and the National Association for Tech Prep Leadership (NATPL) have worked closely together to coordinate their stands supporting the accountability measures of the House and Senate versions of the Perkins reauthorization bills. Although preferring the Senate's proposal (which maintains Tech Prep as a separate

---

[4] Elliott Medrich and Robin White, *The Data Dilemma: Putting Progress Measures Data to Work for Federal, State, and Local Decision Makers* (Berkeley, California: MPR Associates, Inc., August 1999).

funding stream and maintains the 5 percent level of administrative costs), both organizations also appreciate the House version's call for accountability for how the funds are spent.

Research—*How do we know what works?*

Much of the research conducted on Perkins programs is authorized and funded by the federal government. A great deal of research is conducted by the National Research Center for Career and Technical Education and/or published by the National Dissemination Center for Career and Technical Education. The research reports generated by these two entities can be found at www.nccte.org. Other private research organizations such as MPR Associates, Inc. also conduct research under grants from the U.S. Department of Education and other sources.

NCLB and many federal K–12 grant programs call on educational practitioners to use "scientifically based research" to guide their decisions about which interventions to implement. The U.S. Department of Education promotes randomized controlled trials—research's "gold standard"—for establishing what works.

One example of how the U.S. Department of Education's "gold standard" for research was used to discover evidence of effectiveness and success is a study conducted by James Stone III, Director, National Research Center for Career and Technical Education. His research was reported in the NTPN *Connections* newsletter (2005). His study involved more than 4000 students in 240 schools in 2004–2005. The students and teachers were divided into experimental (math-enriched CTE courses) and control groups (conventional CTE courses). Students in the experimental group developed a deeper and more sustained understanding of math than students in the conventional courses. The CTE teachers in the experimental group had math teacher partners. Students in the experimental classes scored higher than the control group on 14 of the 18 measures of global math ability, while there was no difference in the development of occupational skills and knowledge.

Another type of research involves collecting and analyzing the opinions of stakeholders. Several years ago NTPN, in partnership with the Gallup Organization, began offering opinion surveys to Tech Prep consortia. The surveys allowed the consortia to gather and compare the opinions of faculty members, counselors, administrators, and others involved in CTE partnerships. This service evolved into an online survey service that can be used locally or statewide to pinpoint areas in which perceptions of program quality differ among participating groups. This type of survey was recently used in a study commissioned jointly by the Tennessee State Department of Education and the Tennessee Board of Regents.[5] Survey results pointed out significant differences between the perspectives of secondary and postsecondary practitioners. Awareness of these differences has led to increased communication and joint planning.

True experimental research, the federal government's "gold standard" (which calls for the creation of a control group and a means of controlling for independent variables), is largely impractical in statewide data-collection efforts. States can, however, collect student demographic data, educationally related data, student academic outcome data, and wage data that, if analyzed in longitudinal studies, can result in reliable conclusions regarding the effectiveness of educational reform efforts. States, local educational institutions, and partnerships create reports that use descriptive data comparing CTE or Tech Prep students with peers who are not taking career-related courses. Many of these reports show that students whose education is organized around a career focus do as well as or better than non-

Many of these reports show that students whose education is organized around a career focus do as well as or better than non-career-focused students on measures of academic success and retention.

---

[5] Tennessee Tech Prep (http://www.techpreptn.org/ Research%20Page.htm, accessed August 2005).

career-focused students on measures of academic success and retention. One of these local studies is discussed later in this chapter. The authors propose that this type of comparison reporting has value even though it does not meet the federal government's "gold standard" for research.

Program Improvement — *What should we do to make it better?*

Using data for program improvement is the primary focus of this chapter. According to Medrich and White, performance measures are usually designed in a way that enables data to be used for program improvement purposes — for example, by establishing baselines, setting targets, and reviewing progress. The measures are used to identify the strengths and weaknesses of current efforts, to pinpoint areas that should be given more or less emphasis, or to provide a basis for performance-enhancing programmatic adjustments. Sometimes the program-improvement function of performance measurement gets "lost" in the overall data-collection process, and, in these instances, the data are often viewed as compliance requirements and little more.[6]

A couple of years ago, an article about three award-winning high school principals was published in the NTPN *Connections* newsletter.[7] Dr. Elaine Sullivan, principal at Hernando High School in Brooksville, Florida, was the 1998 National Association of Secondary School Principals (NASSP)/MetLife Principal of the Year. Dr. Sullivan shared the NTPN conference opening session stage with former First Lady Barbara Bush in Kansas City. In 1999, Dr. Michael Pladus, principal at Interboro High School, Prospect Park, Pennsylvania, received the NASSP top honor. He presented his story of success that year at the NTPN conference in

---

[6] Medrich and White, *The Data Dilemma.*

[7] David L. Bond, "Principals Using Elements of Tech Prep to Reform Schools," National Tech Prep Network, *Connections,* Vol. 13, No. 4, 2003.

Pittsburgh. Robert Kemmery, principal at Eastern Technical High School, Baltimore, Maryland, was the runner-up for the 2000 Principal of the Year award and spoke that year at the Charlotte NTPN conference. He was also the national winner of the ACTE McDonald's Outstanding Career and Technical Educator for 2002. All three award-winning leaders had in common the use of data for program improvement. Their experiences show that collecting and analyzing the appropriate data help leaders identify needs and measure progress toward meeting improvement goals.

Sullivan led her school toward becoming more adept at using data and arranged for workshops to be conducted on this topic. She stated, "The analysis of data over a period of three, five, and eight years shows significant positive improvement in all aspects of the school's educational services for all ethnic and gender groups." According to Pladus, "We celebrated as our state math scores went up five straight years to a point where they were significantly above the state average, our reading scores were above the state average, and our writing scores were among the very best in our area and the state." Kemmery has about a dozen years' worth of data showing how his school went from "unsatisfactory" to "excellent" in test scores and attendance.

Winning leadership awards and having good data are no accident. Successful leaders study the baseline data and lead their staffs to create action plans for improving student achievement. There will be more on this process later in this chapter.

II. WHAT INFORMATION DO WE NEED AND WHAT DO WE DO WITH IT?

It is important to gather data that reflect whether students are showing improvement and whether they are meeting minimum required achievement levels. This is necessary to maintain

Without consistent data, program benefits cannot be communicated and plans for improvement cannot be created.

the program's integrity. Without consistent data, program benefits cannot be communicated and plans for improvement cannot be created.

The kind of data collected should be based on the goals of the organization that is doing the collecting as well as the requirements of those to whom the organization must report. In education, evaluations should include student outcome data such as academic skill attainment (meeting a minimum criterion or score or showing an improvement from a previously measured baseline), high school completion rates, numbers of students accruing college credits while still in high school, numbers of students who enter college *without* needing remediation, and numbers of students who earn postsecondary degrees. In CTE there are several additional indicators of success such as technical skill attainment, enrollment in advanced skill courses, receipt of certificates and credentials, job placement in chosen careers, and earning levels. In addition, information on demographic characteristics such as gender, ethnicity, and physical disabilities should be collected so that data can be disaggregated as needed.

Collecting data is only part of the process. According to experienced researcher Sheila Ruhland, analysis involves synthesizing and interpreting information to develop reasonable conclusions.[8] Institutions often collect data but seldom take the next step — data analysis. Those responsible for program evaluation often don't know how to use the data.

Database (computer) programs provide a useful way for evaluators to store, analyze, and manage information. Databases can be used to organize data elements relating to students, including demographics, enrollment details, academic performance, course completion, articulated credits earned, and work-based experiences. Some local programs have access to state-administered databases that manage a broad range of student information and provide regular

---

[8] Sheila K. Ruhland, *Measuring Tech Prep Excellence: A Practitioner's Guide to Evaluation* (National Research Center for Career and Technical Education, University of Minnesota, 2003).

reports. In some cases, local programs have modified these databases to meet their unique needs. Some states and local programs use commercially developed database programs, and others have built their own databases to meet specialized needs.

Data collection takes time and costs money. In an environment in which everyone is being asked to do more with less, both human and fiscal resources tend to be directed toward programming and implementation activities, not data collection and analysis. In many local partnerships, the difficulties associated with data-collection processes are compounded by structural barriers ranging from size and scope to jurisdictional boundaries. In larger partnerships, size often makes it impossible to collect new data quickly and efficiently. For some of the largest partnerships, data collection involves multiple school districts and schools, along with several labor market areas. The sheer size of these partnerships makes it virtually impossible to provide training for all of the staff involved in data collection activities.[9]

> In an environment in which everyone is being asked to do more with less, both human and fiscal resources tend to be directed toward programming and implementation activities, not data collection and analysis.

Other barriers to data collection are posed by differences in policies, definitions, and interpretations. Schools, communities, and states define terms differently and collect information in different ways. Even modest movement toward common definitions can lead to less local ownership of data and a greater tendency to focus on *compliance,* i.e., simply collecting and passing on information that someone else wants. In addition, personnel turnover is a barrier to consistent, high-quality data collection.

---

[9] Medrich and White, *The Data Dilemma.*

The Career Pathways Self-Study Instrument — CORD and NTPN announced the launch of the Career Pathways Strategic Improvement Coalition (CPSIC) at the 2004 National Tech Prep Network conference in Minneapolis. To become involved in CPSIC, partnerships agree to complete the Career Pathways Self-Study Instrument, which consists of 18 items covering secondary, postsecondary, business, and partnership components. Each item provides a benchmark. Completion of the instrument involves identifying the extent to which the respondent's partnership meets each benchmark. The respondent chooses from 1 (indicating that the benchmark is not being met at all) to 5 (indicating that the benchmark is being met very well). Accompanying the instrument are rating criteria that specify what each choice (1, 2, 3, 4, or 5) signifies for each item.[10]

> To become involved in CPSIC, partnerships agree to complete the Career Pathways Self-Study Instrument, which consists of 18 items covering secondary, postsecondary, business, and partnership components.

In general, the instrument rates a partnership's success in the following areas:

- *Providing Career Pathways that are guided by 4+2(+2) curriculum frameworks*[11] — It seems likely that Congress will say that all CTE programs must offer Career Pathways as a requirement for receiving Perkins funds. These pathways should begin in the ninth grade and continue through at least the community college level and provide the option of pursuing baccalaureate degrees. Partnerships participating in the self-evaluation should work toward having a complete (eight-year) seamless curriculum in place for each pathway offered.

---

[10] The complete instrument can be seen in Chapter 1; the rating criteria are provided as Appendix 2.

[11] A discussion of curriculum frameworks can be found in Chapter 3.

- *Providing comprehensive student career guidance and counseling*[12]— Partnerships should provide all students with academic and career information that will enable them to make informed choices about programs of study that support transition to further education and work.

- *Meeting rigorous academic and technical skill standards throughout high school and especially in preparation for postsecondary enrollment*[13] — Recent federal legislation, both passed and proposed, requires states and schools to work toward helping all students achieve academic proficiency and, in the process, close the achievement gaps among minorities and other subgroups within the student population.

- *Providing opportunities for dual/concurrent enrollment in college while in high school*[14]— Studies show many benefits to students, parents, high schools, and colleges when students earn college credit while still in high school. Partnerships should seek ways to increase the number of students participating and the total number of credits being earned in this manner.

- *Providing work-based learning and employment opportunities*[15] — Partnerships with strong employer participation can provide the real-world experiences that students need while still in school and the employment opportunities that are sought after graduation, or at multiple exit points. These opportunities should be in the high-wage, high-demand careers for which the pathways were created.

---

[12] A discussion of career guidance and counseling can be found in Chapter 8.

[13] A discussion of improving student performance can be found in Chapter 5.

[14] A discussion of dual enrollment can be found in Chapter 9.

[15] A discussion of work-based learning and employment opportunities can be found in Chapter 8. A discussion of the role of employers can be found in Chapter 7.

- *Providing targeted professional development* — Faculty, administrators, and counselors need training to improve their skills in teaching, advising, and integrating technical and academic instruction.[16]
- *Collecting and using data for program improvement decisions* — This is the topic of the current chapter. Data should be collected on all elements required by relevant federal and state agencies; additional data may be helpful at the local or state level.

An ongoing series of CPSIC workshops is being conducted around the country to help partnerships and states begin to develop Career Pathway improvement plans.

III. HOW HAVE SOME STATES BEEN DEALING WITH DATA COLLECTION?

While meeting certain requirements of the federal government, each state has been responsible for defining its own measures of student success and for the quality of data collected and reported. States have also had to develop their own data-collection systems. Some are home-grown while others use commercially produced software. Often the local system that passes information on to the state system was developed separately from the state system. Many local entities have difficulty following students after they leave educational institutions (secondary and postsecondary), especially in determining whether appropriate employment and wages have been secured. Following are examples of data collection and analysis in six states. In each case, we survey the state as a whole and then focus on a local example within the state.

Texas

Texas has been collecting detailed data on both secondary and postsecondary educational outcomes for over 26 years.

---

[16] See more about the need for professional development in Chapters 5, 7, and 8.

Recently secondary and postsecondary data were combined into a student data warehouse that permits easy monitoring of student matriculation from high school to college. The student data is cross-matched with unemployment insurance wage records in the Adult Learner and Student Automated Follow-up System (ALSAFS) to enable the state to collect data at the student level for correlating educational attainment with future earnings.

Individual student data is annually collected, analyzed, aggregated, and used by districts, institutions, and state agencies to evaluate program effectiveness and student academic achievement. Through this annual evaluation schools and colleges are able to compare their results with state averages, the results of cohort institutions, and their own past performance. State-collected data is a key tool in the evaluation process; it is made public so that communities can know where their schools stand.

Secondary schools report students in the Public Education Information Management System (PEIMS); each student is assigned a PEIMS number based on his or her class-taking. In PEIMS, students are coded as "0" if they take no CTE courses, "1" if they

State-collected data is a key tool in the evaluation process; it is made public so that communities can know where their schools stand.

take CTE courses as electives, "2" if they participate in locally determined sequences of CTE courses, and "3" if they take courses as part of state-approved Tech Prep educational pathways. This enables state data analysts to quickly identify the level of individual student participation in CTE and compare student outcomes such as dropout rates, completion rates, graduation rates, matriculation rates, job placement rates, income levels, and standardized test scores. PEIMS identifiers allow state data analysts to follow those students into postsecondary education so that their future educational and workplace performance can be evaluated. PEIMS allows the results of participating in CTE programs to be evaluated both locally and statewide.

The state system collects student demographic information such as socioeconomic status and family history of college attendance to enable state agency statisticians to eliminate external factors while looking at correlations and identifying causality.

In addition to institutional self-evaluation, state ALSAFS data is used in the planning of institutional self-improvement strategies under Perkins and No Child Left Behind. (Institutions are required to use this data in their annual grant applications.) State data related to PEIMS category is also used in the biannual evaluation of Tech Prep consortia.

Analysis of state longitudinal data indicates that, compared to the student population in general, CTE students, and specifically Tech Prep students, have lower dropout rates, enter and complete college programs at higher rates, do very well on standardized tests, and earn higher salaries when they enter the workforce.

When state-level data (in Texas) is compiled, aggregated, and returned to local colleges and Tech Prep consortia, it is used to determine which programs are effective and which programs should be the focus of improvement efforts. In some cases data is used to determine whether a program should be closed. Among the relevant data are the number of program participants, the number of program completers, and the number of completers placed in further education or work (Perkins quality indicators). Tech Prep consortia also study state-provided charts comparing their Tech Prep students to state averages. Because Tech Prep students do better scholastically and have higher graduation and postsecondary matriculation rates than the student population as a whole, it is obvious when local data indicates otherwise.

> Analysis of state longitudinal data indicates that, compared to the student population in general, CTE students, and specifically Tech Prep students, have lower dropout rates, enter and complete college programs at higher rates, do very well on standardized tests, and earn higher salaries when they enter the workforce.

Consortia have used this data to make sure that Tech Prep students are reported correctly and that high school counselors do not simply report all technical course takers as Tech Prep students.

Golden Crescent Tech Prep Consortium — The Golden Crescent Tech Prep Consortium at Victoria College in Victoria, Texas, saw a need to develop software that would automatically gather student data and make it available to the college so that students would be assured of receiving all the college credits to which they are entitled. In response to that need, consortium leaders developed the Career and Technology Education Management Application ("CATEMA") software, which has been adopted statewide. The system creates student portfolios that list courses taken in high school and identify students' Tech Prep pathways. Colleges can pull up students' data when the students register to ensure that their articulated college credits are transcripted. Colleges can also access the CATEMA database to identify students who are interested in particular college majors and use that information to focus their outreach efforts. This information also helps colleges identify students who have taken Tech Prep pathways.

Louisiana

Louisiana's Career and Technical Education program has implemented software for a statewide data-collection system (CATE) over the last several years. Each year modifications are made to improve the process. Information in current database systems (e.g., demographic data such as name, SSN, race, gender, and grade level; student participation in articulation/dual credit enrollment; and state-required test results) is loaded into the updated software. Efforts are being made to reduce the amount of data that individual schools must enter on career majors, work-based learning activities, receipt of skills certificates, and various survey results. Surveys include the "Student Program Survey," "Student Career Survey," the "Parent Program Survey," and the "Community Program Survey." Job placement information is obtained from the Louisiana Department of Labor.

The system provides detailed reports on five-year education plans, CTE courses taken and credits received, dual enrollment information, work-based and school-based learning activities, participation in or receipt of skill certificates, attendance, discipline records, and graduation information.

The benefit of the updated CATE software system is that it keeps track of all student career and technical activities with minimal data entry while providing schools and districts with information that enables them to assess program effectiveness, meet reporting requirements, and, most important, make improvements that help students.

Patricia Merrick (personal communication, July 2005), Section Administrator for Secondary CTE, Louisiana Department of Education, points out that the CATE system's ability to disaggregate data to the student level makes it an excellent tool for principals, counselors, and teachers to use in talking with parents and advising students. Schools will no longer have to search a multitude of databases to capture information about individual students. This flexibility includes the ability to identify students who need early intervention and students who qualify for scholarships and special diploma endorsements.

> **The benefit of the updated CATE software system is that it keeps track of all student career and technical activities with minimal data entry while providing schools and districts with information that enables them to assess program effectiveness, meet reporting requirements, and, most important, make improvements that help students.**

According to Louisiana State Tech Prep Director Kelley Rhoe-Collins (personal communication, June 2005), the Louisiana Department of Education developed the database to collect data for the secondary Perkins Basic Grant. Tech Prep, which is administered through the Community and Technical College System, has benefited from the department's data and leadership and uses the reports to improve Tech Prep delivery.

In Louisiana, distribution of Tech Prep funds is handled on a competitive basis through evaluation of submitted local application plans. Beyond the information collected through the CATE system, Tech Prep coordinators are asked to respond to a series of additional questions, including:

- How many Tech Prep activities have you developed and/or sponsored? List the types of activities (e.g., faculty workshops and career days).

- Do business, industry, and labor participate in the development of curricular and program design? Are they involved in advisory committees, job shadowing, mentoring, staff development, etc.?

- What indications are there that regional consortia are addressing the goals and related objectives in their local action plans?

Outside evaluators are contracted to perform in-depth site visits at each consortium.[17] The onsite reviews help to answer and validate the responses to the questions listed above.

Acadiana Tech Prep Consortium — Cindy Poskey (personal communication, July 2005) is the high school relations coordinator for the Louisiana Technical College, Teche Area Campus, in New Iberia, Louisiana, and a Tech Prep coordinator for the Acadiana Tech Prep Consortium in southern Louisiana. The data of most interest to her is how the dual enrollment experience affects student plans and success following high school. Her consortium uses personal contacts to determine the depth of impact of the high school experience. They inquire as to whether students followed through with their plans to transition to college or used their skills to move directly into the workforce. Poskey's greatest concern is that parents and students, as well as some educators, still do not consider technical education a means to a rewarding future. She uses the information she gathers to create counseling strategies, including regular workshops for parents.

---

[17] Louisiana Community and Technical College System, *Louisiana Tech Prep 2004 Annual Site Visit Report* (Baton Rouge, 2004).

Florida

In the area of instruction, the Florida Department of Education has created the DART model as a way to analyze data to improve instruction.[18] DART stands for:

D – Disaggregate data: analyze data; tease them apart; display results

A – Assess, identify, and prioritize needs

R – Review Sunshine State Standards and FCAT testing resources to pinpoint deficiencies

T – Target and align curriculum, classroom instruction, and assessment by addressing needs and deficiencies with new or adapted learning activities and available resources

After collection and charting of data, the next steps include:

- Form grade-level teams to study school situations and plan changes

- Form a cross-grade-level team to coordinate efforts and courses to ensure that students are "reading and writing across the curriculum" and across grades

- Review new resources and best practices

- Get help, if desired, from within the district, the Office of School Improvement in the Department of Education, or other regional service providers

Orange-Osceola-Valencia Consortium — Beverlee Andrews (personal communication, June 2005), the Tech Prep coordinator in the Orange-Osceola-Valencia Consortium at Valencia Community College, Orlando, Florida, reports that the state requires local partnerships to report several data elements such as numbers of participating schools and colleges, Tech Prep students, and articulation agreements, along with information on the placement of Tech Prep students. However,

---

[18] Florida Department of Education, *Going Beyond the Numbers to Improve Instruction with DART 2004: A Model for Using FCAT Results to Improve Instruction* (http://osi.fsu.edu/data.nsf/DA?OpenPage, accessed July 2005).

the consortium collects additional data elements that are helpful for program improvement. Those elements include student gender, ethnicity, special needs conditions, grade level, career path, and grade point average; results of program-specific assessments; FCAT scores for reading, writing, math, and science; and postsecondary remediation rates, program enrollment, and completion of degrees or certificates.

Compilation of extensive data allows the consortium to make comparisons between Tech Prep students and non-Tech Prep students across the region and the state. For example, the data indicates that the percentage of Tech Prep students meeting the FCAT reading cut-off score exceeds the percentage of the general student population across the consortium and state by more than 12 percent. FCAT math scores of Tech Prep students are almost identical to the statewide average, but the percentage meeting the cut-off slightly exceeds that of the general population in the two consortium districts.

A valuable piece of information provided by the consortium is the number of tuition dollars saved by students who earn Valencia Community College credits while still in high school. Over the previous ten-year period, Tech Prep high school graduates in the consortium saved over $1.6 million in tuition. This is a great marketing tool for the Tech Prep career paths.

A valuable piece of information provided by the consortium is the number of tuition dollars saved by students who earn Valencia Community College credits while still in high school.

Within the consortium, there is a well-developed database system for identification (by Career Pathway) of Tech Prep students in high school. This data is shared regularly with Valencia Community College for analysis and tracking. In addition, the Florida Education and Training Placement Information Program allows districts, consortia, and the state to follow students from high school into the statewide postsecondary system. According to Andrews, it's more difficult to track the students individually into employment after the completion of educational programs.

Ohio

Nick Wilson (personal communication, July 2005), assistant director for articulation and transfer at the Ohio Board of Regents, states that tracking student transition to and success in postsecondary education is aided in Ohio by access to the Higher Education Information System (HEI). Secondary students can be tracked to any public higher education institution in the state. Available data include time to degree, courses taken, terms enrolled, and remediation levels. As with many other states, postprogram wage data is difficult to track.

During the last three years each Tech Prep consortium has participated in a self-study followed by a visit from an onsite review team. The consortia are evaluated on 32 core standards. They use the results of the study to make strategic decisions; the state provides technical assistance as needed. The state is compiling the best practices from the site visits. The 32 standards are in areas such as the strategic planning process, consortium governance and decision making, financial management system, data collection and evaluation, curriculum development, articulation agreements, instructional needs, contextual learning, technology, continuing professional development activities, marketing and student recruitment, career exploration, underrepresented populations, collaboration and work-based learning, and college transition strategies.

Miami Valley Tech Prep Consortium—Ron Kindell (personal communication, June 2005) is the director of the Miami Valley Tech Prep Consortium (MVTPC) at Sinclair Community College in Dayton, Ohio. Kindell explains that his Tech Prep consortium, like the others in Ohio, is partially funded under a "performance funding" model. Funding points accrue for each of several student milestones: enrolling in an approved pathway (eleventh and twelfth grades), matriculating to a postsecondary institution, beginning postsecondary study without requiring developmental (remedial) coursework, completing at least 60 hours toward a degree, and completing an associate and/or bachelor's degree (double points). This performance data is compiled by gender, race, and disability status. Kindell concurred with Wilson that there is no efficient system for tracking students from education to employment locally or statewide.

In a 2005 article written for the NTPN *Connections* newsletter, Kindell says,

> We need to know whether the pathway methods, practices, and services we employ are working (or not working), as indicated by the steady progress of growing numbers of students toward our primary goal of pathway completion. It is in this area that the temptations of a data swirl are most apt to occur! Therefore, at MVTPC we limit our questions and data to the following: (1) baseline academic performance information, (2) retention in the pathway through high school graduation, (3) matriculation to postsecondary education, continuing in the pathway begun in high school, (4) required remediation, and (5) persistence in college. In the end, data provide us with the success and failure information that is the key to continuous improvement.[19]

We need to know whether the pathway methods, practices, and services we employ are working (or not working), as indicated by the steady progress of growing numbers of students toward our primary goal of pathway completion.

Nationally, Tech Prep and other CTE programs have received much criticism for not conducting research to show that the programs are having a positive impact on student performance. In Ohio, research by Tech Prep consortia has been conducted at the single and multiple partnership levels. In a 2002 study conducted by Sinclair Community College's Office of Institutional Planning and Research, Krile and Parmer concluded that participation in a Tech Prep program (allied health, business, or engineering) has a positive effect on subsequent (Sinclair) college performance. When compared to classmates who did not participate in Tech Prep programs

---

[19] Ronald Kindell, "Does Your Career Pathway Add Up to Success?" National Tech Prep Network, *Connections*, Vol. 15, No. 3, 2005.

prior to enrolling at Sinclair, Tech Prep students had higher entry assessment scores, were less likely to need remedial mathematics, were more likely to receive passing grades in their first college-level math courses, and were more likely to be retained one year after their initial term of entry.[20]

New York

The annual evaluation of New York CTE programs at the secondary level is based on a three-stage process.[21] In the first phase, three types of data are collected through surveys of local education agencies. Data are collected on the academic performance of secondary career education program completers. Data are also collected on the number of students enrolled in CTE and the number of completers. Finally, for program completers, follow-up information is collected approximately six months after program completion, identifying the extent to which completers are employed, are in the military, are enrolled in postsecondary education, are unemployed, or demonstrate other measurable characteristics. In phase two, these data are analyzed by the State Education Department and turned into a report indicating the extent to which eligible (grant) recipients have met the standards of performance for each measure. In phase three, the report is sent back to the eligible recipient. The eligible recipient then brings together an evaluation committee composed of CTE program personnel including teachers, special population representatives, and employers to review the results and

---

[20] Donna J. Krile and Penelope Parmer, *Tech Prep: Pathways to Success? The Performance of Tech Prep and Non-Tech Prep Students at a Midwestern Community College* (Office of Institutional Planning and Research, Sinclair Community College, Dayton, Ohio, 2002).

[21] New York State Education Department, *New York State Plan for the Administration of Career and Vocational-Technical Education under the Carl D. Perkins Vocational and Technical Education Act* (http://emsc32.nysed.gov/workforce/perkins3/perkins2005/docs/applicationdocs04/Current4YearPerkinsPlan.html, accessed July 2005).

develop suggestions for program improvement. The suggestions are then used to amend the local agencies' career education program plans.

Bernie McInerney (personal communication, July 2005), state Tech Prep coordinator, stated that New York requires data reporting in the following areas: academic success (five Regents Exams); technical skill attainment (75 percent or better in Tech Prep courses); secondary level credential (high school diploma); postsecondary credential (college certificate or degree); and employment or military. Each grant recipient must compare its data to a state (quantitative) goal for each area. For each goal not met, program improvement strategies must be described to the State Education Department.

The demographics collected for each student are gender, ethnicity, socioeconomic status, and student characteristics such as physical disability and limited English proficiency. It is anticipated that future data-collection efforts will also include foreign language skills, work-based learning experiences, and college credits earned while in high school.

The annual evaluation of postsecondary CTE programs is accomplished through locally collected data reported to the State Education Department Office of Research and Information Systems. Persistence, completion, and placement data are collected for both postsecondary credit-bearing and non-credit-bearing programs. A postsecondary recipient that is not performing adequately in an occupational area is required to develop a local improvement plan that includes the application of Perkins funds to address the area of need.

Central Southern Tier Tech Prep Consortium — Linda Miller is the Tech Prep coordinator and College and Career Transitions Initiative (CCTI) project director for the Central Southern Tier Tech Prep Consortium at Corning Community College, Corning, New York. Due to the partnership's involvement in Tech Prep and the CCTI grant, Miller reports (personal communication, June 2005) that, based on data collected, the following strategies are being planned and implemented through the Tech Prep management team, Tech Prep superintendents and president, and CCTI core team:

- A first-year experience course
- An annual Tech Prep start-up session
- Work-based learning opportunities by the career development council
- ACCUPLACER assessment in the high schools
- Site manager/cluster advisor/counselor training on data collection and reporting
- STEP coordinators training (System for Tracking Education Performance)
- Tech Prep certificates of completion program
- Continual revision of data-collection forms and processes
- TALK TIME—Secondary and postsecondary faculty gathering by discipline

Miller's most difficult challenge is keeping track of students as they move from high school to college to employment. She attributes this to the lack of a common identifier (i.e., Social Security number or state-issued ID number). Most of the information needed is obtained by self-disclosure via telephone contact with the student. Personally telephoning each student is extremely time consuming and personnel-intensive but has generated a good return rate of usable data.

West Virginia

In West Virginia, the data collected for the Perkins Basic Grant is limited to what is required by OVAE (four core indicators), but according to Dr. Kathy D'Antoni (personal communication, June 2005), state Tech Prep director, there are 20 indicators of a fully implemented comprehensive Tech Prep initiative.

To facilitate institutionalization of Tech Prep across the state, West Virginia implemented a technical assistance tool called STARS (Strategies That Advance Restructuring in Schools). The STARS evaluation guides both program improvement and the awarding of competitive grants (i.e., on the basis of improvements made).

D'Antoni states that collecting data on students as they proceed from secondary to postsecondary is working well, since the state now establishes a college transcript for students while they are still in high school. The most difficult information to obtain is on the employment experiences of former students after they leave the education system.

> D'Antoni states that collecting data on students as they proceed from secondary to postsecondary is working well, since the state now establishes a college transcript for students while they are still in high school.

The 20 STARS indicators cover four broad areas: curricula, stakeholder support, marketing, and assessments. The complete list of 20 indicators can be found at the West Virginia Tech Prep website (http://www.wvtechprep.wvnet.edu/downloads/PDF/starsassessment.pdf).

Western West Virginia Tech Prep Consortium—Jim Hale is the coordinator of the Western West Virginia Tech Prep Consortium at Marshall Community and Technical College in Huntington, West Virginia. According to Hale (personal communication, August 2005) the consortium's Twenty STARS Report is their main tool for initiating program improvement. The consortium executive committee studies the evaluation data and makes recommendations for the next year's grant application and plan. The main emphasis for the last two years has been to develop and offer more associate degrees in technical fields. As part of creating 12 new associate degrees, 48 new EDGE (Earn a Degree, Graduate Early) courses were made available to high school students. Students who score at least 74 percent on an end-of-course test also receive community college credit. In conjunction with the new offerings another emphasis in the consortium plan was to conduct professional development to improve career advising as well as the teaching of math, science, and language arts in all the high schools. A statewide evaluation of the EDGE program revealed that only 7.5 percent of EDGE students required remedial classes in college, compared to a systemwide average of 31 percent.

Hale stated that some data is not readily available due to lack of staff to collect and input data and lack of the software necessary to generate reports. This is especially noticeable when trying to follow-up on students moving from education to employment. Tracking of former students to determine success rates seems to be a common problem across many states and local programs.

IV. SUMMARY

In CTE, data can be collected for accountability, research, or program improvement. The most likely scenario is that data collected is used for all three. Most frequently the data to be collected is designated for accountability purposes and is mandated by federal and state agencies. It is collected by practitioners at the local level and then consolidated at the appropriate state education agency. The items reported depend on the goals of the requesting entity (e.g., Congress or the U.S. Department of Education). For program improvement, the local institution or partnership (or state agency) may decide to collect more information than is mandated by the requesting entities.

Recent reports such as the National Assessment of Vocational Education (NAVE) and the Program Assessment Rating Tool (PART) have been very critical of the Perkins Basic Grant and Tech Prep programs. CTE professionals were no doubt disappointed with the observation that "[vocational courses] have no effect on outcomes such as academic achievement or college transitions."[22] Congress seems determined to give the Perkins legislation one more chance to prove its worth by reauthorizing the program for another six years. However, those same legislators are determined that programs become accountable and show improvement in student academic and career success.

---

[22] U.S. Department of Education, Office of the Under Secretary, *National Assessment of Vocational Education: Final Report to Congress* (Washington, D.C., 2004).

Several agencies, states, national organizations, and even local partnerships have weighed in on what data should be collected and how it should be used to improve student performance and program efficiency. Many states consult data in awarding local grants. Some use self-evaluations, with results reported to the state, and some contract evaluators to perform site visits. In most cases, a combination of methods is used. Also, it is not unusual for successful programs to go beyond what is required and collect information that *they* feel is most helpful for program improvement. The most progressive states have found ways to transition data from secondary to community college to higher education databases as smoothly as the students are transitioned. For most, one of the greatest challenges is tracking the success of students after they leave the education system and begin employment, although some are beginning to solve this problem.

> Congress seems determined to give the Perkins legislation one more chance to prove its worth by reauthorizing the program for another six years. However, those same legislators are determined that programs become accountable and show improvement in student academic and career success.

The Career Pathways Strategic Improvement Coalition developed by CORD and the National Tech Prep Network was designed specifically to facilitate implementation of Career Pathways and to help existing programs improve, whether they are Tech Prep partnerships or more traditional CTE programs.[23]

If Perkins practitioners want to meet the dual goals of continued funding and program improvement, they should consider the following strategies for maximizing data-collection efforts.

---

[23] For more on the Career Pathways Self-Study Instrument, see Chapter 1.

V. WHAT STEPS CAN WE TAKE TO USE DATA FOR PROGRAM IMPROVEMENT?

The following steps are provided as a resource for those responsible for collecting data, analyzing data, and developing improvement plans based on the data.

Creating the environment for data collection

- *Create a data-collection joint committee (representing all relevant levels and agencies).* Instead of having separate data-collection and pathway committees, it may be effective for the data-collection committee to be a subcommittee of the pathway committee.[24]

- *Establish and maintain communication channels with data providers at the state and local levels.* The state agency responsible for collecting and reporting data to the U.S. Department of Education should regularly communicate with regional and/or local data providers through means such as e-mail lists, an online FAQ site, newsletters (paper or electronic), and occasional face-to-face meetings (see next item).

- *Conduct professional development events that focus on data collection.* The face-to-face meetings mentioned in the preceding paragraph are more in-depth than one-way communication such as e-mail and newsletters. They can be half-day or daylong workshops during which case studies are reviewed, sample data-collection forms are discussed, and issues such as reliability and validity are studied.

- *Train practitioners to analyze and apply data.* This is another topic for the professional development events. Working with data means far more than just collecting it. Data is not useful unless it can be interpreted.

- *Work to eliminate the compliance mindset.* Share examples of how data collection and analysis have led to excellence and

---

[24] See also Chapter 7 on building partnerships.

additional funding. Attitudes about data may determine whether the data leads to improvement or stagnation. If the people who collect the data see no purpose or use for it beyond meeting the requirement of some higher authority, the data may be less than high quality and will probably not lead to improvement.

- *Offer feedback to data providers on a regular basis.* Let the people who collect the data know how what they provide fits into the larger picture. How does it affect statewide funding? How does their data compare to that of others? Challenge the providers to meet a certain level of quality.

Deciding what data to collect

- *Involve local practitioners in determining what data elements to collect.* Ownership comes with involvement. Where possible, local practitioners should be given the flexibility to collect data that satisfies their needs and goals (in addition to the needs and goals of federal and state governments). If they are involved in data-related decisions from the beginning, they will see more purpose in their efforts.

- *Determine what is required by the requesting agencies.* Obviously, federal and state agencies that provide funding, or control the allocation of funding, will specify certain data elements that must be collected and reported in a certain manner.

- *Decide what additional data is to be collected for internal use.* Review the goals of the Career Pathway partnership to determine whether the required data is sufficient to measure progress toward all local goals. If it is not, the committee must agree on what additional data to collect.

- *Work with others to agree on common definitions of the data to be collected.* The validity of data, especially when data from several sources are consolidated, is dependent on the use of common definitions. This may mean reviewing definitions provided by authorizing agencies and meeting with other stakeholders to formalize accepted definitions of each data element. These definitions should be agreed upon in writing and clearly communicated to everyone involved.

- *To avoid duplication of effort, find measures that are common to other education and workforce programs.* If NCLB, the Workforce Investment Act (WIA), or other federal or state programs require similar data elements to those required by Perkins (or your local pathway efforts), use common elements and definitions whenever possible. Otherwise you may create unnecessary burdens on those collecting the data and may be required to explain differing conclusions about the outcomes.

- *Avoid collecting data that is not needed.* Collecting data that is not required and not used can be demoralizing to those collecting the data. Each year, the data committee should review what is being collected and how it is being used to make sure there are no wasted efforts.

- Determine whether the elements collected include all the necessary items. The following data elements should be considered essential:

  Demographics such as gender, ethnicity, disability status

  Chosen Career Pathway

  Enrollment in nontraditional programs

  Academic skill attainment (minimum scores on state or national tests of skills in math, communication, science, and other core subjects)

  College credits accrued while in high school

  Technical course assessments that are aligned with the next higher education level and marketable employment

  Enrollment in advanced skill courses

  High school completion

  Need (or lack thereof) for remediation in college

  Continuation in school and in a Career Pathway

  Receipt of certificate or credential

Postsecondary degree completion

Job placement in chosen career

Earnings level

Obtaining the data

- *Involve practitioners in designing data-collection systems.* Data-collection systems include the forms, computer databases, people, and procedures for collecting and submitting data. As with deciding what data to collect, involvement of practitioners gains buy-in that will help ensure the success of the project. Often someone at the local level has had good, or bad, experiences that can be shared, saving time in the decision-making process.

> As with deciding what data to collect, involving practitioners gains buy-in that will help ensure the success of the project.

- *Invest in technology to simplify the collection and analysis of data.* Commercially available software can store, format, and analyze data. An investment in technology may save much in time and financial resources in the long term.

- *Determine the location of all needed data.* This may seem obvious, but not everyone knows the source or location of all data elements. Determination of the location of needed data also affords the opportunity to make sure the right data is being collected. Does the data located meet the definition of the data required?

- *Conduct research.* Research is not something that happens only at the national level. With access to a wealth of data, local partnerships can conduct their own research. The research should be rigorous, valid, reliable, cost-effective, and longitudinal.

- *Coordinate with agencies that have employment and earnings data.* Job placement and earnings data may be the most difficult for some states to obtain. Some state education departments have not yet received access to data from the appropriate state employment agencies, but access should be sought. Following are two national sources for some of this information:

FEDES Pilot — The Federal Employment Data Exchange System Pilot project provides access to employment records maintained by the Office of Personnel Management, the Department of Defense, and the United States Postal Service. Access to federal civilian and military employment records is critical in meeting reporting requirements for people who are not covered by the nation's unemployment insurance (UI) system.[25]

WRIS System — The Wage Record Interchange System is a clearinghouse through which states can obtain UI wage records for people who have been employed in other states. Data available through the WRIS can be used by participating states to meet performance reporting requirements for various workforce investment programs.[26]

Analyzing the data and making a plan

- *Create a joint planning committee.* See the notes above on creating a data-collection committee. This team may be the entire pathway committee, as discussed in Chapter 7, or a subcommittee of that larger group. Either way, those collecting the data should be involved in analyzing the data and making a plan for improvement.

- *Establish baselines and set targets.* The only way to determine whether improvements are being made is to take a snapshot of the current situation. You may know that you are not where you want to be, but make a record of data now so that you can enjoy watching the proof of the improvements. Set aggressive but achievable targets that

---

[25] For more on FIDES, contact Sarah Harlan, Maryland Department of Labor, sharlan@dllr.state.md.us.

[26] For more on the WRIS System, see www.workforceatm.org.

everyone can support. Intermediate goals for each year will help practitioners feel that progress is being made.

- *Identify gaps between various demographic groups.* Most federal programs, and many state programs, want to know how students of differing genders and ethnic groups are performing compared to each other. You need to make sure that no group is being left behind.

- *Identify gaps between the current situation and established objectives.* This relates to establishing baselines and setting targets. One must understand the magnitude of the gap and be realistic about what it will take to reach the desired goal.

- *Identify potential strategies through literature searches for proven practices.* There is a substantial literature reporting on successful initiatives. Some research is funded by the federal government, some by private foundations. Some is conducted by local school districts, colleges, and partnerships. These "best practices" reports, as well as the reports of unsuccessful outcomes, are often a good starting place for beginning an improvement plan.

Implementing the strategies

- *Conduct a small pilot, if feasible.* Once the literature search is complete and a plan has been developed, it may be a wise use of resources to try the implementation on a small scale, e.g., at one school or with one class. Full-scale implementation of a new effort may lead to disappointment and loss of support if the program is a failure. This is an opportunity to apply research techniques.

- *Review the results and refine the approach.* If the pilot results are not exactly what you were expecting, or were hoping for, consult experts and make appropriate changes.

- *Move forward with full-scale implementation.* Once the pathway committee is satisfied that the proposed strategies are appropriate, gain buy-in from all relevant parties and implement widely for maximum positive effect.

Reporting results

- *Share results of program improvement efforts with all stakeholders.* Students, parents, teachers, counselors, administrators, employers, and the entire community should learn how efforts have resulted in student successes. This is a very important step in gaining support. This is often called marketing or public relations, but it is an essential step in continuing programs that help students and the community.

The authors wish to express their gratitude to Linda McDonough, Texas State Tech Prep Director, for her valuable assistance in the writing of this chapter.

Chapter 7 Preview

Postsecondary component:	
10. Provides industry-recognized knowledge and skills.	
Business:	
12. Ensures that students are learning current, in-demand skills.	
Partnership ensures a culture focused on improvement by:	
18. Maintaining ongoing dialogue among secondary, postsecondary, and business partners.	

The call for "connectedness" in education has never been as strong, or as needed, as it is today. Students, parents, community leaders, and policymakers want assurances that every aspect of students' education has meaning and relates to other elements of the curricula and to their lives and work. Accomplishing this goal requires the cooperative efforts of many educational providers and stakeholders.

Career Pathways have the potential to provide those assurances, if all the partners are brought to the table from beginning to end, from the initial planning stages through implementation and evaluation — and if all participants are treated like equal partners.

In this chapter, an award-winning Tech Prep practitioner and an experienced educational researcher challenge the status quo on education-education and education-employer partnerships. They explain goals and strategies for creating the committed partnerships that Career Pathways require. Their concluding remarks on the importance of leadership in sustaining viable partnerships remind us of how vitally important, yet complex, collaboration really is.

D.H.

BUILDING REAL PARTNERSHIPS

Debra D. Bragg and Debra F. Mills

Career Pathways initiatives require strong partnerships that encompass both the secondary and postsecondary levels. While some partnerships — the ones that excel — are held together by deep commitments across levels, others are superficial, linking their participating institutions so weakly that the links break when tested, as, for example, when budgets decline. Too often each institution does what it has always done, with little regard for the collective goals of the partnership.

The process works something like this: First, institutions huddle together *by level,* secondary in one corner, postsecondary in the other. Second, they develop plans that focus entirely on their own needs and the needs of other institutions *at their level.* Finally, they expect institutions at the other level — which were excluded from the deliberations that brought the plans into being — to buy into the plans anyway. The excluded partners might sign on, but they participate only to the extent to which the plans serve *their* agendas. If the plans don't meet their needs, the excluded partners ignore them.

This approach represents a "playing at" partnerships approach. Although this scenario creates a superficial relationship, it does not make for the kind of substantive

169

relationship that can enhance student transitions from the secondary to the postsecondary level. For too long, educational institutions at different levels have tried to connect disparate pieces rather than create a unified whole. This band-aid approach to connecting disjointed pieces is unacceptable in the development of Career Pathways systems. To produce a high-quality workforce, Career Pathways systems must create collective entities whose shared culture embraces both the secondary and postsecondary levels and includes business and industry (employers) as well as the broader community.

Admittedly, our introductory paragraphs take a skeptical view of most existing partnerships. We hope that we have succeeded in grabbing your attention, in making you think about how difficult it is to create long-lasting partnerships. Committed partnerships involve all parties coming together, sharing the work and decision-making in the pursuit of a common goal. Partnerships are tough to pull off.

> For too long, educational institutions at different levels have tried to connect disparate pieces rather than create a unified whole. This band-aid approach to connecting disjointed pieces is unacceptable in the development of Career Pathways systems.

For this chapter, we draw upon our collective experience in working with Tech Prep as program developers, evaluators, and researchers. Our experience with Tech Prep aligns closely with results of national evaluations that have concluded that a major contribution of Tech Prep has been in the creation of productive partnerships.[1] Developing and sustaining those partnerships has not been easy! But challenges in linking secondary and postsecondary education and integrating

---

[1] A. Hershey, M. Silverberg, T. Owens, and L. Hulsey, *Focus for the Future: The Final Report of the National Tech-Prep Evaluation* (Princeton, New Jersey: Mathematica Policy Research, 1998); M. Silverberg, E. Warner, M. Fong, and D. Goodwin, *National Assessment of Vocational Education: Final Report to Congress* (Washington, D.C.: U.S. Department of Education, 2004).

academic and career and technical education (CTE) have been overcome and are now well documented.[2] The contribution of Tech Prep to enhanced relationships between education and employers has also been acknowledged. As we consider the future, we recognize the need to develop robust partnerships that will support and sustain new Career Pathways systems.

Partnerships associated with Career Pathways systems are not designed to represent their partner organizations individually, but to represent *groups* of organizations. Together, multiple partners develop Career Pathways so that students can succeed in occupations aligned along career ladders. Instead of coming to the partnership with a *what's in it for me* mentality, Career Pathways partners ask themselves, *what does my institution bring to the table?* When successful, Career Pathways systems offer students coherent, sequential education and training that help them progress through the P–16 educational system and secure productive employment, ranging from entry-level to high-demand, high-wage occupations.

> Instead of coming to the partnership with a *what's in it for me* mentality, Career Pathways partners ask themselves, *what does my institution bring to the table?*

National and state policies associated with Tech Prep and other CTE transition programs have encouraged partnerships to build new Career Pathways systems.[3] Successful Career Pathways systems begin with a vision that is shared by stakeholders who value each other's contributions and treat each other as equals. Ultimately, successful Career Pathways

---

[2] D. Bragg and W. Reger, "Toward More Unified Education: Academic and Vocational Integration in Illinois Community Colleges," *Journal of Vocational Education Research*, Vol. 25, No. 3 (2000), 237–72.

[3] M. Brooks-LaRaviere, L. Hood, and D. Bragg, *Career and Technical Education Transition Pathways: Postsecondary Perceptions of Programs, Practices and Student Outcomes* (St. Paul: National Research Center in Career and Technical Education, University of Minnesota, forthcoming).

systems are created and sustained by educational practitioners, employer representatives, community leaders, students and parents, and other concerned citizens who share a deep commitment to bettering education for all students.

Three types of partnerships are critical to the formation of new Career Pathways systems: education and employer partnerships, secondary and postsecondary partnerships, and academic and CTE partnerships. All three types are discussed in this chapter.

EDUCATION AND EMPLOYER PARTNERSHIPS

Partnerships involving employers (from business and industry) and education have more than tripled since the mid-1980s.[4] They are committed to helping students become well-educated, well-rounded citizens who have the skills and competencies necessary to secure rewarding careers. Education and employer partnerships are central to forming the workforce development programs that are needed to prepare current and future employees. Workforce development *is* education (and vice versa), and a qualified, world-class workforce is needed to support a democratic society and economic development — locally, statewide, and nationally. There is growing awareness among business and education leaders alike that partnerships that support reform of the entire P–16 educational system and respond to the needs of the community are essential for economic growth.[5]

For several decades, advisory committees have played a valuable role in developing and maintaining CTE programs. They should be the centerpiece of productive education and

---

[4] L. Hood and M. Rubin, *Priorities for Allocating Corporate Partnerships to Improve Education* (Champaign, Illinois: Office of Community College Research and Leadership, University of Illinois at Urbana-Champaign, 2004).

[5] Committee for Economic Development, *Cracks in the Educational Pipeline: A Business Leader's Guide to Higher Education Reform* (Washington, D.C.: Author, 2005).

employer partnerships. When constructed properly, they are representative bodies of education and business leaders who work collectively to improve CTE and other vital aspects of the P–16 educational system. They are committed to avoiding both turf battles and being merely a rubber stamp for the status quo.

The *Pathway Committee:* One Committee to Serve Secondary and Postsecondary Partners

As new Career Pathways systems evolve, their alignment with a reformed P–16 educational system will become increasingly important. In the past, secondary and postsecondary CTE programs used different employer advisory committees, even within the same occupational fields in the same communities. Each employer advisor was committed to one CTE program on one level, secondary *or* postsecondary; rarely were the two levels connected. In that situation, unless some employers served on two advisory committees, one secondary and the other postsecondary, the two groups were entirely disconnected from each other. This approach might have made sense in the past, when secondary CTE graduates headed in one direction and postsecondary graduates headed in another, but today separate and distinct advisory committees are not efficient or particularly useful.

What is called for is a new committee structure that does more than advise and "OK" the decisions of a few educators from a single level. What is needed for each Career Pathway is what we recommend calling a "pathway committee." Pathway committees, which serve both the secondary and postsecondary levels, can play a pivotal role in guiding and sustaining new Career Pathways systems. Employers are key members of the committees. They inform the groups about current employment trends and forecast the future. They also explain how career ladders work in their organizations and in other organizations in the same industries. Career Pathways systems must not be designed to serve one employer only; they must address the employment needs of entire communities.

Career Pathways systems require a joint investment that involves organizations working together to ensure that curriculum is relevant and that it meets the needs of all participating students. Since implementation of Tech Prep began nationwide in the early 1990s, it has become apparent that CTE can and should extend from the secondary to the postsecondary level, creating seamless career transition programs that span two or more institutions. Adopting this perspective, practitioners should create pathway committees that serve their partnerships (Career Pathways that extend from secondary to postsecondary education) and their career fields rather than their organizations exclusively.

Statewide and Regional Career Pathway Committees

Effective implementation of Career Pathways requires both state-level and local (or regional) pathway committees. The state committee addresses broad needs and trends while local and regional committees focus on local needs. This multilayered approach is necessary because of the complexity of the world of business and industry, which also operates on state, regional, and local levels. Moreover, a multilayered approach can provide economy of scale by coordinating the activities of local and regional Career Pathway programs. Statewide pathway committees can bring multiple entities together, including postsecondary institutions (which often operate as independent entities), to develop complementary Career Pathway programs, thus creating Career Pathways systems that have potential to work effectively across entire states.

Local partnerships should be well informed about the activities and long-range plans of the state's economic development department. State-level economic development initiatives in any given industry signal the need for a statewide pathway committee to oversee evolving local programs, give guidance to local pathway committees, and set state skill standards in that industry. Statewide pathway committees can inventory state-level labor market needs and help to coordinate and direct local committee efforts. They can inventory program offerings at the secondary and postsecondary levels, assessing the thoroughness of coverage and identifying similarities and

174

differences among curricula within a given region. They can also explore important questions about the best ways to serve different career fields. For example, are certain career fields better served by several regional committees or a single statewide committee? Or are opportunities to link secondary and postsecondary CTE programs being missed because of lack of state-level leadership?

How Employers Should Influence Educational Change

Some rules are universal. In real estate, the number one rule is location, location, location. With pathway committees, the number one rule is employers, employers, employers! To be effective, these committees must be chaired by businesspeople or cochaired by business and education leaders. Unfortunately, many of the current "advisory" committees are not talking to customers (the business community). By limiting their leadership to educators, they are only talking to themselves. This is a recipe for disaster; business and industry should set the specifications for each pathway. The best way to convince busy industry leaders to serve is to show them that a successful Career Pathways system can improve their bottom lines.

Nine Roles for Employers on a Pathway Committee

Employers should be empowered to engage in a number of roles that support Career Pathways. The work of employer partners should include the following nine roles:

1. *Assess emerging occupations and employer needs.* Employers can forecast where their industries are headed and how advances in technology will affect the labor market. They can identify new or emerging occupations that should be aligned with career ladders associated with their businesses and industries. Because change is a constant in the technological workplace, employers are an indispensable source of up-to-date expertise on new and developing career fields.

2. *Set specifications for curriculum.* Employers can review and critique academic and occupational skill standards to ensure that they meet the needs of students and employers, as well the needs of providers of adult education and training associated with career advancement. Many of the relevant standards can be found in national databases, but the local pathway committee's point of view is necessary to ensure that the skill standards being taught serve local needs. Since most Career Pathways graduates are employed in the communities in which they attend school, the local pathway committee should determine what standards are required at each of the multiple exit points on a given career ladder. The Career Pathway should be aligned with the exit points to ensure that students have a full range of options.

3. *Validate content.* Educators take job specifications, including content and standards, and develop them into curriculum frameworks and course outlines. These are then submitted to employers for validation, that is, to make sure the knowledge and skill requirements represented by the specifications are met in what the students will be taught. Educators should have a deep knowledge of the academic skill requirements of the P–16 system, whereas employers contribute their knowledge of the workplace and labor market. At the same time, to suggest that educators know only academics and employers know only the workplace is too simplistic — an obsolete model. We want a system that calls upon each to be knowledgeable about each other's environments and in which all participants recognize the importance of working together in the development of curriculum frameworks. Reviewing, evaluating, and advising on new curriculum and instructional materials should always be a joint effort involving both educators and employers.

4. *Assess program quality.* Employers on pathway committees can promote continuous improvement by

bringing a workplace focus to the assessment process. For instance, employers are best suited to determine whether the equipment being used in labs in consistent with what actually goes on in the workplace. In addition, employers bring a unique perspective to the evaluation of work-based learning experiences and the workplace readiness of program graduates.

5. *Provide unique education and training experiences for students.* Business partners should provide student internships after the eleventh grade. Internships are an essential component of the Career Pathways experience. A national study of work-based learning conducted by Haimson and Bellotti found that internships helped students clarify their career goals. Students in the study gave high ratings to internships that were customized to their individual needs and that provided one-on-one contact.[6] Students involved in internships placed a high value on acquiring skills in decision making, problem solving, teamwork, interpersonal skills, communication, customer relations, and other complex multistep tasks and job behaviors.[7] Students also reported that internships facilitated the acquisition and production of new knowledge, the application of knowledge to real-world situations, and motivation for taking personal responsibility for their own learning and career development.[8]

---

[6] J. Haimson and J. Bellotti, *Schooling in the Workplace: Increasing the Scale and Quality of Work-Based Learning. Final Report* (Washington, D.C.: Mathematica Policy Research, 2001, ED 455 444).

[7] K. L. Hughes, T. R. Bailey, and M. L. Mechur, *School-to-Work: Making a Difference in Education. A Research Report to America* (New York: Institute on Education and the Economy, Columbia University, 2001, ED 449 364).

[8] M. Hernández-Gantes and D. Sanchez, "Producing Knowledge in Career-Oriented Programs: Students' Perspectives on Schooling Experiences." In *Research for Education in a Democratic Society: Proceedings of the 1996 AERA Vocational Education Special Interest Group*, edited by R. L. Joyner (Washington, D.C.: Vocational

6. *Give credibility to CTE.* Acceptance and continued support of CTE often hinges on a community's knowledge about careers and career-related pathways. (The negative image of CTE stems largely from lack of knowledge about the promising career options that are available to CTE graduates.) Business partners should disseminate accurate information about Career Pathways and the role Career Pathways play in promoting the economic development of local communities. They should publicly endorse local Career Pathway programs and the credentials associated with each program's exit points. Many CTE programs struggle to attract students because the exit point is the AAS degree, which many people still view (quite mistakenly) as a second-rate credential.

7. *Recruit students.* Employers on pathway committees can help "sell" the pathway to students. Many employers are eager to participate in recruitment because they have difficulty finding qualified workers. However, care should be taken to ensure that the employers' recruitment activities do not conflict with the students' long-term educational aspirations. CTE students should not be persuaded to enter the workplace before fulfilling their potential in school.

8. *Mentor and support students.* One of the most important functions of the members of a pathway committee is to serve as role models for students who are considering entering occupations associated with the pathway. Members can serve as mentors and help students in making career choices.

9. *Place graduates in good jobs.* Pathway committees can advise on the current and projected demand for pathway graduates. Employers should articulate their needs and intentions of hiring graduates who demonstrate mastery of academic and occupational skill

Education Special Interest Group, American Educational Research Association, 1996, ED 398 417), 14–27.

standards. They should hire program graduates/ completers and notify instructors of job openings for which students are qualified.

An interesting example of how employers can have a direct effect on what is taught in the classroom was a project conceived and implemented by Betty Musgrave, Tech Prep director for the Mid-South Regional Partnership Coalition in Illinois.[9] The final product was a set of three-ring binders filled with lesson plans. The materials demonstrated the real-world applications of mathematics and communication in the workplace, relating them specifically to Southern Illinois businesses and industries familiar to teachers and students. Employers and teachers collaborated to make the learning contextual, and therefore relevant to students. The 12-step development process outlined by Musgrave involved choosing design teams of employers and teachers; engaging discipline experts to oversee development of the lesson plans; creating guidelines and assigning responsibilities; determining what academic, occupational, and workplace skills are used by the businesses represented on the team; creating workplace problems or scenarios that provide the real-world connection; and reviewing, editing, and piloting the lesson plans. This collaborative project was highly rewarding for participants, and it helped strengthen the relationship between the schools and businesses.

SECONDARY AND POSTSECONDARY PARTNERSHIPS

Historically, the United States has given a great deal of attention to the transition of high school students to four-year colleges and universities. A bachelor's degree is a known quantity for almost all high school students, and it is clearly a desirable credential in today's workplace. But it's not the only

---

[9] A description of the project was published as B. Musgrave, *A Dose of Reality: Twelve Steps in Developing Real-World Lesson Plans* (Waco, Texas: CORD, 2001).

valid option.[10] Many of the fastest growing fields in the United States require postsecondary education but not necessarily four-year degrees. This suggests the need for more partnerships that support student transitions from secondary schools (high schools, career academies, technical schools, and charter schools) to community and technical colleges. Whatever Career Pathways students choose, the doors to advancement must never close. Students who pursue associate degrees must be given ample opportunities to advance by pursuing more education (bachelor's degrees and beyond) and moving up the career ladder.

K–8 and 9–12 Partnerships

By the end of grade 8, students should be prepared to choose Career Pathways and should be academically on track for college within four years. This is a significant challenge that requires strong partnerships between the K–8 and 9–12 levels to ensure that students' academic preparation compliments their career development. Career Pathways systems benefit students by promoting career awareness beginning in kindergarten, career exploration beginning in high school, and career development at the postsecondary level. Each stage parallels the P–16 educational system. To be thorough and effective, career preparation must be systematic, comprehensive, and cumulative, with each grade level building on the one before it. At present, many career development programs consist merely of a career interest inventory given in grade 8 and job shadowing in grade 9. While both are valuable activities that stimulate students' thinking about careers, they do not constitute a system.

---

[10] Michael E. Wonacott, "Credentials: One Size Fits All?" *The Highlight Zone: Research @ Work,* No 2. (NCCTE, 2000).

High School and Community and Technical College Partnerships

Partnerships between high schools and community and technical colleges are crucial because they provide a stepping stone that enables students to transition to the workforce smoothly and enhance their quality of life. A breakdown can dead-end students at high school graduation, seriously diminishing their prospects for rewarding careers and relegating them to the ranks of the working poor. Consequently, one goal of any partnership between high schools and community or technical colleges should be to help each high school graduate enter postsecondary education with a clear career focus and ready to learn at the college level, without requiring remediation.

For new Career Pathways, the relationship between the secondary system and the community or technical college may be the most important link in the chain. The fastest growing fields require some postsecondary education but not necessarily four-year college degrees.[11] One ramification of this fact is that many high school graduates would serve their own interests best by entering two-year colleges immediately after high school graduation (not six to eight years later).[12] Community and technical colleges are not only educationally sound, they are relatively inexpensive — giving parents another important reason to give them serious consideration.

Research shows that the high school senior year is often wasted.[13] As a countermeasure, some high schools and colleges are jointly attempting to "push down" the curriculum by

---

[11] K. Gray and E. Herr., *Other Ways to Win: Creating Alternatives for High School Graduates* (Corwin Press, Inc., 1995).

[12] C. Adelman, *Moving into Town — and Moving On: The Community College in the Lives of Traditional-Age Students* (Washington, D.C: U.S. Department of Education, Office of Vocational and Adult Education, 2005).

[13] National Commission on the High School Senior Year, *Raising Our Sights: No High School Senior Left Behind* (Washington, D.C.: Author, 2001).

181

giving students dual enrollment and dual credit options (see Chapter 9). High school graduates who have taken advantage of dual credit opportunities can enter the postsecondary level with college transcripts already started. This is a very attractive option for many students and their parents. Devising more dual credit agreements will help create partnerships in which student pathways traverse two levels.

Development of new secondary and postsecondary articulated curriculum frameworks should involve the collaboration of secondary, postsecondary, and business partners. When college credits are at stake, educators can no longer count on curricula consisting of disjointed pieces. A better alternative is a model called "learning the landscape," in which progressive curriculum frameworks are developmentally appropriate at each level of student maturity.[14] Making "learning the landscape" a reality calls for a systems approach that promotes the design of new, collaborative learning environments.[15] When high school graduation requirements do not align with postsecondary entrance requirements, many students struggle to make the transition from one level to the next.

K–12 and University Partnerships

High school graduates should be able to enter four-year colleges and universities with some idea of their future careers, and without the need for remediation. Traditionally, high school principals and guidance counselors have tended to focus their attention on high school students who seemed headed for four-year colleges and universities. But focusing on that relatively small number of high-achieving students is no

---

[14] J. Greeno, "Number Sense as Situated in a Conceptual Domain," *Journal for Research in Mathematics Education*, Vol. 22, No. 3 (1991), 170–218.

[15] A. L. Brown and J. C. Campione, "Guided Discovery in a Community of Learners." In K. McGilly (Ed.), *Classroom Lessons: Integrating Cognitive Theory and Classroom Practices* (Cambridge, Massachusetts: MIT Press, 1994), 229–70.

longer acceptable. Today's counselors must be well informed about what it takes for the "neglected majority" of students to be successful in transitioning to college.

Pathway committees should include representation from four-year colleges and universities to ensure that the groups' perspectives remain sufficiently broad. All institutions that represent student exit (or credentialing) points must work together so that students can move into and out of the P–16 system at different entry and exit points and not be penalized or stopped in their forward movement.

Community/Technical College and University Partnerships

Traditionally, the associate of applied science (AAS) degree has tended to be thought of as a terminal degree. But Career Pathways are changing that perception. In the Career Pathways concept, nothing is terminal. There is always an avenue for further progress. Today's students need multiple entry points into and exit points out of the P–16 system to match progressive career-ladder opportunities. Students need to be able to continue from high school to college and from the AAS degree to the baccalaureate degree without being penalized. It is true that many students who earn AAS degrees then go directly to work.[16] Nonetheless, immediate employment is not their only option. For a growing number of postsecondary students, completing the AAS degree is the mid-point toward completion of a bachelor's degree, either immediately following the AAS degree or following a few years of full-time employment. Because transfer agreements do not cover AAS degree programs but rather focus on the transfer of students with AA or AS degrees, some students pay a penalty when they attempt to transition to the bachelor's level. They find that they need additional coursework to be on

[16] D. Marcotte, T. R. Bailey, C. Borkoski, and G. S. Kienzl, "The Returns of a Community College Education: Evidence from the National Education Longitudinal Study," *Educational Evaluation and Policy Analysis*, Vol. 27 (2005), 157–75.

track for baccalaureate degrees. This must change; students should be able to reenter the education system without penalty. The community college component of Career Pathways programs should be aligned and articulated with baccalaureate programs. This goal is much easier to accomplish if the program is developed with the last two years of the bachelor's degree already in view (i.e., 4+2+2 — four years of high school [grades 9–12] linked to two years of community or technical college [grades 13–14] linked to the last two years of a baccalaureate degree [grades 15–16]). To ensure unity of purpose among all educators involved, representatives of all three of these educational levels (grades 9–12, 13–14, and 15–16) should be "at the table" when curriculum is developed.

In times past, most students pursued traditional degrees. More recently, *certificates* have emerged as a new form of credentialing that is closely tied to the knowledge and skills needed for many occupations and professions.[17] Many Career Pathways provide a means for students to earn industry-recognized credentials rather than degrees. The American community college system, which provides much of the nation's workforce development training, encompasses many programs that award industry-specific certificates. Usually these credentials are offered on a noncredit basis through cost-recovery units such as corporate or contract training departments that operate separately from the rest of the college. This separation can hinder the development of Career Pathways systems and impede the integration of academics, CTE, and contract training, making it difficult to create an educational approach that is responsive to the labor market.[18]

---

[17] A. P. Carnevale and D. M. Desrochers, *Help Wanted . . . Credentials Required: Community Colleges in the Knowledge Economy* (Washington, D.C.: Educational Testing Service and American Association of Community Colleges, 2001).

[18] J. L. Alssid, D. K. Gruber, D. Jenkins, C. Mazzeo, B. Roberts, and R. Stanback-Stroud, *Building a Career Pathways System: Promising Practices in Community College-Centered Workforce Development* (San Francisco: Workforce Strategy Center, 2002).

A full-fledged Career Pathways system that can serve all students, both young people and adults, involves a marriage that integrates the two sides of the house (credit and noncredit). When college credit is given for certifications, the student is not penalized for returning to the educational system to complete an associate or bachelor's degree.

ACADEMIC AND CTE PARTNERSHIPS

Another type of partnership that is critically important to the development of Career Pathways systems is that between academic education and CTE. More and more educators are recognizing that preparing students for postsecondary education and careers involves engaging *all* students in rigorous academic coursework. Consequently, CTE curricula offered at both the secondary and postsecondary levels should be integrated with, or at least complementary to, core academic curricula.

Though public policy has not dictated how practitioners are to integrate academics and CTE, it has established the expectations that (1) core academic curriculum will be predominant and (2) if CTE is to continue to exist at the K–12 level, it must be integrated, or at least closely coordinated, with core academics. Applied academics and multidisciplinary courses are examples of course-level integration in which academic content is infused with CTE concepts (or vice versa). Linked courses, learning communities, work-based learning, and other integrated approaches require the collaboration of multiple instructors. Instructional strategies that support integrated curriculum are contextual teaching and learning, problem-based instruction, and integration through learning technologies.[19]

---

[19] N. Badway and W. N. Grubb, *Curriculum Integration and the Multiple Domains of Career Preparation: A Sourcebook for Reshaping the Community College* (Berkeley, California: National Center for Research in Vocational Education, University of California at Berkeley, 1997); R. L. Lynch, *New Directions for High School Career and Technical*

In Career Pathways systems, academic and CTE educators collaborate, as equal partners, in the development of integrated academic and CTE curriculum that serves the needs of all students. Because different students have different career goals, Career Pathways systems must provide a menu of career options. For this to be accomplished, faculty members, administrators, and counselors at both the secondary and postsecondary levels must understand that the overarching goal of Career Pathways systems is to provide opportunities that allow all students to progress through the P–16 educational system as far as they can.

The curriculum should support entry points and, more important, exit points that are well understood and supported because faculty members work together to plan and implement the curriculum, from start to finish. Partnerships between academic and CTE faculty members begin at the secondary level and extend to the postsecondary level. This means, for example, that it is not enough for high school science and health occupations teachers to work together; postsecondary faculty members in these same disciplines should be involved as well.

Our vision goes beyond the partnering of working professionals. In the best of cases, students become partners, actively participating in and facilitating their own learning. In the past, we have considered academic and CTE faculty members the primary, if not the *only*, partners in formulating curriculum and instructional materials and strategies. But in Career Pathways, students should be equal partners in this process. Clearly, if students are not interested in the curriculum, and they don't see it as more interesting and advantageous than conventional academic approaches, they are not likely to enroll in it. And even if they do enroll, they are not likely to excel. New Career Pathways can overcome the complacency of the past by engaging students as equal partners.

Education in the 21st Century (Columbus, Ohio: ERIC Clearinghouse on Adult, Career, and Vocational Education, 2000, ED 444 037).

Collaborative learning processes involving students are encouraged when teachers are visibly supportive of one another, that is, when teachers are active collaborators. We would argue that the less isolation and the more cooperation that are evident among faculty members, the more students will value active, collaborative learning environments too. Collaboration promotes student retention because collaboration makes schools (and colleges) places where students want to be. By modeling collaboration, education professionals demonstrate to students that active learning is a highly valued endeavor.

To promote integration, partnerships require a common understanding among school and college educators (including teachers, counselors, and administrators) who are collaborating and communicating their expectations to each other and to students (and parents). One way to encourage partnerships focused on the creation and ongoing delivery of integrated curriculum is to form school-based and college-based teams whereby teachers of different disciplines meet regularly to plan, implement, and advocate for integrated curriculum. These teams can be at one level (i.e., *horizontal* teams), or they can span several levels up and down the system (i.e., *vertical* teams), with both types encouraging communication and collaboration. Curriculum integration requires both types, horizontal and vertical. It simply cannot and will not happen if only one or two teachers know the plan. Success requires faculty leaders who appreciate the importance of integrated curriculum and are committed to its implementation. In a study of the development of integrated mathematics curriculum, Hernandez and Brendefur found that interdisciplinary teacher teams could be successful in writing curriculum when the following circumstances exist: support from the school's community, regular meetings with all the team members present, conversations focused on student understanding, writing tasks that promote conceptual and integrated understanding of the concepts, and collaborative writing that includes reflective thought.[20]

Finally, we acknowledge the irony in our insistence that faculty members who work within the same institution be treated as equal partners. This irony reflects an unfortunate truth: Because of issues involving status and image, academic and CTE teachers do not always see themselves as peers. From our perspective, the differences in status between academic and CTE curricula are illusory, perpetuated by an educational system that has become disconnected from the "real world." In the future, all students, regardless of background and academic ability, should engage in college and careers, and the P–16 educational system must change to accommodate them. By building new Career Pathways systems through partnerships between academic and CTE instructors at the secondary and postsecondary levels, as well as between educators and employers, we can create an educational environment in which these new systems flourish.

CONCLUSIONS AND IMPLICATIONS FOR PRACTICE

New Career Pathways systems represent a major change in the way P–16 education is constructed, organized, and operated. They require new partners and new forms of partnerships. They demand that faculty members, counselors, and administrators gain additional knowledge of how the educational system aligns with the labor market. Career Pathways systems require careful thinking about core curriculum that integrates academic education and CTE to meet the needs of all students, without leading any students into dead ends. They mandate that secondary and postsecondary educators collaborate, creating seamless transition opportunities from high school to two-year and four-year colleges and universities. And, finally, the success

---

[20] V. Hernandez and J. Brendefur, "Developing Authentic, Integrated, Standards-Based Mathematics Curriculum: [More Than Just] An Interdisciplinary Collaborative Approach," *Journal of Vocational Education*, Vol. 28, No. 3 (2003), 259–84.

of Career Pathways systems depends on deep commitments in business and industry.

We have reserved the discussion of leadership to the conclusion of our chapter because of its importance in the development of all forms of partnerships. Simply put, leadership begins at the top, and top-level leaders must provide visible, vocal support for the partnerships that form the backbone of new Career Pathways systems. Vision begins at the top, and CEOs of the organizations involved must spend time together developing their shared vision for Career Pathways systems. Partners must recognize that the actions of their top leaders will have a profound impact on the success of the new systems. Laying a foundation for a Career Pathways system requires these components:

- *A common vision among all stakeholders:* Everyone must be "on board" for a new system of education—Career Pathways systems. Leaders should lead by example and nurture leadership in others by advocating and developing ownership for Career Pathways systems.

- *A governance structure or process for implementation:* Build a winning team and set up and support an organized structure for partnership meetings. The team needs workable strategies that lead to desired outcomes. Strategies should include:

  - Identify Career Pathways by focusing on industries that have labor market needs and can fuel the economic development in your local or regional area.

  - Establish or expand pathway committees to include all levels of education (secondary and postsecondary). Business representatives play a strong leadership role in these committees, detailing the career specifications for the workforce, validating the content of the curriculum, assessing the quality of programs, and giving creditability to the pathways. Committee members should not be allowed to feel that their time is wasted; they must take pride in what is accomplished.

189

- Implement a Career Pathways curriculum with multiple entry and exit points. Curriculum should be built on standards (academic, skill/technical, and employability/workplace) that are logical for several partnering institutions. Alignment of calendars may be essential for students who travel between high schools and colleges for dual credit courses and/or new organizational models such as middle or early college high schools.

- Professional development: Educators need the tools and techniques to make the necessary changes. Often faculty calendars must be aligned between institutions, and staff development opportunities must be added to orient faculty members to new Career Pathways and provide counselor training.

- Create a community awareness campaign and share information with parent and community organizations.

- *Action research:*
  - Collect and analyze appropriate data to identify student outcomes and enhance their educational experiences.
  - Meet regularly to share results and study concerns that are impeding the performance of the system.[21]

Tech Prep initiatives (and many others) have built successful partnerships between secondary and postsecondary for years. Many of those involved in Tech Prep may be asking, "How is this any different?" Career Pathways partnerships differ from Tech Prep partnerships in these respects:

- *All occupations*—The local partnership offers students a menu of options that goes beyond the technical pathway focus of Tech Prep. Career Pathway systems encompass *all* occupations.

- *All students*—Career Pathways partnerships serve all students, not just a select group.

---

[21] Adapted from Carl. D. Glickman, "The Courage to Lead," *Educational Leadership,* Vol. 59, No. 8 (May 2002), 41–4.

- *One curriculum* — Each pathway offers a curriculum developed with all partners at the table. This curriculum is "stretched" over the educational institutions in the partnership.

- *Multiple exit and entrance points* — All partners in Career Pathways systems implement components so that students can enter and exit the pathways without penalty; this should include the baccalaureate level.

- *One pathway committee for each pathway or cluster* — Pathway committees should focus on specific Career Pathways as a whole, not just particular institutions.

Each participating institution should recognize that it is only one piece of the Career Pathways puzzle. For many institutions, this requires a fundamental change in mindset. Partnerships are based on relationships and relationships are nurtured through time spent together. This involves interaction among all participants — business and education personnel, faculty members, middle managers, counselors, and, of course, CEOs. It also involves interaction between the secondary and postsecondary levels. Without doubt, transition from high school to college can be improved through better cooperation and communication between secondary and postsecondary systems.[22] Over time, Career Pathways can lead to an elaborate system of intertwined networks in which participants stay well informed, have the tools necessary to navigate the system successfully, and feel ownership in their successes. When fully developed, Career Pathways systems become an essential part of the P–16 educational system, empowering all students to stay in school and get as much education as they need and want, and equipping them to participate in a global economy that requires world-class workers and informed, productive citizens.

---

[22] T. R. Bailey, K. L. Hughes, and M. M. Karp, *What Role Can Dual Enrollment Programs Play in Easing the Transition Between High School and Postsecondary Education?* (Washington, D.C.: Office of Vocational and Adult Education, U.S. Department of Education, 2002).

Chapter 8 Preview

2. Career Pathways include comprehensive student career guidance and counseling.

Partnership ensures a culture focused on improvement by:

16. Using data for planning and decision-making.

18. Maintaining ongoing dialogue among secondary, postsecondary, and business partners.

Far too often, students select courses and career options based on what their friends are doing. Counselors must have the time, the cooperation, and the tools to help students make choices that will ensure success in later life.

Successful Career Pathways will depend on an effective, comprehensive career guidance system that uses the expertise and commitment of all pathway partners to ensure that:

- *All eighth graders (and their parents) are prepared to choose initial fields for Career Pathways in the ninth grade.*
- *Career Pathway students in the ninth and tenth grades are provided with experiences and contexts that will help them to fully understand the opportunities and environments associated with their career fields of interest.*
- *Career Pathway students, by the end of the tenth grade, are encouraged to reconsider their initial career field choices and reconfirm or change their pathways.*
- *Career Pathway students continue to reevaluate their career field choices throughout the remainder of high school through internships and mentoring experiences.*
- *All students will examine higher education opportunities and make sure they are on track to meet requirements for admission to the postsecondary institutions of their choice.*

Counselors cannot accomplish these tasks alone. They can design an effective guidance system, but implementing the system will require the assistance of teachers, administrators, parents, post-secondary personnel, employers, and community leaders. The authors of this chapter, leaders in counseling education and practice, provide resources, procedures, and practical advice to help counselors design and lead career guidance teams. D.H.

HELPING STUDENTS MAKE CAREER CHOICES

Pat Schwallie-Giddis, Elizabeth Creamer, and Linda Kobylarz

In the Career Pathways process, secondary counselors must wear many hats. Of course, their first priority is to advise students, but they must also be involved in public relations, marketing, and labor market research. They must be relentless in combating biases, stereotypes, and misinformation. They must be thoroughly familiar with federal and state policy to ensure that their programs meet all guidelines for accountability.[1] They must be great communicators who can establish and maintain networks of productive connections in their schools, districts, and communities.

Every worthwhile endeavor within a Career Pathways partnership will require a catalyst to get the process moving along; the counselor must often take the initiative in being that catalyst.

---

[1] For more on alignment of Career Pathways programs with federal and state policy, see Chapter 4.

This chapter provides practical advice for secondary counselors. It focuses on five areas: the makeup and function of the career guidance team, communication, marketing, student advisement, and work-based learning. The chapter concludes with an overview of Virginia's Career Coaches Initiative.

THE CAREER GUIDANCE TEAM

Every Career Pathways program should have a career guidance team, chaired by the counselor (or department chair) at the secondary level.[2] The team should consist of 12–15 members chosen by the institutions they represent— businesses, community colleges, secondary schools, and other partner organizations. The team should meet quarterly or at least twice each semester and over the summer as needed. Activities of the team should include evaluation of performance data, program review and revision, review of curriculum frameworks, and analysis of community acceptance. Following are brief descriptions of the roles of the guidance team's members:

- **Counselor**—The counselor should lead the team. This will include scheduling and overseeing meetings. The counselor should work with teachers and administrators in setting up a comprehensive guidance program that helps students make preliminary career choices, preferably during the eighth grade. The counselor should claim ownership in specific pathways, become knowledgeable about occupations to which those pathways lead, and establish relationships with area businesses and industries that provide jobs in the relevant occupations. Industry-specific information gathered by counselors should be made available to teachers and students, as a resource in the

---

[2] The career guidance team is not the same as the pathway committee described in Chapter 7. The career guidance team can be a subcommittee of the pathway committee or a separate group. In either case, the career guidance team reports to the pathway committee.

career exploration process. As a follow-up to students' first exercises in career exploration, the counselor should schedule students for individual sessions to talk about their goals and how those goals relate to their schedules for each year of high school. The counselor should set up small-group sessions in which students with similar interests

> **The counselor should work with teachers and administrators in setting up a comprehensive guidance program that helps students make preliminary career choices, preferably during the eighth grade.**

discuss their future and explore options for mentoring and other work-based learning opportunities. All of these efforts should be shared in the guidance team meetings.

- **Teachers** — The teacher representatives on the career guidance team should assist in the development of a process for integrating career information into the curriculum frameworks. They should also coordinate with the other members in arranging for career development activities such as visits from guest speakers, job shadowing, and other experiences that might be integrated with classroom learning.

- **Administrators** — The administrators on the team must represent and/or be liaisons to the principal's office to ensure that all activities planned are consistent with the overall governance of the school. They should also be thoroughly knowledgeable about how the plans and activities of the career guidance team affect and/or are affected by overall school finances.

- **Employers** — The primary role of the employer representatives is to ensure that the program is consistent with up-to-date information on the requirements for job entry, the knowledge and skills required for success, and the benefits derived from various career choices. They can also help in providing for activities that complement the guidance program, for example, job shadowing opportunities, guest speakers at events such as career fairs, and summer internships.

- **College representatives** (two- and four-year) — The college representatives should work closely with the counselor in providing Career Pathways students and their parents with accurate information on what it takes to make a smooth transition from secondary to postsecondary, without requiring remediation. They should take a keen interest in what goes on in their feeder high schools and take an active role in aligning secondary and postsecondary (which is an essential component of Career Pathways).

- **Parents** — The attitudes of parents have a profound effect on the career choices of their children. Parents are also experts on their own children's interests and aptitudes. For these reasons, parents should be integral to the work of the career guidance team.

- **Community leaders** — Career Pathways partnerships are *community* partnerships. They are intended to serve the economic development interests of entire communities. Thus, community leaders should be involved in the work of the career guidance team, as well as in the process of evaluating the effectiveness of the partnership.

STAYING INFORMED

To be effective in the Career Pathways process, secondary counselors must be well informed about the labor market. In fact, they must be experts — which requires an ongoing effort to gather and assimilate information. Following is a sampling of the information that counselors should have about the labor market, along with descriptions of two especially valuable resources.

A Sample of What Counselors Should Know About the Workplace

Almost every day there is something in the news about jobs, the economy, layoffs, huge companies buying smaller ones, or competition from other countries.[3] Students frequently ask counselors about the best bets for future jobs. Counselors can find a lot of information about employment projections and trends. Most of it is free and on the Internet. However, making sense of it all can be challenging. It is important that counselors provide accurate and current information to students so that they can make the best possible decisions about education and careers. Following are some good basics about labor market information and projections.

The Basics: Working Vocabulary

Labor market information (LMI) is systemized data, produced on a regular basis, about jobs. It encompasses topics such as economic conditions, workforce demographics (population, education, and income), and employment trends. At the federal level, LMI is collected by the Bureau of Labor Statistics (BLS), the Bureau of the Census, and the Department of Education's Office of Adult and Vocational Education. LMI is also collected by state labor and education agencies.[4]

To be effective in the Career Pathways process, secondary counselors must be well informed about the labor market. In fact, they must be experts—which requires an ongoing effort to gather and assimilate information.

There are more than 145 million people in the U.S. labor force today. Most of them have *jobs,* i.e., paid positions with specific duties, tasks, and responsibilities in particular workplaces. In the year 2012, we expect to see more than 50 million job openings for new workers. Jobs are grouped into *occupations*. An occupation is a cluster of jobs with common

---

[3] This section was adapted from the article "Where the Jobs Are" by Linda Kobylarz (www.acrnetwork.org/ncdg). Additional labor market information can be found in Chapter 2.

[4] For more, visit www.bls.gov/emp. *The Occupational Outlook Quarterly* is also an excellent resource for job outlook information. It is available online (www.bls.gov/opub/ooq/ooqhome.htm) and in print (800-512-1800).

characteristics that require similar skills. (For example, athletic trainers, audiologists, and certified nursing assistants all use some of the same basic skills.) Most people work in 10–12 occupations over a lifetime. All of the jobs people have and the occupations in which they work make up their *careers*. A career also includes how a person prepares for jobs (education and training), as well as how work is interwoven with other areas of life such as family, community, and leisure. For LMI reporting purposes, occupations are grouped, or "clustered," according to their common knowledge and skill requirements.[5]

Industries are collections of companies and establishments that do the same kind of work. For example, companies in the computer industry make, sell, and service computers. Large companies often do business in more than one industry. BLS develops projections for 262 industries or industry groups that make up the U.S. economy as a whole.

Education, Skills, and Wages

Some jobs pay more than others, for a variety of reasons. Mostly it has to do with the value the employee can bring to the employer and the availability of jobseekers with the skills employers need. Professional baseball players earn high salaries for two reasons: (1) They attract thousands of paying customers and (2) there are only a few really skilled baseball players. The people who take up tickets at the stadium, while important to the smooth operation of the stadium, don't bring nearly as much value to their employers, and there are lots of people who have the skills to do that job. Consequently, the baseball player gets paid much more than the ticket taker.[6]

So, *skills* are the key to good wages. Skills are the combination of knowledge and abilities needed to do a

---

[5] For more on career clusters, see Chapter 3.

[6] For more information about wages, visit http://www.acinet.org/acinet/. Click on *Wages and Trends* or visit www.bls.gov/oes.

particular job. The more skills people have, the more likely they are to find satisfying jobs that pay well.[7]

Education and training are the main ways to acquire work skills. There are many education and training options for students to pursue after high school. Two-year and four-year colleges, CTE programs, apprenticeships, the military, and on-the-job training are all viable routes.

Studies show that people with postsecondary credentials earn more money over the course of their careers than those without the credentials. Compare the median weekly earnings listed in the following table.

Level of education attained	Median weekly earnings in 2003 (dollars)
Doctoral degree	$1,349
Professional degree	$1,307
Master's degree	$1,064
Bachelor's degree	$ 900
Associate degree	$ 672
Some college, no degree	$ 622
High-school graduate	$ 554
Some high-school, no diploma	$ 396

Source: Bureau of Labor Statistics; earnings,
March 2003: Bureau of the Census

LMI numbers tell the *availability of jobs in different occupations, how fast their numbers are growing, how much they pay, and where they are located.* Here are two keys to understanding LMI numbers:

- Information about changes (increases or declines) is expressed two ways: numeric change and percentage change.

---

[7] To learn more about occupations and the skills they require, visit www.onetcenter.org/. Many states and schools have access to a computer information delivery system [CIDS] that will provide occupational information.

- Numeric change means the actual number of people employed or expected to be employed (e.g., 100,000).
- Percent change is the rate of growth or decline in employment (e.g., 13%).

- Just because a high *percentage of growth* is shown, it does not necessarily mean that there will be plentiful jobs for that occupation. Consider this example of two views of projected employment growth for 2002–2012 (*Occupational Outlook Quarterly*, Spring 2004).

Occupation	Numeric employment growth	Percent employment growth
Environmental engineers	18,000	38%
Accountants and auditors	205,500	19%

Even though the percent change is greater for environmental engineers, there will be more jobs for accountants and auditors. So a high growth rate does not always translate into lots of jobs. It is important not to jump to conclusions. Get the whole picture before giving information to students.

The numbers can also tell a lot about **competition for job openings.** When the number of jobs is small, as in very popular fields such as sports and entertainment, a person has to be **very** good to compete for the jobs. When the number of jobs is large, the competition is not so fierce (unless, the number of people qualified for those jobs is also large). The supply of workers versus the demand for workers is an important factor.

Employment and industries are always changing; some are growing some are shrinking. **Trends** tell us what happened from one year to the next **in the past**. **Projections** seek to predict what the pattern will be **in the future**.

A long-term rising trend can mean more opportunities when a student is ready to look for a job. A declining trend can be a sign that the student should use caution and get more information before choosing that occupation or industry.

Highlights 2002–2012 Projections

Industry growth is projected to be concentrated in the service-producing sectors. Among the fastest growing are: professional and business services, education, health services, transportation and warehousing, and information services.

Among goods-producing industries, construction is projected to gain about 1 million jobs. Employment in manufacturing is expected to decline slightly.

Sixteen of the 20 projected fastest-growing occupations are in healthcare or computers. Earnings are highest for workers in computer-related jobs.

Top 20 occupations with most new jobs, highest paying—bachelor's or graduate degree:

Teachers (postsecondary, elementary, secondary, special education)
• General and operations managers • Accountants and auditors
• Computer systems analysts • Computer software engineers
• Applications and systems software • Management analysts
• Lawyers • Physicians and surgeons • Financial managers • Network systems and data communications analysts • Sales managers
• Computer and information systems managers • Network and computer systems administrators • Chief executives • Computer programmers • Medical and health services managers

Top 20 occupations with most new jobs, highest paying—less than bachelor's degree:

Registered nurses • Truck drivers, heavy and tractor trailer • Sales representatives • Maintenance and repair workers • First-line supervisors of retail sales workers • Electricians • Computer support specialists • Police and sheriff's patrol officers • Licensed practical and licensed vocational nurses • Executive secretaries and administrative assistants • Carpenters • Correctional officers and jailers • Automotive service technicians and mechanics • First-line supervisors/managers of office and administrative support workers • Plumbers, pipe fitters, and steamfitters • First-line supervisors/managers of construction trades and extraction workers • Self-enrichment education teachers • Heating, air conditioning, and refrigeration mechanics and installers • First-line supervisors/managers of production and operating workers

Source: *Occupational Outlook Handbook, Winter 2003-04 – Charting the Projections: 2002–12*

Resources

America's Career Resource Network (ACRN)

One of the best sources of information on careers and career planning is the website of America's Career Resource Network (ACRN; www.acrnetwork.org). The site provides this overview statement about ACRN:

America's Career Resource Network (ACRN) consists of state and federal organizations that provide information, resources, and training on career and education exploration. The network is funded by a grant from the U.S. Department of Education, and operates in every state and territory.

ACRN is focused on helping students and adults make the best possible decisions about education, training, and career development. ACRN helps learners identify their skills and interests and plan an education and training pathway that makes the most of their natural abilities and leads directly to fulfilling work.

For teachers and counselors, ACRN provides guides and curricula that help them incorporate career development into a high-quality academic program. For students, ACRN emphasizes the connection between academic work and future career options, helping learners of all ages to focus on achievement.

The site provides sections for students, parents, teachers, counselors, and administrators. Each section is subdivided into topics, resources, and links. The subsection provides much information, including numerous articles on No Child Left Behind and academic achievement, that would be useful to counselors. Sample lessons show how career development concepts can be easily integrated into core academics, making the academics more relevant to students' career interests.

The National Career Development Guidelines (NCDG)

Counselors in Career Pathways programs should consider using the National Career Development Guidelines (NCDG) as a framework for building and evaluating comprehensive career development programs. The guidelines cover three domains: personal social development, educational achievement and lifelong learning, and career management. Under each domain are 2–5 goals (11 in all). The goals define broad areas of career development competency. The NCDG domains and goals are listed below. Clearly, they support the Career Pathways process.

Counselors in Career Pathways programs should consider using the National Career Development Guidelines (NCDG) as a framework for building and evaluating comprehensive career development programs.

Personal Social Development

- Develop understanding of self to build and maintain a positive self-concept
- Develop positive interpersonal skills including respect for diversity
- Integrate personal growth and change into your career development
- Balance personal, leisure, community, learner, family, and work roles

Educational Achievement and Lifelong Learning

- Attain educational achievement and performance levels needed to reach your personal and career goals
- Participate in ongoing, lifelong learning experiences to enhance your ability to function effectively in a diverse and changing economy

Career Management

- Create and manage a career plan that meets your career goals
- Use a process of decision-making as one component of career development
- Use accurate, current, and unbiased career information during career planning and management

- Master academic, occupational, and general employability skills to obtain, create, maintain, and/or advance your employment
- Integrate changing employment trends, societal needs, and economic conditions into your career plans

The NCDG give counselors a framework for organizing their activities and services. Following are examples of specialized services that counselors can and should provide. They are listed under the three NCDG domains.

Personal Social Development

- Administer, analyze, and discuss career assessments (e.g., interests, aptitudes, abilities, and work values) with students
- Help students develop conflict resolution skills
- Help students develop behavior management skills for school, social, and work situations
- Provide assistance to students in solving problems at school and work

Educational Achievement and Lifelong Learning

- Help students identify strategies for improving educational achievement and performance
- Help students identify their learning styles and make connections to effective study skills
- Ensure that students know the requirements for graduation, assist them with appropriate course selection, and recommend remedies when graduation is in jeopardy
- Provide information about postsecondary education and training options and financial aid and assist students with the transition process

Career Management Domain

- Assist students with identifying career goals (e.g., Career Pathway) and developing plans to reach those goals
- Help students develop effective decision-making skills

- Help students identify and learn to use a variety of career information resources (i.e., occupational, educational, economic, and employment) to support career planning

- Help students identify and learn about Career Pathways

- Provide opportunities for students to explore occupations (including nontraditional) and discuss occupations of interest

- Help students develop job seeking skills (e.g., resume writing and job interviewing)

- Help students identify their general employability skills (e.g., time management, organization, problem solving, critical thinking, and interpersonal)

- Help students understand how employment trends, societal needs, and economic trends can affect their career plans

COMMUNICATION

Facilitating Communication Between Secondary and Postsecondary

One of the main reasons students often encounter barriers in making the transition from secondary to postsecondary is that, in general, the secondary and postsecondary levels do not communicate and/or collaborate regularly. This so-called *great divide* creates many problems, for example, frequent mismatches between high school graduation requirements and postsecondary entrance requirements, and lack of vertical alignment between secondary and postsecondary standards.

The success of Career Pathways programs depends on productive interaction between the secondary and postsecondary levels. Secondary counselors have an important role to play in making that interaction a reality, especially when programs are in the planning stages. For instance:

- They can invite postsecondary counselors to "get acquainted" events such as coffees, open houses, luncheons, and kick-off meetings. Where possible, they should include postsecondary counselors in the planning of those events. Secondary counselors should work at engaging postsecondary counselors at the secondary level so that they have a clearer picture of where their students are coming from.

> The success of Career Pathways programs depends on productive interaction between the secondary and postsecondary levels.

- Secondary counselors should provide postsecondary counselors with the names of Career Pathways students in their schools. This will help the postsecondary counselors work with their departments or programs in recruiting students into career areas in which the students have already shown interest.

- Secondary counselors should review any changes made by postsecondary institutions in requirements for specialty fields to determine whether the new requirements call for revision of the corresponding secondary curricula.

- Secondary counselors should call one or two meetings annually to discuss procedures, problems, and changes that affect postsecondary enrollment and completion. This can be especially effective if the secondary counselors have already built relationships with their counterparts at the postsecondary level, whether through one of the aforementioned events or some other means.

Communicating with Area Employers

Counselors should survey area employers annually to *identify recent graduates who have been employed*. If any recent graduates have not been retained, the counselors should request information as to why. This will help to identify areas in which the Career Pathway program is not meeting employer standards or not keeping pace with changes in industry.

Counselors should *keep employers informed about Career Pathway programs* through personal contact, newsletters, and/or electronic communication.

They should also *encourage and work with employers in providing mentors.* This involves not only setting up mentoring relationships but facilitating training opportunities for new employees who would like to become mentors. Ideally, novice mentors would be given opportunities to meet with and learn from more experienced mentors. Counselors should take the initiative in coordinating these opportunities with the mentors' employers.

Counselors should take a leading role in arranging for field trips, but they should go beyond that. They should *work with teachers in providing preparation and follow-up for field trips.* It is not enough for students merely to visit worksites. They should spend time beforehand learning about what they are about to experience. After the field trip, they should also spend time reflecting on the experience. How did it change their presumptions about the career(s) represented? Did the employees seem to enjoy their work and find it interesting? How much money could they make? Students should be given the time and resources to explore the ramifications of those questions. When well planned and executed, field trips can be life-changing experiences. Counselors should be proactive in working with employers and teachers to ensure that field trips make lasting impressions on students.

Counselors should *seek opportunities for employers to interact with Career Pathway teachers.* These can be luncheons, discussions at conferences, or almost any kind of networking event. In the long run, students benefit from that interaction.

Communicating with Community College Counselors

Secondary counselors should keep in regular contact with their counterparts at area community colleges. They should determine which institutions their students are most likely to attend after graduation and then make sure a counselor or administrator from each of those institutions is invited to serve on the career guidance team and/or the curriculum development committee. Secondary counselors should also visit each area community college at least once a year (preferably more often) to inquire as to how recent high school graduates are

> Counselors should seek opportunities for employers to interact with Career Pathway teachers.

performing. They should also invite the college counselors to visit their schools and become familiar with the counseling services they provide for Career Pathways students. One of the many benefits of this kind of regular interaction is that parties at both levels are aware of important trends and changes. Lack of interaction can cause indifference, even hostility.

Bridging the Gap Between Academic and CTE Teachers

In the Career Pathways process, students' chosen pathways provide career *contexts* for learning academic concepts. In practical terms, this means that the teaching of technical and academic content must be integrated. For most teachers, both CTE and academic, this is a stretch. Unfortunately, many academic teachers hold to the negative stereotypes of CTE (as do many administrators), and many CTE teachers feel unqualified to teach academic content. Many schools, even by their physical layouts, create environments in which CTE and academics are thought of as completely separate spheres of activity. Counselors must take the initiative in changing the preconceptions of both academic and CTE teachers by encouraging interdisciplinary communication and collaboration.

MARKETING

Disseminating Information about Career Pathways

Counselors should take the lead in providing information to parents, employers, and the media regarding the Career Pathways *concept* and the success of Career Pathways students. This information can take any of several forms—editorials or newspaper stories, television spots, newsletters, conferences with parents and employers, and online articles. There must be consistent, ongoing effort to bring positive attention to students who have planned well and are successfully moving through the Career Pathways process. The success of those students should be highlighted at every opportunity.

Secondary counselors should also try to ensure that their schools have career centers, either free-standing or as designated areas within their schools' media centers. Students should be able to go to those centers for brochures and other printed items containing employment information. The centers should provide assessment tools and, if possible, computerized career guidance systems to help students identify their interests, aptitudes, and skills and identify the careers in which those skills are most useful and in demand. Parents should also be made aware of the materials and services provided by the career center.

Dispelling Negative Misconceptions about Career and Technical Education

One of the greatest frustrations experienced by CTE educators is that parents, students, guidance counselors, principals, many other teachers, and even many employers have a negative image of CTE. Despite irrefutable evidence to the contrary, most people still think the only way to succeed in today's world is to get at least a bachelor's degree. (This belief is especially pervasive among parents, and parents are not going to think otherwise unless someone persuades them to.) Most people consider CTE a "dumping ground" for students who lack the intelligence to succeed in the college-prep path. This is unfortunate, for several reasons. For example, it causes many students to follow the college-prep path even though they are much better suited to CTE. It also discourages students from giving serious, realistic thought to how they plan to make their living as adults. And it can diminish the enthusiasm of the CTE students themselves.

The negative image of CTE represents a battle that Career Pathways counselors must be willing to fight, no matter how unfavorable the odds might seem. Bettina Lankard Brown has offered the following excellent strategies for combating the negative image of CTE.[8]

1. **Give students something to brag about.**

   - *Provide stimulating, innovative activities that students can appreciate, learn from, and share with their peers.* (Like everyone else, students get excited at the prospect of learning something that not many other people know.)

   - *Get state-of-the-art equipment or at least provide students access to it.* (Cutting-edge equipment doesn't just improve learning; students think its "cool.")

   - *Highlight the marketability of CTE program completers.* (Technical employment is the fastest-growing segment of today's labor market. Most technical occupations require only associate degrees, and the salaries are much better than most people realize.)

2. **Bring parents on board.**

   - *Address misconceptions about the need for all students to seek college degrees.* (Far too many high school graduates pursue college simply because they think it's the thing to do. For many of those students, associate degree programs are a far better option, but they don't know it.)

   - *Describe CTE options that might better meet the needs of their children.* (People who hold CTE in low esteem

> The negative image of CTE represents a battle that Career Pathways counselors must be willing to fight, no matter how unfavorable the odds might seem.

---

[8] Bettina Lankard Brown, "The Image of Career and Technical Education," *ACVE Practice Application Brief* no. 25 (2003) (http://www.cete.org/acve/docgen.asp?tbl=pab&ID=115; accessed August 2005).

usually don't know what the real options are for graduates with good technical skills. They don't know where the good jobs are, what they pay, and what it takes to get them.)

3. **Target marketing to those who have the greatest impact on student choices.**

   – *Look to student organizations for influence.* (When student organizations promote CTE, other students listen. Student organizations can also do a lot to elevate the appeal of CTE among minority and female students, who tend to be underrepresented in technical fields.)

   – *Cultivate support of business/industry representatives.* (Many businesses are more than willing to send representatives to speak with students and their parents.)

4. **Work with the media.**
   The image of CTE will never improve unless individual CTE success stories are communicated to the public.

Removing the Perception That Anything Other Than a Four-Year Degree Is Second Rate

Counselors should make every effort to enlist the help of the career guidance team in changing the widespread perception that some careers are categorically better than others. The reality is that all careers have value, and the more we talk about that concept and share our views with others, the more quickly we can begin to change people's misperceptions.

Every counselor should read *Getting Real: Helping Teens Find Their Future* by Kenneth Gray (SAGE Publications, 1999) and *Other Ways to Win: Creating Alternatives for High School Graduates* by Kenneth Gray and Edwin Herr (SAGE Publications, 2000). As Gray and Herr point out, every student should leave high school with a plan for success. But determining what constitutes "success" is a personal matter that should be decided by the student. If counselors are serious about changing people's perceptions about education and jobs, they should focus on the benefits that students enjoy as they pass each milestone associated with *their chosen Career Pathways* — rather than assessing them strictly on the basis of whether they go to college.

STUDENT ADVISEMENT

Getting Parents More Deeply Involved in Their Children's Career Planning

Many studies have shown that families, especially parents, "play a significant role in the occupational aspirations and career goal development of their children. Without parental approval or support, students and young adults are often reluctant to pursue — or even explore — diverse career possibilities."[9] In fact, parental involvement improves virtually every aspect of students' performance in school. "The research overwhelmingly demonstrates that parent involvement in children's learning is positively related to achievement. Further, the research shows that the more intensively parents are involved in their children's learning, the more beneficial are the achievement effects. This holds true for all types of parent involvement in children's learning and for all types and ages of students."[10] For this reason it is imperative that secondary counselors communicate effectively with parents of both current and prospective Career Pathways students.

Counselors should take the lead in organizing events for joint parent-student planning (e.g., Saturday seminars and workshops). These events require much forethought and preparation to ensure that participants have access to the best

---

[9] Jeffrey Taylor, Marcia B. Harris, and Susan Taylor, "Parents Have Their Say…About Their College-Age Children's Career Decisions," *Career Development and Job Search Advice for New College Graduates* (http://www.jobweb.com/resources/library/Parents/Parents_Have _Their_242_01.htm).

[10] Kathleen Cotton and Karen Reed Wikelund, "Parent Involvement in Education," *School Improvement Research Series*, Close-Up #6 (Northwest Regional Educational Library) (http://www.nwrel.org/scpd/sirs/3/cu6.html).

available tools and information. In addition to focusing on Career Pathway options, labor market information, and the importance of setting personal goals, the events should provide opportunities for working professionals to describe the pathways they followed in reaching their current positions. One interesting and encouraging outcome of this process is that students can see that the path to success invariably involves overcoming obstacles. Students should also see that the pathways followed by many (if not most) people, even the most successful, have led to unexpected destinations by way of many unexpected detours. And students will benefit from hearing successful adults talk about what they would have done differently if, as youngsters, they had known what they know now. When well planned and executed, these events will be very popular among parents and students alike and will produce excellent results.

Helping Students and Parents Make Preliminary Pathway Decisions — Without "Tracking"

Career awareness activities should begin as early as the elementary grades and continue into the middle school years. Teachers and counselors must work together to create ways to help students see the relationship between what they learn in school and how that information is used outside the classroom. By the eighth grade, students should be exposed to the differences between pursuing a career and merely getting a job. Parents should also be informed about what is meant by the term *career cluster* and have at least minimal exposure to the 16 generally recognized clusters.

> Whatever choice a student makes at the end of the eighth grade should be reviewed each year thereafter to see whether that is still the Career Pathway that the student wants to pursue.

During the eighth grade, students should be given both interest and aptitude assessments to help them begin to make initial career choices. It is extremely important that the results of these assessments be explained to both the parents and the

213

students so that they can see that this is just the beginning of the exploration phase; it is merely a place to start. The beginning of the career decision process involves many factors, and the more information students can get about themselves and their interests, abilities, and preferences, the better their choices will be. This is an ongoing process that should continue throughout the secondary school experience and be reevaluated every year. Whatever choice a student makes at the end of the eighth grade should be reviewed each year thereafter to see whether that is still the Career Pathway that the student wants to pursue. No decision made in eighth grade, or at any time in high school, should be seen as a "track" that students can't change.

As students have more and more opportunities to explore careers through job shadowing, mentoring, part-time jobs, and volunteering, they will develop a clearer sense of what they like and don't like. These are valuable experiences that help students determine whether they are in the pathways that are right for them. The key to the success of this process is to be sure that a student's career plan (which begins in eighth grade) is reviewed each year by the student, the parent, and a school representative (ideally the counselor). This will ensure that the student is not stuck or labeled as "tracked" into only one career choice for the entire secondary school experience. It should also be made clear by the counselor and the teachers that a Career Pathway provides preparation for a whole group of related occupations, not just preparation for one job. In fact, when the business representatives are speaking with students, they should emphasize the breadth of career preparation that the Career Pathways program provides.

Helping Career Pathways Students Take the Next Step After High School Graduation

By the middle or end of the eleventh grade, students should be developing a clear understanding of the knowledge and skill requirements of the career specialties within their pathways. The counselor should make that information available through interviews with employers, written materials, the Internet, guest speakers, field trips, and (where possible) summer employment. This is where the cooperation of college representatives, employers, and community leaders becomes essential. School administrators should be supportive of innovative activities designed to help students dig a little deeper in becoming acquainted with their career options.

> One of the benefits of the ninth- and tenth-grade portion of the Career Pathways process is that it gives students an opportunity to conclude that they are *not* in the right pathways.

At the beginning of the twelfth grade, the counselor should conduct one-on-one or group sessions with students to help them review their career plans and set postgraduation goals. Those goals serve as powerful motivating factors. Part of the counselor's job is to help students understand what it will take to reach their goals — what skills, how much and what kind of education, and how long. The counselor should help each student select a career field and write a corresponding education and training plan. The plan then provides benchmarks for assessing the student's progress. Each student's progress should be reviewed periodically, at least once or (preferably) twice a year. Then, if necessary, the student's plan should be revised to reflect where he or she is on the road to reaching personal goals.

Students should be encouraged to identify barriers that might hinder them from taking the next step. They should be helped to understand how various factors — family circumstances, financial need, occupational requirements, personal desire, and personal motivation — might affect their

215

decisions. Of primary importance is whether the student is prepared academically to pass the college entrance exam. Just qualifying for high school graduation may not be enough. If students learn by the eleventh grade that they are deficient in certain academic areas, they still have time to rectify the situation so that they will not require remediation in college.

Dual Enrollment and Students' Decisions Regarding Higher Education

Counselors should encourage Career Pathways students to take advantage of dual enrollment opportunities. Dual enrollment allows students to get a taste of what it takes to do college-level work. Credits received through dual enrollment reduce the time required to complete college programs and/or allow students to take more advanced courses in their chosen majors. Dual enrollment credits can reduce the cost of college attendance and give students a "can do" attitude about their college programs. Experiences gained through dual enrollment courses can also show some students that college is *not* the best route for them; in many cases those students are better off pursing alternative routes such as apprenticeships. Whatever direction students take, dual enrollment courses provide additional experiences that help them assess their interests and abilities.[11]

> Counselors should encourage Career Pathways students to take advantage of dual enrollment opportunities.

"Learning to Learn" and Career Counseling

Our country's economy has undergone many dramatic changes in the last few years. Those changes have resulted in vastly different requirements for employment. "Job security" is a thing of the past. Everyone should be prepared for the

---

[11] For more on dual enrollment, see Chapter 9.

inevitability of change. Considering today's high-tech, global economic environment, counselors should focus their attention on helping students lay a foundation that will qualify them to pursue *ranges* of careers, rather than narrow, task-specific jobs. The emphasis must now be on helping students lay a strong foundation of academic skills that will allow them to adapt to changes in the workplace by developing new skills quickly, as the need arises. This process of adaptation is a lifelong activity. To maintain career success over a lifetime, people must "learn to learn." They must learn to adapt quickly to changing occupational environments.

> Counselors should focus their attention on helping students lay a foundation that will qualify them to pursue *ranges* of careers, rather than narrow, task-specific jobs. The emphasis must now be on helping students lay a strong foundation of academic skills that will allow them to adapt to changes in the workplace by developing new skills quickly.

One of the many ways counselors can help students lay a strong foundation that equips them for high achievement in school and (eventually) success in the workplace is by contributing to the development, refinement, and/or teaching of the ninth-grade introductory Career Pathways courses. Those courses, typically titled "Personal Management for Career Success" or something similar, are designed to help students begin the process of exploring career options, learning employability skills, and understanding the importance of core academic skills in the modern workplace.

Student Portfolios in the Guidance and Placement Process

Counselors should insist that students keep their portfolios up to date and in good order. A student portfolio is a record of a student's progress in achieving the goals associated with his or her Career Pathway. Information in the portfolio should include assessment scores, lists of courses taken, grades received, and descriptions and documentation of occupational experiences (including work-based learning or other special training). The portfolio should also include information on special accomplishments, rewards, or recognitions that the student has received. Extracurricular activities and any other voluntary experiences should also be a part of each student's individual portfolio.[12]

WORK-BASED LEARNING

Every student should have an opportunity to learn about the workplace and careers first-hand, before joining the workforce full time as an adult. Every student should also learn "soft skills" or "employability skills," and the best place to do that is at real worksites. Through work-based learning experiences, the student learns the importance of teamwork, effective communication, workplace ethics, and problem solving. Through work-based learning experiences the student also learns whether he or she has the skills, interest, and temperament for a particular career. Work-based experiences can greatly enhance a student's understanding of career requirements, both mental and physical.

> Every student should have an opportunity to learn about the workplace and careers first-hand, before joining the workforce full time as an adult. Every student should also learn "soft skills" or "employability skills," and the best place to do that is at real worksites.

Counselors should strive to ensure that work-based learning experiences have clear objectives and that students understand the objectives and are assessed on their success in

---

[12] For more on student portfolios, see Hope J. Gibbs, "Student Portfolios: Documenting Success," *Techniques,* May 2004 (http://www.acteonline.org/members/techniques/may04_feature3.cfm). The American School Counselor Association's *Get-a-Life Personal Planning Portfolio for Career Development* is a commercially available planner that helps students in grades 5–12 make career decisions and formulate educational plans. See http://www.schoolcounselor.org/store_product.asp?prodid=91.

meeting them. Work-based learning experiences should not be thought of as extracurricular. They should be closely aligned with and support the curriculum. Counselors should help students put their work-based learning experiences into the perspective of their long-range plans. This can be accomplished through group sessions in which students share information about their work-based learning experiences, assess their own job performance, and articulate their feelings about their career choices.

Where possible, in addition to job shadowing and field trips, counselors should try to set up full-fledged mentoring relationships. Mentoring is the most effective form of worksite learning experience, particularly when mentors are well trained and genuinely interested in students' progress. Mentors can serve as valuable role models. They can not only expose students to the requirements and regulations of their chosen fields but also acquaint them with other specialties within those fields (for example, the many Career Pathways within the clusters of business or medicine or law). Mentors should be aware of their responsibilities in exposing students to their fields and be willing to devote the time and effort necessary to expand the students' knowledge about the entire range of requirements within those fields.

> Mentoring is the most effective form of worksite learning experience, particularly when mentors are well trained and genuinely interested in students' progress.

VIRGINIA'S CAREER COACHES INITIATIVE

In an effort to help students make career choices and to increase the number of high school graduates prepared for employment and/or community college enrollment in CTE, Virginia has created a new statewide initiative called Virginia Community College System (VCCS) Career Coaches.

Project Background

Career coaches are community college employees placed in high schools to help high school students define their career aspirations and recognize community college and other postsecondary programs and services that can help them reach their goals. Career coaches identify for students and their parents career exploration and planning opportunities and secondary-to-postsecondary transition programs such as Tech Prep, dual enrollment, and the recently launched Bridges Partnership Program.[13] Career coaches also advise students on Career Pathways that are accessible through secondary and postsecondary CTE programs, apprenticeships, and industry certifications and licensures. Central to the interaction between career coach and student is the development of a career plan for each student. A primary goal of the Career Coaches initiative is to increase the number of high school graduates prepared for employment and/or community college enrollment in CTE fields.

The initiative was launched with fewer than five career coaches. Currently, 16 career coaches report to 14 community colleges and are based in 19 high schools throughout the Commonwealth. VCCS and the Virginia Department of Education (VDOE) are collaboratively funding the initiative through a two-year Perkins special projects grant. Interest in the program by college and school division partners has been such that, by September 2005, 22 additional career coaches will join the program, for a total of 38. Most of these new coaches will be locally funded by VCCS colleges through their Tech Prep and postsecondary Perkins grants. In at least one Tech Prep region, allied business and industry and economic and workforce development partners have committed funds to expand the number of career coaches based in their region.

---

[13] The Bridges Partnership Program provides early college placement testing and assessment for targeted high school students along with academic interventions as necessary to ensure that students can begin community college programs without remediation. The program is affiliated with the League for Innovation in the Community College.

Program Model

Many of the career coaches have educational backgrounds and work experience in either high school or college counseling. However, in their role as career coaches, these professionals have a unique function. Career coaching is an extension of the coaching that all students receive (or should receive) at some point in their adolescent development, whether from parents and other relatives, teachers, or athletic coaches and trainers. Contemporary culture offers fewer and fewer opportunities for high school students to be naturally coached. Consequently, there is increasing interest—on the part of secondary and postsecondary educators and their business and industry partners—in developing a cadre of practitioners who support career development just as fitness trainers support athletic development. Like a fitness trainer, a career coach conducts much of his or her work "in the field," meeting with students in school lunch rooms and computer centers, and visiting businesses and industries and colleges to establish experiential learning programs.

> Contemporary culture offers fewer and fewer opportunities for high school students to be naturally coached. Consequently, there is increasing interest—on the part of secondary and postsecondary educators and their business and industry partners—in developing a cadre of practitioners who support career development just as fitness trainers support athletic development.

Career coaches carry out many functions besides coaching. They develop interpersonal relationships that permit students to discover how to move in the direction of their dreams. Other areas of the career coach's job include the following.

- **Consulting**—To increase the impact of the 37 career coaches who will be in the field by fall 2005, the new VCCS career coaches are encouraged (and will be trained) to serve not only as coaches but as consultants within their assigned high schools and school divisions. In this capacity they will support teachers, administrators, and business partners who are also engaged (officially or not) in coaching students in their career planning.

- **Teaching** — A career coach teaches students about career planning; teaches teachers about career coaching and career resources; teaches business partners about adolescent development, career coaching, and educational preparation; and teaches administrators about the practice of career coaching.

- **Administration** — Career coaches administer their own coaching programs. This includes developing strategic plans with their assigned high schools and community colleges and developing program resources and program evaluation methods. Local career coaching programs are administered within the context of the larger administrative structure for the statewide career coaching initiative.

- **Marketing** — Career coaches market their program and their skills so that others will come to see the value of those skills and of their coaching activities. Coaches develop marketing activities directed at businesses and community organizations, teachers and administrators, and students and their parents or guardians.

- **Relationship** — Career coaching is built on relating to others — students, parents, teachers, administrators, other career coaches, business partners, and the community at large. It is in relating to others that the fundamental nature of career coaching is demonstrated. Coaches help students discover their strengths, overcome obstacles, build inner resolve, and develop a sense of social presence.

- **Instrumentation** — Career coaches develop instruments designed to account for program activity, demonstrate program effectiveness, and maintain the integrity of the relationship between coach and student. The VCCS "starter kit," which career coaches adapt to their own situations, includes student intake forms, templates for student career plans, and tools for student and program assessment.

- **Community of practice** — VCCS is committed to a plan of professional development that will increase the coaches' awareness of career-exploration resources and encourage mutual support among the coaches. As part of this commitment, VCCS is developing a "network-centric" model of professional training and collegial support through an online community in which career coaches and co-participants in career coaching can interact and learn. The network is under construction at http://vacareercoaches.org/.

Professional Development

VCCS career coaches have been trained in the above-described model of career coaching as well as in Career Pathways, career planning, and career resources through two statewide professional development courses held in April and July 2005. The curriculum for the first course was jointly developed by the University of Virginia's Workforce Development Academy, the Coaches Training Institute, and high school and community college practitioners. The program for the July 2005 workshop on the role of career coaching in Career Pathways was developed by CORD. The next planned step is to develop a formal training curriculum that includes classroom, video, and online instruction.

Evaluation

The VCCS system office is tracking student participation and maintaining data to measure the following outcomes:

- Increase in student enrollment in secondary to postsecondary transitional programs such as Tech Prep, dual enrollment, and the Bridges Partnership Program
- Increase in the number of students who graduate from high school with college credits
- Increase in the number of students who graduate from high school with industry certification or licensure
- Increase in the number of students who participate in work-based learning activities such as business incubator

projects, problem- and case-based learning, service learning, and internships and co-ops

- Increase in the number of high school graduates who enroll in community college CTE programs

Relationship to Career Pathways

The Career Coaches program is the primary strategy through which VCCS is moving to integrate systematic and sequential career planning services in its Tech Prep Career Pathways. In close conjunction with the launch of the Career Coaches program, VCCS held a series of statewide focus group meetings of secondary and postsecondary educators that established common Career Pathway elements for the state. These statewide Career Pathway elements include articulation and dual-enrollment, business and industry partnerships, career coaching, work-based learning, integrated curriculum, and transitional services. In less than a year, career coaching (initially the least familiar of these program elements to Tech Prep practitioners) has become a significant transformational force.

CONCLUSION

In the Career Pathways process, secondary counselors have big shoes to fill. They have many roles to play, and they can't wait around for others to make the first move. They must be high-energy initiators, motivators, and communicators. They must work hard to stay on top of trends and projections in business and industry. They must know enough about jobs — many jobs — that they could almost step in and do the jobs themselves. They must be able to build relationships that overcome natural barriers — between school and the workplace, between secondary and postsecondary, between academics and CTE, and sometimes even between students and their own parents. They must be willing to take up the fight in changing the way people think about career education.

That's a tall order. But it can be done. And when it is done right, the results can be dramatic, as the Career Coaches program in Virginia is proving. Effective counseling in Career Pathways produces tangible results—more students thinking about careers at the *beginning* of high school, more students making smooth transitions from secondary to postsecondary, more students beginning their college careers with college credits already in hand, and more students leaving high school with a clear sense of direction and the tools necessary to reach their goals.

Chapter 9 Preview

Secondary component:

7. Provides opportunities for students to earn college credit through dual/concurrent enrollment or articulation agreements.

Postsecondary component:

8. Provides opportunities for students to earn college credit through dual/concurrent enrollment or articulation agreements.

Dual enrollment provides several incentives for Career Pathway students to do well in high school and transition to college after high school graduation:

1. *By enrolling in college courses while still in high school, students who have already completed their graduation requirements do not waste time in their senior year.*

2. *High school juniors and seniors have an opportunity to "experience college." They experience a different environment in which they are treated more as adults. And they discover that they can compete at the college level.*

3. *They discover early whether they have deficiencies that might prevent college entrance, and have an opportunity to correct those deficiencies so that they will not be required to take developmental (remedial) courses in college.*

4. *They have an opportunity to earn up to one year of college credits by the time they graduate from high school. This "jump start" is not just a morale booster; it can result in significant savings in college expenses.*

This chapter explains the differences between articulation (which is predominant in typical Tech Prep consortia) and dual enrollment. Sometimes the authors use the terms "articulation" and "Tech Prep" interchangeably. The reader should not assume that the comparison is "Tech Prep versus dual enrollment"; rather, the authors' purpose is to show how most Tech Prep consortia could improve student incentives and opportunities by converting from articulation to dual enrollment.

But converting to dual enrollment in Tech Prep is not a simple process. It is most effectively accomplished after a new 4+2 curriculum framework is created, as described in Chapter 3.

D.H.

DUAL ENROLLMENT/ DUAL CREDIT: ITS ROLE IN CAREER PATHWAYS

Katherine L. Hughes, Melinda Mechur Karp, David Bunting, and Janice Friedel

As Dan Hull points out in *Career Pathways: The Next Generation of Tech Prep*,[1] Tech Prep has been widely effective in many ways but now faces challenges. Hull calls for Tech Prep to be seen as a change agent—for Tech Prep practitioners to use their knowledge and partnerships to bring about program improvement through the creation of Career Pathways. This chapter focuses on a particular feature of Career Pathways: dual enrollment, also called concurrent enrollment.

An important goal of Tech Prep has been to connect students' high school and postsecondary course-taking—to create curricular alignment so that high school students can transition seamlessly to college, and enter with advanced standing. Achieving this goal, however, has been difficult for

---

[1] Dan M. Hull, *Career Pathways: The Next Generation of Tech Prep* (Waco, Texas: National Tech Prep Network, 2004).

some Tech Prep partnerships, as we will elaborate on below. Still, the current popularity of dual enrollment demonstrates the continued interest in accelerating some high school students' studies. And, the essential characteristics of an ideal Career Pathway, as defined by CORD and the College and Career Transitions Initiative, and approved by the Office of Vocational and Adult Education, U.S. Department of Education, include the provision of opportunities for high school students to earn college credit. Thus, to understand the role that dual enrollment can play in the next generation of career and technical education (CTE) programs, it is instructive to examine how dual enrollment is being promoted and developed around the country, at the state and local levels.

Dual enrollment programs allow high school students to enroll in college courses and earn college credit that is placed on a college transcript. In some programs, students earn high school and college credit simultaneously; these programs may be referred to as dual credit. Dual enrollment is not always for dual credit. Though dual enrollment has existed for many years, it is becoming increasingly widespread and student enrollment has been growing. In Florida, for example, the number of students participating in dual enrollment grew from 27,689 in 1988–1989 to 34,273 in 2002–2003.[2] Forty states have policies addressing dual enrollment.[3] Over 50 percent of colleges in the United States allow high school students to enroll in college courses.[4]

---

[2] Florida Board of Education, untitled, undated presentation of dual enrollment participation data (http://www.flboe.org/news/2004/2004_03_10/DualEnrollment_Pres.pdf; accessed July 2005).

[3] Melinda Mechur Karp, Thomas R. Bailey, Katherine L. Hughes, and Baranda J. Fermin, *State Dual Enrollment Policies: Addressing Access and Quality, Community College Research Center Brief Number 26* (New York: Community College Research Center, Teachers College, Columbia University, 2005).

[4] Tiffany Waits, J. Carl Setzer, and Laurie Lewis, *Dual Credit and Exam-Based Courses in U.S. Public High Schools: 2002–03* (NCES 2005-009) (Washington, D.C.: U. S. Department of Education, National Center for Education Statistics, 2005).

Traditionally, dual enrollment has been targeted at academically advanced students. However, policymakers and educators now believe that dual enrollment is not only for high-achieving students. Instead, they argue that dual enrollment programs may meet the needs of a range of young people, technical students included.[5] The federal government has called for the expansion of dual enrollment to new student populations on a number of occasions.[6]

The chapter is organized as follows. We differentiate between dual enrollment and the articulation model found in many Tech Prep programs, highlighting the advantages and disadvantages of using one versus the other of these models. We then discuss some issues that practitioners face when implementing technically oriented dual enrollment programs, focusing on questions of program model and state policy context. We then highlight one program model, Iowa's career academies, that demonstrates the role that dual enrollment can play in helping CTE students move seamlessly from high school to college and credentials. Finally, we offer recommendations for those seeking to include dual enrollment as part of a Career Pathway.

---

[5] See, for example, Thomas Bailey and Melinda Mechur Karp, *Promoting College Access and Success: A Review of Dual Credit and Other High School/College Transition Programs*. Report prepared for the Office of Vocational and Adult Education, U.S. Department of Education (New York: Community College Research Center, Teachers College, Columbia University, 2003); National Commission on the High School Senior Year, *Raising Our Sights: No High School Senior Left Behind* (Princeton, N.J.: The Woodrow Wilson National Fellowship Foundation, 2001); Katherine L. Hughes, Melinda Mechur Karp, Baranda J. Fermin, and Thomas R. Bailey, *Pathways to College Access and Success* (Washington, D.C.: U.S. Department of Education, Office of Vocational and Adult Education, forthcoming).

[6] U.S. Department of Education, Office of Vocational and Adult Education, *The Secondary and Technical Education Excellence Act of 2003: Summary of Major Provisions* (Washington, D.C.: Author, 2003); U.S. Department of Education, Office of Vocational and Adult Education. *OVAE Review*, April 2005 (http://www.ed.gov/news/newsletters/ovaereview/orev043005.html; accessed July 2005).

TECH PREP AND DUAL ENROLLMENT: TWO MODELS FOR STUDENT ACCELERATION

Tech Prep consortia work with partnering high schools and colleges to identify opportunities for curricular alignment. In the traditional model of Tech Prep, this involves identifying opportunities for the partnering college to offer courses on the high school campus that are part of a connected sequence of courses at the college. High school students who successfully complete the high school course may be exempted from the equivalent college course upon matriculation into the postsecondary institution.

For example, a college offering an associate degree in culinary arts may collaborate with a high school creating a culinary arts program. In looking at syllabi, the two institutions may determine that two semesters of high school culinary arts courses could be based on the college curriculum, so that the high school students would gain the same competencies that they would taking Culinary Arts 101 at the college. The two institutions may come to an agreement that any high school student who completes the two courses and matriculates into the college may enroll directly in Culinary Arts 102.

In this way, Tech Prep articulation agreements help connect students' high school course-taking to future education in their career fields. They may also lend coherence to students' high school curricular experiences by rewarding students for taking multiple courses in the same subject area and encouraging students to build their skills in a sequential, progressive manner. Finally, these agreements may help accelerate student progress toward degrees or certificates, because students should not spend time in college relearning the skills already mastered in their high school Tech Prep courses.

In our research around the country, however, we have heard that the promise of articulation agreements is often not realized. For a variety of reasons, articulation of high school and college coursework does not lead to high levels of curricular coherence for students or widespread acceleration toward degrees. A national evaluation of eight consortia also found that students tended not to benefit from the articulated credits, sometimes because student participants were unaware that they could earn college credits from their high school Tech Prep coursework.[7] Thus, there are reasons to be concerned about this model of Tech Prep.

First, though conceived as curricular pathways or discrete CTE programs, Tech Prep frequently devolves into a series of electives. Pathways may exist on paper, but, in practice, students take only one or two courses in the program. Instead of a coherent multiyear program, Tech Prep courses remain one of a variety of elective course options. In other words, although many students are enrolling in Tech Prep, fewer are completing Tech Prep sequences.

This has a number of ramifications for students' educational and Career Pathways. Engaging with technical coursework for only one semester, rather than through a sequence of courses, may not allow students to develop a progressively complex understanding of the technical area. Students do not have the opportunity to recognize that technical skills build upon one another over time, nor are they likely to make connections between technical and academic courses. Also, when students do not complete a Tech Prep sequence, secondary and postsecondary curricula remain unconnected.

> **Engaging with technical coursework for only one semester, rather than through a sequence of courses, may not allow students to develop a progressively complex understanding of the technical area.**

A second concern with the articulated Tech Prep model is the nature of credit-earning it promotes. Articulation agreements are institution-specific. This means that if a student takes an articulated Tech Prep sequence offered through a community college, there is no guarantee that any other

---

[7] Debra D. Bragg, *Promising Outcomes for Tech-Prep Participants in Eight Local Consortia: A Summary of Initial Results* (St. Paul, Minn.: National Research Center for Career and Technical Education, 2001).

postsecondary institution will recognize the competencies he or she learned in that sequence. Hence, unless students matriculate into their high school's postsecondary partner, they are unlikely to reap the college-credit-earning benefit of participating in Tech Prep.

Moreover, even when students take a full Tech Prep sequence in high school and matriculate into the partnering college, they may not receive credit for their articulated classes. Many articulation agreements rely on something called "credit-in-escrow." This means that students must meet a complex set of requirements to receive credit on their college transcripts for their Tech Prep courses. Though these requirements vary, depending on the institutional agreement, they are often quite onerous. At one consortium in our research, we found that to have their Tech Prep courses placed on their college transcripts, Tech Prep students had to enroll in the college within two years of high school graduation, declare their major in the same field as their Tech Prep courses, submit a petition to the registrar's office asking for their credits, and take at least six credits at the college. The result of this policy is that, while thousands of high school students are enrolled in Tech Prep courses, only a handful receive college credit each year.

The practitioners we have spoken with express frustration at these aspects of articulated Tech Prep models. They support the goal of creating a seamless transition from high school CTE into college majors that lead to occupational certifications and degrees. And they recognize that by working together, secondary and postsecondary institutions can help students make connections between their coursework and their occupational goals. But they often feel that this Tech Prep arrangement discourages such connections, in large part because of ambivalence in presenting Tech Prep programs as coherent program sequences, and because Tech Prep courses do not easily lead to college credit. Many consortia have begun to look for alternative models through which to accelerate their students' learning. Some consortia no longer rely on articulated courses, instead integrating dual enrollment courses into their Tech Prep pathways.

Like articulated Tech Prep, dual enrollment programs are predicated on close cooperation between high schools and colleges. In dual enrollment programs, high school students enroll in college courses. Because these courses are the same as those offered on college campuses — usually using the same syllabi and textbooks — high schools and colleges do not need to engage in a process of matching competencies, such as that done for some Tech Prep and other articulation agreements. Instead, it can be assumed that a student taking Culinary Arts 101 through a dual enrollment program is mastering the same skills as a regularly matriculated student taking Culinary Arts 101 as part of his or her college course load. Thus, the college credit earned through dual enrollment courses is immediately placed on students' college transcripts.

High schools and colleges partnering for dual enrollment do have decisions to make together. Dual enrollment programs can vary along a range of features and adhere to a variety of program models (see text box, following page).[8] Partnering institutions must decide the location of the course (high school or college), who will teach the course (college faculty or high school faculty certified as college adjuncts), what the student mix will be (high school students only, or high school students mixed with college students), how the courses will be financed (who will pay tuition?), and which students will be permitted to enroll.

---

[8] For a full description of these program models, see Thomas Bailey and Melinda Mechur Karp, *Promoting College Access and Success: A Review of Dual Credit and Other High School/College Transition Programs.* Report prepared for the Office of Vocational and Adult Education, U.S. Department of Education (New York: Community College Research Center, Teachers College, Columbia University, 2003).

Ten Features Along Which Dual Enrollment Programs Can Vary

- **Target population:** Do programs target a specific type of student and, if so, which type?
- **Admissions requirements:** What criteria must students meet to be eligible for participation?
- **Location:** Are dual enrollment courses offered at the high school, the college, or both locations?
- **Student mix:** Do dual enrollment students take courses with regularly matriculated college students, or do they have their own separate courses?
- **Instructors:** What credentials must dual enrollment teachers hold?
- **Course content:** Are dual enrollment courses identical to regular college courses? If not, are processes in place to ensure that their content is college-level?
- **Credit-earning:** How do dual enrollment students earn credit? Is it dual credit? Is this regulated by the state or institutionally determined?
- **Program intensity:** Does state policy encourage or mandate *singleton, comprehensive,* or *enhanced comprehensive* programs?
- **Funding:** How are dual enrollment programs funded? What happens to full-time enrollment (FTE) and average daily attendance (ADA) funding for dual enrollment students?
- **Mandatory nature of state dual enrollment policy:** Are dual enrollment programs required by state policy, or simply permitted at an individual institution's discretion?

Source: Melinda Mechur Karp, Thomas R. Bailey, Katherine L. Hughes, and Baranda J. Fermin, *State Dual Enrollment Policies: Addressing Access and Quality* (Washington, D.C.: U.S. Department of Education, Office of Vocational and Adult Education, 2004). See also the 2005 *Update* to this report.

Partners must also determine whether dual enrollment programs will adhere to a singleton, comprehensive, or enhanced comprehensive program model. Singleton programs are single-course electives. Comprehensive programs include a series or sequence of dual enrollment courses and usually encompass much of students' junior and senior years of high school. Enhanced comprehensive programs also include multiple dual enrollment courses over a number of semesters or years, and provide support services to help students enter and succeed in postsecondary education as well. These services may include counseling, assistance with financial aid applications, or work-based learning experiences.

Dual enrollment programs often focus on academic courses, such as English composition or statistics. But they are also a useful model for offering technical coursework. Many high schools do not have up-to-date equipment for CTE; college partners often do. Moreover, many high-wage, high-growth technical fields require high levels of academic skills. Technically oriented dual enrollment programs can address both types of coursework by building program pathways that include college-level academics and college-level technical classes. Comprehensive programs include the curricular sequencing necessary for developing students' technical skills, and enhanced comprehensive programs include services tailored toward easing CTE students' transition into postsecondary education and employment. The Iowa career academies discussed later in this chapter are one example of dual enrollment as CTE.

ADVANTAGES AND DISADVANTAGES

From our perspective, dual enrollment has three distinct advantages — and one possible disadvantage — in creating seamless transitions for CTE students, as compared to articulated models of Tech Prep. These stem from the fundamental difference between the two arrangements, namely, whether or not high school students are enrolled in the partnering college. In many current Tech Prep arrangements, high school participants are not considered college students. Their Tech Prep courses are, first and foremost, *high school* courses. Dual enrollment students, in contrast, are students in two institutions. They are high school students who are also simultaneously enrolled in college.[9]

By considering participants college students, dual enrollment programs eliminate one of the thorniest issues facing articulated Tech Prep models—that of credit transfer. Dually enrolled students earn college credit that appears on a college transcript, just as would any other college student. Therefore, if they choose to matriculate into a different postsecondary institution, they can request the transcript and have their credit applied toward a major at their new college in the same way that transfer students might. (It should be noted that credit is not guaranteed to transfer—but it is no less likely to transfer than credit earned by a freshman transferring to a new institution as a sophomore.)

For students who matriculate into the institution at which they took their dual enrollment course, credit transfer is even simpler. Because it is already on their transcript, they automatically receive credit toward their college degree. This credit may count toward their majors, if they continue to pursue a degree related to their CTE coursework. Or, if they choose to pursue a different career, their dual enrollment credit may count as an elective course. Either way, there are no additional hurdles to navigate. Thus, dual enrollment students enter college with a head-start toward a degree. They may also understand that their high school coursework was connected to their college course-taking, because they see the tangible connection between what they did in high school and what they plan to achieve in college. And, because dual enrollment credits, in many cases, may count toward students' majors, those credits are the first step in a sequence of career-specific courses leading to a credential.

---

[9] Dually enrolled students are not always considered identical to regularly matriculated college students. They are often considered nonmatriculated students or special registrants, and they are ineligible for federal financial aid. Nonetheless, dually enrolled students are typically counted in colleges' FTE headcounts and, for practical purposes, are considered college students.

The second important advantage is that dually enrolled students, because they are considered college students, have access to all of the support services available on the college campus. These may include tutoring and advising. Tech Prep students, by contrast, do not usually have access to those services.

Support services provide dual enrollment students with additional resources to ensure that they will be successful in their college-credit classes. Access to tutoring and other academic supports is particularly important for students in rigorous technical fields such as health, because high school-based staff may not have the specialized knowledge to help students. Academic and career counseling at the college may also help students with their overall transition to college. Such services can help students understand the educational and career trajectories they might take to build upon their high school experiences. Students who take advantage of college-based advising are likely to have more information that enables them to engage in planful behavior. They may, for example, come to understand that their intended major requires them to take additional math and science in high school to prepare for high-level technical courses in college. Or they might better understand how their coursework connects to their future jobs, or the types of degrees they need to pursue to enter their chosen professions.

High school counselors are often overworked and unable to provide students with the personal attention they need to select a college, navigate the admission process, and apply for financial aid. Moreover, many high school counselors are unfamiliar with the variety of career options and the educational backgrounds necessary to enter technical fields. Thus, dual enrollment students can use college counselors as an additional resource for determining their post-high school plans.

As college students, dual enrollment participants often have access to college facilities, such as libraries, and may even receive priority registration for future semesters. Spending time on the college campus may help students learn about "college life," thereby smoothing their transition into postsecondary education. And for students hoping to pursue majors with waiting lists, such as those in the health professions, early registration may make it easier for them to meet their degree requirements in a timely manner.

A third potential benefit of dual enrollment as part of a Career Pathway or other CTE program is that it can raise the prestige of such programs. Given the current national emphasis on raising academic standards, courses with college-level curricula add rigor to CTE programs. In addition, as opportunities for college-credit-earning such as AP and dual enrollment become more popular with students and parents, the inclusion of transcripted college credit in CTE programs would serve to make those programs more attractive.

There is one potential drawback to dual enrollment, however. Because dual enrollment students are enrolling in college courses, they often have to meet the same entry standards that regularly matriculating college students do. Eighty-five percent of colleges nationwide have admission requirements for dually enrolled students.[10] In addition, high schools[11] and states sometimes impose additional eligibility criteria. Thus, when compared to Tech Prep, in some locales students may have to meet higher academic requirements to participate in dual enrollment. This has the effect of restricting access.

These requirements vary widely. At some colleges, students must pass some or all placement tests to take a dual enrollment course — even if it is in a technical field. In others, students may have to gain regular admission to the college. Other colleges permit technical students to take only certain courses (leading to certificates rather than degrees, for

---

[10] Brian Kleiner and Laurie Lewis, *Dual Enrollment of High School Students at Postsecondary Institutions, 2002–2003* (Washington, D.C.: U.S. Department of Education, National Center for Education Statistics, 2005).

[11] Tiffany Waits, J. Carl Setzer, and Laurie Lewis, *Dual Credit and Exam-Based Courses in US High Schools, 2002–2003* (Washington, D.C.: U.S. Department of Education, National Center for Education Statistics, 2005).

example), while others allow high schools to determine which students are ready for college-level coursework. These requirements are particularly troublesome when dual enrollment is targeted at CTE students. CTE students are sometimes disengaged from traditional academic work, or learn better when academics are placed in context, and therefore could benefit mightily from technical dual enrollment—and yet their previous academic performance may prevent them from entering the program.

The question of dual enrollment entry standards is a contentious one. Colleges are justified in expecting that high school students enrolled in their courses meet the same standards as regular college students. Moreover, allowing students to enter college courses without going through the admissions process may ignite the criticism that technical education is less rigorous than traditional academics. Ensuring that students in technical dual enrollment programs are prepared to do college-level work through admission requirements could demonstrate the quality of CTE, as well as help ensure that students are not set up for failure when they enroll in college courses.

Finally, eligibility criteria are only a potential drawback, and actually present an opportunity. One of the essential characteristics of an ideal Career Pathway is that it meets postsecondary entry and placement requirements. Career Pathway programs aim to ensure that high school students are prepared to meet the standards set for college entry. Thus, such programs offer secondary and postsecondary partners the opportunity to clearly align not only their curricula in the technical area, but their academic exit and entry requirements as well.

STATE POLICIES AND DUAL ENROLLMENT

For those making efforts to move from the traditional articulated Tech Prep model to technical dual enrollment, certainly an important step is to examine one's state policies for dual enrollment. While not all states have policies addressing dual enrollment, in those that do the policies will provide some parameters for program implementation.

State policies regarding dual enrollment vary widely.[12] Some policies are quite comprehensive, while others do little more than grant institutions the option of offering dual enrollment if they so desire. Policies can range along the ten features highlighted earlier (in the text box).[13] For the purposes of this discussion, we focus on the features most relevant to the creation of CTE pathways that include dual enrollment. However, since dual enrollment has traditionally focused on advanced students, in many states the needs of technical students are not explicitly addressed by current policies.

State policies addressing eligibility requirements are the first feature that may influence technical students' access to dual enrollment. Most states with dual enrollment policies address the question of which students may take college courses. Some states regulate only the age of dually enrolled students, while others set forth specific admission requirements. Other states' policies allow institutional discretion over student eligibility. As noted earlier, eligibility requirements may prevent CTE students from taking dual enrollment courses. And when a state makes those requirements part of its official policy, institutions have little flexibility to tailor admission requirements to the types of programs they offer.

Some states have created policies that support the inclusion of a broad range of students in dual enrollment. In some cases, students must demonstrate that they do not need remediation in the subject of their dual enrollment course. A student who wants to take a college-credit math course (perhaps as part of a technical sequence) need only place out of remediation in

---

[12] See Melinda Mechur Karp, Thomas R. Bailey, Katherine L. Hughes, and Baranda J. Fermin, *State Dual Enrollment Policies: Addressing Access and Quality* (Washington, D.C.: U.S. Department of Education, Office of Vocational and Adult Education, 2004). See also the 2005 *Update* to this report.

[13] Ibid.

math; poor history or English performance would not prevent his or her participation in dual enrollment. Another possibility is to create two admission standards—one for academic courses and another for technical courses. Students with low grade point averages may be able to take technical courses, even if they are not deemed prepared for college-level liberal arts classes. This solution, however, risks sending a message that technical courses are less rigorous than academic courses.

Second, policies addressing program structure may play a role in establishing dual enrollment for CTE students. Most states do not have in-depth policies addressing program structure. In the case of dual enrollment as part of a Career Pathways initiative, the lack of policy may have positive or negative consequences.

Leaving program model decisions up to individual institutions likely benefits CTE programs, as it provides them with the flexibility to create programs that best prepare students for careers. However, if policies do not provide support for the additional effort that must go into creating comprehensive and enhanced comprehensive programs, CTE programs may suffer. Technically oriented dual enrollment programs should be comprehensive or enhanced comprehensive. This is because dual enrollment is only one component of Career Pathways and therefore must be integrated into the larger CTE program. Dual enrollment teachers should have a connection to the high school, so that they understand students' previous CTE experiences and can link the content of a college course to prior learning. And, if students take more than one dual enrollment course, those courses must be deliberately selected so as to extend high school learning in an ordered manner.

Such programs take additional staff time, as they require coordination and collaboration between the college and the high school, additional planning time for teachers, and extra time for creating meaningful curricular pathways. Policies typically do not address these needs. For example, states usually do not provide incentive funding for programs attempting to create curricular pathways. Because singleton programs are simpler (and probably cheaper) to implement, colleges may be more likely to implement them than more comprehensive efforts such as technically oriented curricular pathways. Thus, the lack of policy in this area can serve as a disincentive.

Policies addressing other aspects of program structure also influence technical dual enrollment. Some states require that dual enrollment courses be offered only on college campuses; programs must then develop ways to transport students from the high school to the college during the school day. Similarly, regulations regarding who is eligible to teach dual enrollment may limit the pool of available faculty members to such an extent that there is no one to teach a technical dual enrollment course offered at a high school. State policies rarely address the inclusion of support services in dual enrollment programs. They do not prevent support services, but do not encourage them either. Thus, programs may find it difficult to include such services — especially services tailored to the needs of CTE students.

Third, state funding of dual enrollment often serves as a disincentive to the creation of comprehensive or enhanced comprehensive programs. Though state policies vary widely (and we do not have space to address the intricacies of funding streams in this chapter), suffice it to say that policymakers struggle with funding dual enrollment programs in ways that benefit students, high schools, and colleges equally. States often seek to ensure that students need not pay for their dual enrollment courses. This necessitates, however, the state or an educational institution paying program costs.

Some states allow both institutions to receive full funding for dual enrollment, essentially paying twice for the same students. Other state policies stipulate that only one institution can receive funding, or that both institutions may receive partial funding, for dually enrolled students. In such arrangements, the net result for the institutions is a loss of funds, thus potentially discouraging institutional participation. Additionally, even when both institutions receive funds for dually enrolled students, they do not usually receive additional funding for activities supporting comprehensive dual enrollment programs. So again, funding may discourage the creation of technical curricular pathways that include dual enrollment. Moreover, we are not aware of any funding arrangements that account for the more expensive nature of technical courses. In other words (as is often the case with the funding of higher education generally), institutions do not receive additional funds for students enrolled in technical courses, even though technical courses are often more expensive than academic courses. This, too, may discourage widespread institutional participation in technical dual enrollment.

This limited discussion of state policy might give the impression that state policies, on the whole, discourage CTE students from participating in dual enrollment. But this is not the case. Many states provide limited guidance for dual enrollment programs. Institutions that are committed to creating dual enrollment pathways for CTE students face few constraints. In fact, some of the most innovative dual enrollment programs we have seen have been in locales in which there is no state policy; though institutions in these cases must fund their programs creatively, they also have leeway to develop and refine the programs in ways that best meet the needs of their students. This should also be the case in states where policy is not terribly stringent; flexibility within the regulatory constraints is possible. Second, it is rare for all of the negative situations described above to occur at once. Again, this leaves programs with significant flexibility.

Finally, although we have focused on the possible downsides of state policy, there are many potential positives. First is that the existence of policy provides a framework for engaging institutions in collaborative efforts and a starting point for discussion regarding program implementation. Second, policies can be created that support technically oriented, comprehensive dual enrollment programs. Iowa is one example of this. In the next section, we describe Iowa's dual enrollment policies, some of which were specifically designed to support CTE. We also describe a program that both informed and has grown with the support of these policies, Kirkwood Community College's Career Edge Academies.

DUAL ENROLLMENT IN IOWA

Iowa has a long history of educational governance structures supporting local control, innovation, and cooperation across educational sectors and with public agencies and private enterprises. The vast majority of Iowa's 359 public comprehensive high schools are rural, and those communities are committed to the viability and survival of their schools. Each school district is locally governed by an elected board. The local board determines the curriculum to be offered and sets high school graduation requirements; school accreditation standards are set in Iowa Code and include vocational education program standards.

The enabling legislation for Iowa's system of public comprehensive community colleges was passed in 1965. Legislative leadership demonstrated its wisdom by creating nonduplicative educational systems that cover all regions of the state and are responsive to local community, business, and student needs. (There are no vocational area schools or vocational high schools or institutes; both the high schools and community colleges are comprehensive in mission.)

Since the late 1980s, the state of Iowa has fostered dual enrollment opportunities for high school students through policy and legislation, visionary leadership, and educational collaboration. A major outcome is a system for career development, future workforce development, and economic development in Iowa.

Iowa's public policy has encouraged the development and implementation of CTE programs that are linked across the secondary and postsecondary sectors in multiple ways: through the articulation requirement for access to the state's secondary vocational program appropriation; the state's vocational program approval process, which also requires documented articulation; the Postsecondary Enrollment Options Act or PSEO (Chapter 261C, Iowa Code); Supplemental Weighting (Chapter 257, Iowa Code); and, most recently, career academies (Iowa Code 260C.18A 1.c).

PSEO was enacted in 1987 to promote rigorous academic pursuits and to provide a wider variety of options to high school students. It enables eleventh- and twelfth-grade students, along with ninth- and tenth-grade students identified as gifted and talented, to enroll part-time in college credit courses offered by two- and four-year colleges. In keeping with the emphasis on local control, the state does not set student eligibility requirements but allows school districts to determine eligibility, as well as determine which college courses may be made available to high school students, based on local curricular offerings. The local high school also decides whether to award high school credit in addition to the college credit.

The legislation does stipulate a funding arrangement: high schools must pay the partnering college a maximum of $250 for college tuition, textbooks, and fees. Students must reimburse the district if they do not complete or successfully pass the course. This amount fails to cover all of the college's costs of offering courses to high school students, yet no additional fees can be collected from the students or the high school. This arrangement serves as a disincentive to high school and college participation. Hence, in 1998, supplemental weighted funding began to allow local school districts to receive additional state funding (1.48 funding) for high school students enrolled in community college courses. This funding stream is critical to the growth and sustainability of dual enrollment in Iowa, particularly the more costly CTE programs. To qualify for supplemental weighted funding, the local school district must verify that the college courses meet six criteria:

- Supplement, not supplant, existing high school courses
- Are not required by the local school district to meet minimum state accreditation standards
- Are for college credit and apply toward an associate of arts, associate of science, associate of applied arts, or associate of applied science diploma
- Are taught by a teacher meeting community college licensing requirements
- Are taught using the community college syllabus
- Are of the same quality as a course offered on a community college campus

The state policy for supplemental weighted funding has led to an increase in the number of contractual agreements between high schools (or consortia of high schools) and community colleges for the provision of college credit classes to high school students. In 2003, 17,883 unduplicated high school students were enrolled in Iowa's 15 community colleges, an increase of about 6 percent over 2002. In the same year, approximately 16 percent of the total community college headcount enrollments were high school students, and those students earned an average of seven credit hours. About 12 percent of all eleventh and twelfth graders in the state are enrolled in community college courses.

The most recent public policy supporting dual enrollment was legislation passed in 2002 for the development and implementation of career academies. The legislation defines a career academy as a program of study that combines a minimum of two years of secondary education with a postsecondary career preparatory program in a nonduplicative, sequential course of study that is standards-based, integrates academic and technical instruction, incorporates work-based and worksite learning where appropriate and available, uses an individualized career planning process that involves parents, and leads to an associate degree or postsecondary diploma or certificate in a rewarding, high-skill career field. Several existing funding streams, as well as a specially created innovative economic development funding stream, are available to support career academies.

CAREER EDGE ACADEMIES – KIRKWOOD COMMUNITY COLLEGE

The career academy legislation is an interesting instance of an existing program—the Kirkwood Community College Career Edge Academy program—influencing the development of state policy. The Kirkwood program was the model for the legislation. In 1998, Kirkwood Community College in east central Iowa was approached by a local school district regarding the need to create dynamic learning opportunities for high school students that would better prepare them for their future. In particular, it was felt that too many students were leaving high school underprepared for academic success in college and without career direction, so there was a need to make the last two years of high school more meaningful and career-focused. As it was felt that these programs would benefit students at all high schools in Kirkwood's seven-county service area, and that this presented an opportunity for collaboration, a council of key stakeholders was established to discuss and develop this new vision.

The program is a true partnership among Kirkwood Community College; the 33 school districts in Kirkwood's seven-county service area; The Workplace Learning Connection, an intermediary linking business and education; the Grant Wood Area Education Agency, an intermediary support service provider; and area business partners. Through the work of the stakeholder council it was agreed that each academy, regardless of location, would meet the following Career Edge core elements:

- **2+2+2 program design** — Students would see how their two years in high school would provide a seamless transition to a community college program and/or a four-year college or university. Students would have multiple options to continue their education or enter the workforce immediately after high school.

- **Dual credit** — Students would earn both high school and college credit, the college tuition being paid by their school districts. These earned college credits would be placed on the students' transcripts.

- **Career Pathway** — Students would follow Career Pathway plans involving both high-quality career and academic coursework at the secondary and postsecondary levels. This planned instructional sequence would guide the students in their course selections and lead to advanced placement in postsecondary programs.

- **Work-based learning** — Each academy would involve strong linkages with business and industry through job shadowing, internships, tours, and guest speakers arranged through The Workplace Learning Connection. Because The Workplace Learning Connection works with over 700 regional employers, students would learn about career opportunities within their communities or regions and the essential skills for those careers.

- **Skills certificates** — Each academy course would provide students with certificates to validate competency and share with future employers.

- **Scholarships** — Each academy would provide scholarship opportunities to enable students to continue their education at Kirkwood Community College.

- **Advisory committee** — An advisory committee would be established for each academy. Each committee would consist of business and industry representatives, students, and faculty members from both the high school and college ranks.

- **Career Edge website** — The website *www.careeredge.info* would provide academy and career information for students, parents, and counselors. Students could view a model Career Pathway plan and design an individual pathway plan based on their high school curriculum.

Each career academy was to be closely affiliated with a Kirkwood academic department, providing strong faculty support, mandatory professional development for teachers, and ongoing academy coordination. The academy selection process was based on current and future employment needs, income potential in the career fields under consideration, student interest, faculty support, and commitment from a Kirkwood department. The development process involved the selection of an academy champion who would convene interested schools and facilitate the development process. High schools select which Career Edge Academies to offer. The following 10 Career Edge Academies are in operation, most in multiple locations:

- Advanced Manufacturing Academy
- Automotive Technology Academy

- Automotive Collision Academy
- Computer Programming Academy
- Engineering and Engineering Technology Academy
- Graphics and Media Communication Academy
- Health Science Academy
- Human Services Academy
- Information Systems Management Academy
- Local Area Network Academy

The structure of each academy is slightly different. In general, academy students take a series of college courses over the course of a school year and participate in work-based learning activities and support services that complement their coursework. In the Health Science Academy, for example, students attend college classes at the end of each school day. The program meets at area high schools, college satellite campuses, and local health care facilities. Academy instructors are practicing nurses who have been certified as college adjuncts by Kirkwood.

Health Science Academy students complete 10.5 college credits over two semesters. They take seven courses: Professionals in Health, Health Skills 1, Health Skills 2, Basic Medical Terminology, First Aid Concepts, Cardiopulmonary Resuscitation (CPR) for the Health Care Provider, and Nurse Aid. Students who successfully complete the Nurse Aid course are eligible to take the national licensing examination to become certified nursing assistants. Academy curricula are developed by the college's nursing faculty and mirror the content taught on campus. Course instructors are given class materials, including syllabi and lesson outlines, by the college department. These courses also serve as prerequisites for entry into many health-related majors at Kirkwood, including nursing, physical therapy assisting, and dental hygiene.

Work-based learning is integrated into the Health Science Academy. As part of their coursework, students are required to engage in clinical practice at local hospitals and nursing homes. This includes working at the hospital before school hours under the supervision of the course instructor. Students also attend a career day at a local hospital and have the opportunity to participate in job shadowing experiences arranged by the Workplace Learning Connection.

A variety of strategies are used to recruit students into the academy programs, including brochures, posters, the Career Edge website, student/parent orientation sessions, and a Career Edge Academy program of study that can be inserted into the high school's regular program of study. High school counselors, teachers, and current academy students are all considered essential in student recruitment.

While interest is the primary criterion for admission, student success is also important. To gauge the potential for success, several participating schools have designed an academy eligibility rubric that incorporates student attendance, student behavior, prerequisite courses, and academic assessments. The rubric is shared with students who express interest in the academies. It helps them plan by enabling them to compare their current scores with academy entrance criteria. The rubric is continually refined. Students do not have to take college placement tests to enroll in a career academy.

As noted above, leadership and collaboration have been vitally important to academy development and success, particularly the commitment of Kirkwood Community College's academic departments and support services. Most applied science and technology departments have added department coordinators whose responsibilities to the Career Edge Academies include working with department faculty on an initial academy design, connecting community college and high school faculty, securing state program approval, ensuring that academy faculty meet certification requirements, coordinating professional development for academy faculty, and seeking funds for program development and student scholarships, among others.

Other Kirkwood partners essential to the success of Career Edge Academy programs include the offices of resource development, government relations, admission, marketing, and enrollment services. As an example, Kirkwood's resource development office has been instrumental in writing grant proposals and seeking corporate investment in these programs. To date, over $2.3 million in grants and corporate gifts have been secured. The internal collaboration and commitment are very important to the long-term success of the programs.

Funding to develop, improve, and sustain Career Edge Academy programs has come from federal, state, and local sources, including Perkins funds, U.S. Department of Labor funds, the state supplemental weighted funding, and Grow Iowa Value Funds, which provide support to community colleges for workforce development. Local business partners have also provided funds for the academies. Rockwell Collins, a world leader in avionics that develops much of the instrumentation for airplanes, supports both the Engineering Technology Academy and the Computer Programming Academy by providing five years of support for a half-time college-level electronics instructor at the partnering high school, as well as $20,000 annually to support student scholarships.

The career academies have proven popular: over 1100 area high school students enroll annually from nearly 40 high schools and earn both high school and college credit in one of the ten programs. Data collected by Kirkwood find that nearly 50 percent of the Health Science Academy students continue their education at the college immediately after high school, mostly in health- and human services-related programs. This compares favorably with the 32 percent of all high school graduates from Kirkwood's seven-county service area who continue at Kirkwood immediately after graduation. Other data show that career academy students are transitioning to college well-prepared: of twenty students in the Engineering Technology and Local Area Networking Academies who continued at Kirkwood, none needed remediation in writing and only two students needed remedial work in mathematics.

Career Edge Academy students benefit from their participation in the program in a variety of ways. First, they earn transcripted college credit that can be used at Kirkwood or at other colleges and universities. Second, they are college students with access to the full range of college services, including career counseling; academic advising; computer labs;

library services; math and writing labs; and free admission to athletic events, the college wellness center, and performing arts events. Moreover, the academies often offer additional support services geared specifically toward dual enrollment students. These include work-based learning opportunities, as described earlier, as well as college orientation sessions.

Another benefit that academy students enjoy is their ability to register for their freshman-year courses earlier than other incoming students. This is helpful for students pursuing courses of study (e.g., health) that have waiting lists for certain classes; early registration means that academy students are less likely than other freshmen to be shut out of these courses. Thus, they are less likely to experience delays on the way to earning their degrees. And of course, by earning college credit while in high school, all academy students have the opportunity to enter college with advanced standing. Career academy students are also given special consideration when applying for some Kirkwood scholarships.

Finally, because academy courses are college courses, academy students become acclimated to the expectations of college classes and may be more likely than their peers to be successful as college freshmen. Career academy students may enter college with preexisting relationships with college faculty members. These relationships can help them adjust to college life more easily than other students.

RECOMMENDATIONS

We have described the ways that dual enrollment can be integrated into a Career Pathway, and why this arrangement might be preferable to more traditional Tech Prep models. We have also offered an example of a successful technically oriented dual enrollment program. As dual enrollment becomes a more prominent feature of CTE programs, practitioners will benefit from following these recommendations.

Create strong collaborative relationships and facilitate collaboration by clearly establishing the roles and benefits for each institution in the partnership. Collaboration is a difficult process and one with which some programs struggle. It is important that collaboration occur between different levels of the partnering institutions; the top levels of leadership and administration must collaborate on governance of programs, while faculty members must work together on curriculum. Collaboration is an ongoing process, and collaborative relationships must be continually nurtured.

The Career Edge Academies at Kirkwood Community College offer an excellent example of collaboration. The roles and expectations of each partner in the program are clear to all involved. Descriptions of the responsibilities for program activities are formally distributed to specific individuals throughout the partnership. For those involved at the college, in particular, academy program responsibilities are written into their job descriptions. Such clarity helps the program run smoothly and makes all partners feel that they are valued and respected members of the partnership. It also helps ensure that the academies are part of a larger workforce development system, rather than an isolated program. The high school district leadership recognizes and appreciates the college's leading role in coordinating the numerous details of the program.

Support broader integration between the secondary and postsecondary sectors. The word "collaboration" does not fully describe the type of institutional relationships that dual enrollment and Career Pathways require. These programs call for deeper institutional changes; participating high schools and colleges must be willing to overcome their structural differences and integrate their goals, practices, and services. This is the only way to create a truly seamless education system.

Alignment of high school graduation requirements with college entrance requirements is an important step. The success of the Career Pathway model depends on the ability of the high school portion of the pathway to equip students to enter the postsecondary portion without requiring remediation. When secondary and postsecondary institutions work together to create dual enrollment opportunities for Career Pathway students, they are better equipped to communicate regarding students' college readiness.

Kirkwood Community College's Career Edge Academy program is unique in that its dual enrolled students do not necessarily have to pass the college's placement tests. Program administrators from the college trust their high school counterparts to select students who would benefit from participation. And, as described above, some academies have developed selection rubrics to use as student placement and advisement tools.

> The word "collaboration" does not fully describe the type of institutional relationships that dual enrollment and Career Pathways require. These programs call for deeper institutional changes; participating high schools and colleges must be willing to overcome their structural differences and integrate their goals, practices, and services.

Simplify the credit earning and credit transfer process. A hallmark of dual enrollment, as opposed to the traditional model of Tech Prep, is that it allows students to earn transcripted college credit, rather than credit-in-escrow. We strongly support transcripted credit, rather than credit-in-escrow. We also advocate efforts to increase the transferability of college credit, for example, common course numbering across state college systems, which helps students keep their credits when they change institutions. Finally, dual credit, in which students receive high school *and* college credit for their program course work, as opposed to receiving one type of credit or the other, is preferable. Dual credit truly accelerates students' progress, since earning the two types of credit for one course saves time and money. In addition to simplifying participation for students, dual credit prods institutions to work together to align curricula. Students in Iowa's Career Edge Academies earn both high school and college credits for their program courses.

Creating Career Pathways that include dual enrollment is not easy. But such programs stand to benefit students in a variety of ways and thus are a promising extension of the good work already accomplished by Tech Prep.

For Program Information

Career Edge – For the New World of Work
Contact: David Bunting, Executive Director
of Secondary Programs
Kirkwood Community College, (319) 398-7170,
dbuntin@kirkwood.edu
1030 5th Avenue S.E., Cedar Rapids, Iowa 52403

Dr. Hughes and Ms. Karp gratefully acknowledge the U.S. Department of Education, Office of Vocational and Adult Education, for its support of research that informed some of the arguments made in this chapter.

Chapter 10 Preview

Postsecondary component:
8. Provides opportunities for students to earn college credit through dual/concurrent enrollment or articulation agreements.
9. Provides alignment and/or articulation with baccalaureate programs.
10. Provides industry-recognized knowledge and skills.
11. Provides employment opportunities for high-wage, high-demand careers in the chosen Pathway and provides multiple exit points.

Partnership ensures a culture focused on improvement by:
17. Providing targeted professional development for faculty, administrators, and counselors to improve teaching/learning and integration of technical and academic instruction.
18. Maintaining ongoing dialogue among secondary, postsecondary, and business partners.

In the early years of Tech Prep (1990–1998) much of the activity centered on improving the role of the high school for "neglected majority" students (changing high school voc ed and helping struggling students with contextual teaching of academics). Community colleges were engaged in the consortia mainly through articulation agreements.

In the late 1990s, changes in the global economy made it apparent that rewarding careers would require some postsecondary education, and that the level and rigor of associate degree programs would have to increase. But more and more students entering the colleges were found to require remediation in core academic subjects, which led to the obvious conclusion that high school graduation standards were not aligned with college entrance requirements. More community college presidents recognized the potential benefits of a strong, meaningful partnership with feeder high schools.

Today it is more obvious than ever before that community colleges will have to assume a greater leadership position and "bend a little more" to make these Career Pathways partnerships a win-win experience for all institutions, students, and faculty who are involved.

This chapter was authored by the presidents of two colleges that have been building local partnerships for over a decade — and they have the results to prove it! D.H.

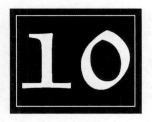

COMMUNITY COLLEGE LEADERSHIP IN CAREER PATHWAYS

Ed Massey and John Sbrega

The next phase in the evolution of Tech Prep will be Career Pathways, in which integrated 4+2+(2) curriculum frameworks prepare students to transition smoothly from high school to college, eventually securing employment in rewarding, high-demand occupational fields. The Career Pathways concept calls for *partnerships* comprising both secondary and postsecondary educational institutions, especially two-year postsecondary institutions. Consequently, as the Career Pathways initiative unfolds, community college presidents will be positioned to dramatically boost the partnering institutions' ability to take students and communities to the next level of student achievement and workforce development.

This chapter provides a look at how community college presidents can be leaders in this new phase of Tech Prep. The chapter also provides examples of presidential involvement in education reform initiatives that have resulted in significant reductions in remediation and dropout rates, increases in the numbers of program completers, and other strides and improvements. As "tone-setters" at two-year postsecondary institutions, community college presidents can do much to build and sustain successful Career Pathways partnerships.

THE CHALLENGE

Isolation Versus Collaboration

Historically, problems and deficiencies affecting education have been dealt with by individual educational sectors working in isolation. This approach has largely failed. Many of the problems educators face are simply too involved for any one system to resolve. When the problems are big, it becomes difficult to say who should step forward and claim ownership. One of the most damaging symptoms of working in isolation is poor communication. This is not only a serious problem in its own right but one that tends to create other problems. Lack of communication leads to lack of awareness, which in turn leads to a lack of understanding. Lack of understanding of intent can lead to a lack of trust and mutual support, not only between institutions but between people within the same institution. Lack of communication at the top tends to filter downward. When educational administrators don't communicate with one another, their faculty members and counselors tend to follow suit.

No one has been more aware of the need to improve communication among the different sectors of our public education system than community college presidents. As isolation has increasingly limited their potential sphere of influence, many have come to the realization that the creation of high-quality educational environments is impossible without effective collaboration. Over the past twenty years, duplication of effort and disconnected attempts to solve problems have produced an educational system that is far less effective than it could be. Postsecondary has misunderstood what secondary *does,* and

> Postsecondary has misunderstood what secondary *does,* and secondary has misunderstood what postsecondary *wants*.

secondary has misunderstood what postsecondary *wants*. Problems at all levels have been compounded by the isolation of the entities that have been working to resolve them. Awareness of the need for communication between sectors has stemmed from recognition of the fact that in today's world the most pressing needs in education span the entire pre-K–20 system.[1] Today's most pressing needs affect, or are affected by, every person in the educational enterprise. Examples of these include the need to

- Reduce postsecondary remediation rates,
- Reduce high school dropout rates,
- Improve academic performance and formulate higher standards in all sectors,
- Produce students who are well prepared to enter the workforce *and* continue their education at the postsecondary level,
- Restructure curriculum to reflect the contemporary workplace,
- Improve instructional delivery through contextual teaching,
- Give more emphasis to math, science, and technology,
- Address economically disadvantaged students in the community, and
- Increase the availability of baccalaureate degrees.

The coming of the information age has added a critical new need to that list—the need for our educational system to provide training for "skilled" occupations. Changes in the workplace necessitate changes in the way educators *prepare* people for the workplace. Consider the impact of the following recent labor-market trends on the roles and responsibilities of our educational system:

---

[1] Many states use the term "pre-K–16" to refer to the full range of their educational systems, i.e., from prekindergarten through the baccalaureate degree. By legislation, Florida refers to its system as "pre-K–20," i.e., prekindergarten through the doctoral level.

- The proliferation of new occupations with technical and scientific cores

- Declining employment among the ranks of the semiskilled and unskilled

> Changes in the workplace necessitate changes in the way educators *prepare* people for the workplace.

- The infusion of analytical and technical content into jobs that traditionally have not been considered technical[2]

- 4 million more jobs — soon to be 10 million — without qualified people to fill them[3]

The shift from isolation to collaboration enables educational leaders to face these challenges with an expanded solution base and network of support.

THE COMMUNITY COLLEGE PRESIDENT AND THE NEW EDUCATIONAL PARADIGM

Over the last 20 years, American society has become a "more decentralized, networked organizational arrangement" in which teaching and learning have been reorganized around "learning communities and the proliferation of educational partnerships and networks connecting schools, colleges, businesses, and community organizations." In his recent book *The World Is Flat,* Thomas L. Friedman stresses the importance of upgrading and expanding education at the high school, community college, and university levels.[4] According to Friedman, the achievement of American students parallels that of students from other industrialized countries until the eighth grade. But by the senior year, American students have often fallen behind. The Career Pathways model will help to reverse

---

[2] National Center on the Educational Quality of the Workforce, 1992.

[3] Roger Herman, Joyce Gioia, and Tom Olivo, *Impending Crisis: Too Many Jobs, Too Few People* (Oakhill Press, 2002).

[4] Thomas L. Friedman, *The World Is Flat: A Brief History of the Twenty-First Century* (New York: Farrar, Straus and Giroux, 2005).

that trend by infusing rigor throughout grades 9–12, increasing dual enrollment opportunities, and expanding and improving training for the "skilled" category of careers, thereby increasing our nation's global competitiveness.[5]

In light of the new educational paradigm, community college presidents must consider the following questions:

> The primary role of community college presidents in the new educational paradigm is to *build and lead meaningful multilateral partnerships across the pre-K–20 system.*

- Should the community college president take the lead in seeking effective ways to address workforce shortages and deficiencies?

- Should the community college president assume the responsibility of bringing together the other educational sectors to determine how to improve and strengthen the quality of education at all levels?

- What type of collaborative group can be created that will transcend the parties involved and provide long-term continuity despite changes in personnel?

- Could this group be led to identify sector-specific issues that — *addressed collectively* – would result in positive legislation, funding, and performance outcomes?

- How could this group expand partnerships with area businesses and industries to produce workforce-ready students?[6]

The answer to the first two questions is an emphatic *yes.* The community college president should be willing to assume a leadership role in improving our educational system's ability

---

[5] David Jacobson, "The New Core Competence of the Community College," *Leadership Abstracts* (League of Innovation, 2005).

[6] Ed Massey, "Partnering for Change," The Leadership Dialogues: Community College Case Studies to Consider (University of Florida, 2004).

to produce capable citizens and workers who can meet the pressing social and economic needs of the 21st century. The primary role of community college presidents in the new educational paradigm is to *build and lead meaningful multilateral partnerships across the pre-K–20 system*. Much of the confusion created by the persistent chasms between sectors within our educational system can be reduced if we conceptualize a unified pre-K–20 system, and act accordingly. Tech Prep was a major step in that direction. The development of Career Pathways, as defined in Chapter 1, is the next important step.

Community college presidents should assume the responsibility of bringing together key representatives of the other educational sectors, along with business representatives and community leaders. Community college presidents are accustomed to looking beyond the internal interests of their institutions. Community colleges have always had a dual focus—part internal, part external. Their mission dictates that, in addition to supporting and sustaining their own students and faculty and staff member, they are charged with responding to the workforce development needs of the communities they serve. Because of their experience in "reaching out," community college presidents have the experience and skills necessary to break through the barriers of educational isolation. This is precisely what the Career Pathways concept demands—strong links between pre-K–12 systems and postsecondary institutions.

One goal of the Career Pathways concept is seamless secondary-to-postsecondary transitions. Smooth transitions are a goal of community colleges as well. Thus, this too is an area in which community college presidents should lead. Because of the growing interest in Career Pathways, community college presidents have an unprecedented opportunity and responsibility to insist that their "colleagues in learning" (in all educational sectors) do their part to ensure smooth transitions for Career Pathway students. In the new educational paradigm community college presidents can and should work directly with superintendents, principals, and other high-ranking postsecondary administrators to make seamless pathways a reality for all students. This is a difficult task, and many presidents are still bloody and scarred from previous battles in this domain. But they must be willing to keep trying. The success of Career Pathways — and the resulting benefits to students — will be directly proportional to the willingness of community college presidents to organize educational partners from every sector of the pre-K–20 spectrum. (A successful Career Pathways Organizational Model is presented in a subsequent section of this chapter.)

DEVELOPING AND SUSTAINING CAREER PATHWAYS: THE COMMUNITY COLLEGE PRESIDENT'S ROLE

The actions and attitudes of community college presidents regarding Career Pathways will have a strong impact on leaders in other educational sectors and on the people within their own organizations. Whatever is important to presidents has a tendency to become important to the people who work under them. If community college presidents expect others to recognize the importance of the major tenets of Career Pathways — high academic achievement, strong employability and technical skills, and a globally competitive workforce of lifelong learners, among others — they must communicate a clear vision. But that vision cannot be merely their own. It must be a *shared* vision. Thus, community college presidents must cultivate personal networks of key community players (educators and business leaders) whom they can lead in the joint development of a shared vision that corresponds to the unique dynamics of their communities.

> **Community college presidents must cultivate personal networks of key community players (educators and business leaders) whom they can lead in the joint development of a shared vision that corresponds to the unique dynamics of their communities.**

This section describes five general areas in which community college presidents should lead. Our remarks

include descriptions of activities at Bristol Community College
(BCC) and Indian River Community College (IRCC).

1. Partnering

Community college presidents should organize local forums
that bring to the table key partners such as business leaders,
chamber members, economic and workforce development
leaders, and educators. The forums' discussions should focus on
topics such as (1) educational shortcomings identified in
national reports on the status of education and (2) how
collaboration between the educational sectors and the business
community can address those shortcomings. The forums must
not be simply cordial social gatherings. They must be hard
hitting, driven by a willingness to face the well-documented
reality that our country could lose its competitive edge in the
global marketplace if we don't get serious about changing the
way we educate students. The forums have a serious mission:
They must result in frameworks that both increase academic
rigor *and* address local workforce development needs. The
community college president must be willing to tackle these
difficult challenges, aided by strong alliances in the community.

One result of the forums will be the formation of a Career
Pathways Coalition. The mission of the Coalition will be to
establish common goals regarding curriculum, counseling,
sharing of resources, government policy, grant procurement,
and other areas in which concerted action can help to ensure
the success of the Career Pathways program.

In building these strategic partnerships, community college
presidents include "real world" players who can significantly
strengthen the *career* component of Career Pathways. These
partnerships can benefit their communities by:

- Creating a strong workforce of high-wage earners who can
  sustain a healthy economy.

- Facilitating positive community relations between
  successful businesses and well-trained employees.

- Reducing employer training costs.

- Reducing the shortage of skilled workers.

- Improving the quality of high school and community college graduates, who in turn improve the quality of life in their communities.

- Encouraging the use of business-validated curriculum standards.

- Encouraging and coordinating collaboration between business and education.

Convincing business and industry leaders of the value of these benefits will not be difficult.

2. Funding

Collaboration is perhaps the single most important ingredient in procuring external grants and contracts. RFPs (requests for proposals) often require evidence of partnering. One benefit of the Career Pathways Coalition described in the previous section is that, through it, alliances will emerge, making the Coalition a strong force in securing grants. By joining forces, the individual sectors involved will be able to compete for awards that might otherwise be unattainable. BCC and IRCC have both learned from experience that strong coalitions have an advantage in the pursuit of grants.

Evidence of this advantage can be seen in BCC's ability to leverage its Women in Technology program to secure over two million dollars in funding from the National Science Foundation's Advanced Technological Education program. This series of grants supports student recruitment, scholarships, and transfer agreements. BCC's Computer-Integrated Manufacturing and Women in Technology programs were able to secure funding through their participation in an international workforce conference in China. In addition, winning the prestigious Bellwether Award and the WEPAN Prize enabled the BCC Tech Prep program to secure local, state, and federal grants.

IRCC's coalition, formed in 1991, has created an environment in which relationships flourish. Grant-procurement collaboration has resulted in more than $156 million in state, local, and federal grants. These grants

include funding for programs for economically disadvantaged
students (e.g., Gear Up, Upward Bound, Talent Search, Student
Support Services); the development of a biotechnology
curriculum; and an international award-winning web-based
program called Living Science (www.living-science.org), in
which students in the classroom interact with scientists in
laboratories using an interactive mediapage.

Federal and state funding agencies prefer partnerships over
individual entities because partnerships stretch dollars and
serve relatively large numbers of
people. Partnerships also widen
the dissemination of results and
expand the possibilities for
replication. Time invested by the
community college president in
forming these coalitions will
greatly improve prospects for
obtaining the funding necessary to
implement a successful Career
Pathways program.

> **Federal and state funding agencies prefer partnerships over individual entities because partnerships stretch dollars and serve relatively large numbers of people.**

3. Industry Validation and Assessment

As leaders within Career Pathways partnerships, community
college presidents should assume a prominent role in the
formation of the advisory groups necessary for validation of
industry-specific certifications for pathway curricula. When
community college presidents approach external entities (both
public and private) about accreditation, certification, and/or
credentialing, they tap into a reservoir of expertise that can
ultimately enrich Career Pathways programs and strengthen
student credentials. Those external entities often become
lasting partners. Perhaps most important, presidents can
enhance the acceptance and sustainability of their Career
Pathways by arranging assessment and accountability
components through the certification process. BCC and IRCC
have both increased their success in these areas by aggressively
expanding their partnerships and linkages. In the Career
Pathways environment, community colleges must be willing to

"share" their business partnerships with secondary schools to create 4+2+2 curriculum frameworks. A good example is the IRCC International Marketing framework shown as Figure 3-6 in Chapter 3.

Community college presidents must do their part in ensuring that assessment components are in place to measure the effectiveness of each Career Pathway. This can be accomplished by:

- Checking the alignment of Career Pathways with relevant occupations at the local, state, and national levels.

- Developing relationships with organizations such as the Southern Regional Education Board (SREB) to identify performance measures, collect data, and monitor program improvement.

- Using the Career Pathways Self-Study Instrument (described in Chapter 1).

Community college presidents can play a vital role in implementing effective evaluation processes that strengthen each Career Pathway partnership, provide assurances about the quality and effectiveness of Career Pathways in general, and facilitate what Dan Hull describes as the logical progression from Tech Prep to Career Pathways.[7]

4. Promotion

In addition to building strategic partnerships, a major role of community college presidents is to capitalize on every opportunity to focus attention on the Career Pathways concept. At BCC, the Tech Prep registration form specifically defines six fields of study that include 24 Career Pathways. BCC Tech Prep students are able to take five college courses free of charge on a space-available basis starting in their junior year of high school. Tech Prep site coordinators help organize course selection for each Tech Prep student by referring to pathway grid charts.

---

[7] Dan M. Hull, "Career Pathways: The Next Generation of Tech Prep," *Connections*, vol. 14, no. 5 (http://www.cord.org/uploadedfiles/Vol14No5.pdf; accessed July 2005).

To promote the Career Pathways concept to secondary schools, parents, the community, and the college, IRCC created the Clark Advanced Learning Center on its campus. The Center is designed around an integrated curriculum with dual-enrollment options leading to careers and continuing education in digital media, entrepreneurship/e-commerce, medical professions, information technology, and environmental technology.

Leading by example, community college presidents must provide compelling evidence, through actions and words, that Career Pathways are a high priority for their institutions. This can be accomplished by highlighting Career Pathway successes and allocating resources for professional development activities for Career Pathways personnel. Community college presidents must take a broad, long-term view, favoring education for *careers* over training for task-specific jobs (i.e., traditional voc-ed). The presidents must use every opportunity, from public presentations to social functions, to educate their communities about the real academic and technical skill demands of today's workplace.

> **Community college presidents must provide compelling evidence, through actions and words, that Career Pathways are a high priority for their institutions.**

5. Empowering

Another way community college presidents can contribute to the success of Career Pathways is to support and empower the Tech Prep staff members at their institutions. Those individuals focus their outreach efforts on secondary schools and provide training for secondary personnel. For example, since 1988, BCC and IRCC's Tech Prep programs have offered professional development opportunities for secondary teachers in portfolio development, curriculum guides, math, robotics, women in technology, engineering, and biotechnology.

With committed support from their community college presidents, Tech Prep personnel will be able to garner allies from principals, guidance counselors, and high school teachers. The resulting alliances will eventually include faculty members from baccalaureate-granting institutions. *The efforts of Tech Prep personnel to salvage the careers of aimless students depend on active, consistent presidential support.*

Studies show that students who participate in dual-enrollment programs, particularly students who belong to historically underrepresented populations, are more likely to graduate from high school and enroll in postsecondary education than nonparticipants.

> **The efforts of Tech Prep personnel to salvage the careers of aimless students depend on active, consistent presidential support.**

Community college presidents should support the expansion of dual-enrollment opportunities and custom-designed service-learning components as complements to Career Pathway curricula. Exploring ways for ABE (adult basic education), GED, and ESOL students to participate in Career Pathways is also recommended.

Even though existing legislation prevents Tech Prep from reaching overtly into middle and junior high schools, innovative ways to attract those students must be created as well. Exploration of career interests and portfolio development are integral components of the transition into *high school*. Promotion of those activities will attract new Career Pathways students and help potential dropouts get back on track.

THE CAREER PATHWAYS ORGANIZATIONAL MODEL

The Career Pathways Organizational Model included in this chapter can be used as a guide for the leadership activities of the community college president as well as for the community college as a whole. As Jim Collins states in his book *Good to Great*, the first question to ask is not *what* but *who*. [8] Community college presidents must lead in the formation of strategic

---

[8] Jim Collins, *Good to Great* (HarperCollins, 2001).

partnerships that bring the right people to the table. As stated previously, these partnerships must not be limited to educators but be representative of employers and other community leaders. The Career Pathways Organizational Model is offered as a starting point for building strong and vital partnerships within communities. The model is based on the premise that a unified effort can accomplish far more than the isolated efforts of individuals or groups. The formation of partnerships benefits the entire educational enterprise by merging the component sectors in thought, discussion, and action.

The community college president is well-positioned to lead in the merging of constituent sectors. The resulting group will transcend the potential of its individual members, establish a shared vision for long-term goals, prevent the domination of special interest groups, connect educational leaders (all sectors) with business leaders, and focus on the final product—a well-trained and globally competitive workforce. Community college presidents must step forward and do their part to level the "global playing field."

When educational leaders at the highest levels promote systematic, sustainable improvement, it sends a strong and powerful message that all educators should do likewise, whatever it takes. Creating a shared vision and laying out a clear plan for achieving it also demonstrates to all stakeholders—parents, teachers, principals, business leaders, and legislators—that working together is the key to securing adequate funding, raising completion rates, and improving student access to the best possible educational opportunities. To resolve problems and face challenges effectively, educators must be united and well informed.

> A unified effort can accomplish far more than the isolated efforts of individuals or groups.

In implementing the Career Pathways Organizational Model, the different sectors must work together to maximize both state and local resources. Joint-use facilities, joint-use programs, and colocated institutions allow for flexible, effective delivery of education. Partnering with area universities increases student access to associate-to-baccalaureate opportunities; partnering also increases prospects for obtaining educational funding. The bottom line is this: *Working together will improve all facets of education.*

The evolution of Tech Prep into Career Pathways requires the concerted efforts of leaders in every sector of the pre-K–20 system. Trust and collaboration can exist only if each sector's role is clearly understood and accepted by all. Each sector must assume ownership, participate in pre-K–20 Career Pathways partnerships, and be willing to make the necessary curriculum changes. Staff professional development must be provided to eliminate the deficiencies of the current system. The goal is to eliminate duplication of effort and pool resources and energy throughout the pre-K–20 system. The alternative is for that system to continue to fall short of its potential.

Implementation of the Career Pathways Organizational Model will serve as a change agent in the conversion of traditional CTE programs to Career Pathways. The model expands our view of the educational process to include not only students and teachers, but parents, employers, policymakers, and community leaders. The resulting pre-K–20 system will not merely prepare students for the next level of education, it will prepare them for life. The current two-path system, Tech Prep and college prep, limits students' future opportunities and options, but the Career Pathways Organization Model provides a roadmap for developing systemic solutions that are broader in concept and address a broad range of societal issues. The authors support the 18 CPSIC benchmarks and support the Career Pathways Organizational Model as a starting point.

Strengthening the Framework

The model can integrate new and existing partnerships. Those partnerships represent a united force made up of business and industry partners, educators, parents, chambers of commerce, workforce boards, and others who will demand the most from education. The partners will develop a network of opportunities for students of all ages by linking existing organizations, activities, and programs. The model does not require starting from scratch. The participating entities can expand the existing consortium structure and maximize educational opportunities by providing up-to-date technical and labor market information, enhanced counseling, character education, work-based experiences, and state-of-the-art technology. The goal is to support all pre-K–20 students, including adult learners, as they make career, education, and life choices.

Career Pathways Organizational Model

What follows is our recommendation for the administrative organization of a Career Pathway partnership. It can be adapted to any partnership. Members of secondary and postsecondary institutions are active members within all levels.

STEERING COMMITTEE
Community College President
and Board
District Sec. School Supts.
and Board
CEO of Workforce Board
University Representatives
Business Representatives

ADVISORY COMMITTEE
Tech Prep Consortium—District Technical/Career Directors
Tech Prep Coordinator
Community College Provosts/VPs/Deans of Arts and Sciences,
Applied Science and Technology, and others areas
Secondary Principals/Deans of Curriculum/Instruction
University Deans/Department Chairs

IMPLEMENTATION COMMITTEE
Tech Prep Coordinator
School District Technical Directors
Individual Secondary School CTE and ESE Coordinators
K–12 School District Personnel and Correlating Advisory Boards

Roles of the committees—Steering Committee: Serves in a leadership role to establish the vision and long-range strategic goals; Advisory Committee: Advises and makes recommendations to the implementation committee regarding career guidance, planning, and/or faculty and staff development; Implementation Committee: Implements and/or supports recommendations from the steering and advisory committees.

CONCLUSION

Because it links theory and application across the entire spectrum of the American educational enterprise, the Career Pathways concept is nothing short of revolutionary. It promises a globally competitive workforce and a better life for all American students and workers. The Career Pathways Organizational Model has the potential to produce mutually beneficial partnerships that can facilitate curriculum development, enhance prospects for funding, accommodate validation and assessment of progress, and promote the Career Pathway program in a way that will ensure acceptance and success among the partners.

To compete in the global marketplace, America must not only raise educational levels across the board but also create and maintain a well-trained, well-educated workforce that meets the needs of the 21st century. Career Pathways can play a powerful role in the development and maintenance of that workforce.

Community college presidents have the experience, connections, and influence necessary to energize Career Pathways. They can be a pivotal force in breathing life into Career Pathways partnerships. Much, however, remains undone. If the Career Pathways concept is to fulfill its potential, community college presidents must step forward and do their part. *Our students deserve nothing less.*

The authors wish to express their gratitude to Ted Boudria, Tech Prep Coordinator, Bristol Community College; Elizabeth "Libby" Livings-Eassa, Tech Prep Coordinator, Indian River Community College; Bryan Beaty, Executive Assistant to the President, Indian River Community College; and Hope Cotner, Director, Community College Initiatives, CORD, for their assistance in preparing this chapter.

Chapter 11 Preview

Partnership ensures a culture focused on improvement by:

18. Maintaining ongoing dialogue among secondary, postsecondary, and business partners.

Imagine what a task it would be to create Career Pathways if we had no experience or models in:

- *Secondary-postsecondary partnerships*
- *Articulated, aligned secondary-postsecondary curricula*
- *Contextual teaching and learning*
- *Cooperation and integration between academic and career and technical education*

This is exactly where we were twenty-one years ago when a visionary leader (Dale Parnell) wrote "The Neglected Majority" and, six years later, the U.S. Congress included Tech Prep in the reauthorized Perkins legislation.

Following that beginning, state leaders (like Kathy D'Antoni) and local leaders (like Ron Kindell) took Parnell's vision and made a reality of the Tech Prep: Associate Degree. Today, there are 977 Tech Prep partnerships to provide experience and examples for creating the new vision of Career Pathways. While I cannot imagine that one of the current Tech Prep partnerships could honestly score a "5" on all eighteen of the Career Pathways benchmarks, I am assured that among them there are experiences and successful strategies that can benefit all (existing and new) partnerships that are creating Career Pathways.

In this chapter, Parnell summarizes the vision and salient features we must capture and improve upon, while D'Antoni describes how Tech Prep leaders are paving the way for Career Pathways and how one state (West Virginia) has already put in place the policies and procedures that will produce excellence in this initiative.

D.H.

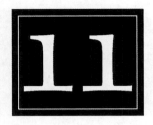

THE COLLEGE TECH PREP PROGRAM AND CAREER PATHWAYS

Dale Parnell and Kathy J. D'Antoni

PART 1: THE COLLEGE TECH PREP PROGRAM[1]

by Dale Parnell

There is nothing particularly unusual about the idea of establishing Career Pathways as a way to structure high school curricula. High school students have long experienced curricular pathways designed to serve students who aim for baccalaureate degrees and beyond. The curricular requirements for college prep pathways have been established primarily by universities to give high school students clear signals about the

---

[1] *Author's note:* When Dale Parnell and I wrote the "how to" Tech Prep book in 1990, Dale insisted that it be called "Tech Prep/ Associate Degree." Otherwise, Tech Prep would have been regarded as a high school reform movement. Eight years later many practitioners did treat Tech Prep as a secondary program, so Dale just started calling it "College Tech Prep." Several states later adopted this term. D.H.

preparation required for entry into four-year colleges and universities.

Community colleges and other postsecondary technical schools that offer sub-baccalaureate degrees such as associate degrees have generally not given clear enough signals to high school students and their parents about what constitutes excellent preparation. If you ask the typical high school student about the high school preparation required to earn an associate degree, you are likely to get a blank stare. On the other hand, there is usually not much question about preparatory programs for careers requiring bachelor's degrees.

Our research in the mid-1980s indicated that roughly 75 percent of high school students were unlikely to earn baccalaureate degrees. Yet high school curricula were dominated by college prep programs. Even today, in 2005, the U.S. Census reveals that fewer than 30 percent of American adults hold bachelor's degrees, yet the college prep pathway continues to dominate. This leaves open the question as to how the majority of students in a typical high school can best be served. Our further research indicated that the majority of high school students, which we called the "neglected majority," were primarily enrolled in general education programs that prepare students neither for work nor for college. To most students, the purpose of a high school education was unclear. The concept that there is a neglected majority in education is just as powerful today as it was 20 years ago.

Unfortunately, to a large extent the concept of excellence in education has been associated exclusively with preparation for a four-year college education. Shouldn't all students experience programs of excellence rather than just some of them? John Gardner said it best some 44 years ago in his book *Excellence: Can We Be Equal and Excellent Too?* (1961):

> The society which scorns excellence in plumbing because plumbing is a humble activity and tolerates shoddiness in philosophy because it is an exalted activity will have

neither good plumbing nor good philosophy. Neither its pipes nor its theories will hold water.[2]

Every high school and college program must develop standards of excellence. Excellence is just as important to the aircraft technician as it is to the engineer. The notion of excellence must be applied to every course and every student. Can the development of Career Pathways for all students not only give purpose and meaning, but also promote the concept of excellence for all students? The answer is yes.

The greatest challenge for secondary education—and to a large extent the same challenge faces the comprehensive community college—is how to meet the great range of individual differences facing teachers in every classroom. The breadth of diversity among students today is daunting and demands alternative educational approaches. There are vast individual differences among students of any age in terms of learning speed and comprehension of theoretical knowledge.

Educators have allowed one definition of excellence to dominate our schools. We have insisted that all students wear one size of educational program shoes. It is clear that one curriculum pathway will not fit the diversity of individual differences any more than one size of shoe will fit all sizes of feet. In particular, the two middle quartiles of a typical high school student body (the "neglected majority") have not been well served by college prep curricula and the accompanying theory-based teaching.

Unfortunately, vocational education was born with a fundamental defect called "prestige deficiency." Despite the best efforts of many educators, and despite a new name— career and technical education (CTE)—the general public still clings to the image of vocational education as a program for "not-so-smart" students and the neighbor's kids. As a consequence, high schools have tended to separate students who "think" (head skills) from those who "work" (hand skills). But the complexities of life in the 21st century demand

---

[2] Quoted in Dale Parnell, *The Neglected Majority* (Washington, D.C.: Community College Press, 1985), 46.

educational programs that teach students to do both, to "think" *and* to "work," by integrating academic with vocational pursuits.

The College Tech Prep (CTP) pathway grew out of the answers to four fundamental questions:

1. Can education better prepare students for the increasing volume of technical and mid-range jobs requiring some postsecondary education but not necessarily baccalaureate degrees?

2. Can education develop and sustain a program of excellence that better meets the needs of a typical high school student body, in terms of diversity, academic talent, and learning styles?

3. Can the establishment of a College Tech Prep pathway address the image problem?

4. Can high school students develop career maturity, as well as academic maturity, in a purpose-driven educational experience?

The Image Problem

One of the original purposes of the CTP pathway was to address the negative image of CTE. Because of that image, the academic value of CTE courses is usually overlooked. For example, a high school course in business letter writing can be rigorous and can help students improve their overall writing skills. Likewise, a course in business mathematics can be rigorous and can help students master computing percentages or applying statistical methodology. But because those courses are viewed as vocational, they often are not included in the college prep curriculum or recognized as courses with standards of excellence. CTE's persistent image problem is a hindrance to education in general and to CTE in particular.

Education Preparation and Job Growth

Much of the job growth in the coming years will occur in occupations that require some postsecondary education and training but not necessarily baccalaureate degrees. One of the problems experienced in many community colleges is that excellent technical education programs cannot be adequately completed in a two-year block of time, particularly if the student has had inadequate secondary school preparation. The senior year in high school has been seen by some students as a waste of time. The CTP pathway was developed to make better use of grades 11 and 12 by coordinating those two years with the first two years of postsecondary. The resulting 2+2 structure helps to ensure that students make good use of the senior year and transition smoothly to postsecondary. The end result is that two-year postsecondary graduates are well prepared for the demands of today's high-growth job market.

It is important to point out that the secondary portion of the CTP pathway is designed to help high school students develop broad-based competence in Career Pathways and avoid the pitfalls of narrow job training. The high school experience should open students' eyes to multiple career opportunities rather than narrow their focus to specific job training. The CTP pathway leaves the highly specific areas of technical education to the postsecondary experience, during which students also continue to develop their academic competence.

Meeting Individual Needs

The current estimated 20 to 25 percent high school dropout rate remains a big challenge for high school educators. This is a statistic that is hard to nail down, but it is well known that the dropout rate, particularly for Hispanic and African-American students, is much too high, as much as 40 to 50 percent in some schools. The CTP pathway was developed, in part, to help more students understand the "why" as well as the "how" of their high school education. The largest volume of dropping out occurs between grades 10 and 11. The CTP pathway is designed to help students connect their high school experience with real-life issues and thus be more motivated to stay in school.

In the development of the CTP pathway we found that one of the barriers students face is program fragmentation.

279

Students are expected to go from subject to subject, grade to grade, and school to school with little sense of how one thing is connected to another. For the most part it is left up to the student to grasp that a formula learned in a math class might also be useful in a graphic arts class, that English courses have prerequisites, and that certain subjects must be completed for graduation. This kind of fragmented structure is rarely effective in motivating students to strive for higher levels of achievement or helping them understand the purpose of their education. The CTP pathway concept is aimed at reducing the fragmentation and helping students make the connections.

The Pedagogical Foundation

A Career Pathway can offer purpose and structure for the student, but that is not enough. If a Career Pathway is to fulfill its promise of improving student achievement, it must be connected to purposeful classroom teaching and student learning.

The CTP pathway was designed to provide both a purposeful curricular structure and purposeful substance for teaching and learning. The two are inextricably linked; both are essential for purpose-driven education. It is the highest form of irony when students ask the question, "Why do I have to learn this?" and receive the answer, "We don't really know, but you might need it someday."[3] Students must be able to connect school with their real-life experiences and their real-life experiences with school. If students are to be motivated to

> The CTP pathway was designed to provide both a purposeful curricular structure and purposeful substance for teaching and learning. The two are inextricably linked; both are essential for purpose-driven education.

---

[3] Dale Parnell, *Why Do I Have to Learn This? Teaching the Way People Learn Best* (Waco, Texas: CORD Communications, 1995).

high levels of achievement, they must feel the touchstones of reality and purpose in their total educational experience.

The term "contextual teaching" refers to an educational strategy that focuses on helping students find meaning and purpose in their daily classroom experiences. (Contextual teaching presents new information in contexts that are familiar to students and show how the information is useful outside the classroom.) The CTP approach to high school education advocates contextual teaching as the most effective method for helping students (especially the "neglected majority") develop higher levels of achievement. When students are not informed of the practical value of information taught in the classroom, they become bored. As one high school student told us, "I know it is up to me to get an education, but a lot of times school is so dull and boring. You go to this class and that class, study a little of this and a little of that, and nothing connects." The problem with classes that are written off as "boring" is not in what is being taught but in the failure to connect subject matter and application.

> The term "contextual teaching" refers to an educational strategy that focuses on helping students find meaning and purpose in their daily classroom experiences.

Let no one misinterpret the basic tenets of contextual teaching. The content of knowledge is important, but the context of application is also important. Helping students understand the context or application of knowledge can make the difference between whether or not the content is learned at all. When we merely attempt to pour knowledge into the human brain, as though through a funnel, making no attempt to connect that knowledge with real-life situations, our efforts are wasted.

> The content of knowledge is important, but the context of application is also important.

The need for connectedness in education stems from the most fundamental facts about how the human brain operates.

The brain is constantly in the process of sending and receiving messages. It naturally looks for patterns and attempts to make associations. When the brain receives information that it can't connect with something familiar, it sends no messages about that information. It merely discards it. Psychologists, philosophers, and educators from William James to John Dewey to Jerome Bruner to Howard Gardner have made the case, in one way or another, that the success of the teaching and learning process depends on students' ability to make connections.

A vital aspect of the CTP pathway is that it is designed to help students use the magnificent power of the brain to make the connections between:

- Knowing and doing,
- Academic and career education,
- School and other life experiences,
- One subject matter discipline and another,
- Knowledge and the application of knowledge, and
- Subject matter and the context of its use.

The educational establishment can issue reams of position papers on the number and length of school days, site-based management, high-stakes tests, and other "hot" topics of the moment, but it is not likely to make much difference in overall student achievement. The difference will be made when all students are helped to make connections and see purpose in their daily learning and in the educational pathways they are following.

PART 2: CAREER PATHWAYS AND TECH PREP

by Kathy J. D'Antoni

School systems that embrace the Career Pathways concept will give *all* their students the opportunity to experience purposeful education through individual educational plans based on the students' goals and desires. Each student would graduate from high school with the academic and technical foundation and career maturity necessary to be successful at the next level. This is not occurring today, even among our brightest and best, as is attested by ever-increasing high school dropout rates and postsecondary remediation rates.

The report *Betraying the College Dream* (2001) published by Stanford University states that the following generally holds true in our secondary schools:

- The coursework between high school and college is not connected.

- Students graduate from high school under one standard and then are required to meet a whole new set of standards in college.

- No one is held accountable for student transitions from high school to college.

- Inequalities exist throughout the education systems in college preparation course offerings and connections with local postsecondary institutions.[4]

For the past decade, the Tech Prep initiative, using the Career Pathway concept, has been diligently working to address these problems for students enrolled in career and technical education (CTE). Under the auspices of Tech Prep, consortia are conducting the following activities:

- Alignment of secondary and postsecondary courses

- Setting standards at secondary and postsecondary education levels based on employer input

- Monitoring student transitions from high school to college

- Providing opportunities for students to earn college credit while still in high school.

- Providing career development activities to foster career maturity.

---

[4] Andrea Venezia, Michael W. Kirst, and Anthony L. Antonio, *Betraying the College Dream: How Disconnected K–12 and Postsecondary Education Systems Undermine Student Aspirations* (Stanford University, Final Policy Report from the Bridge Project, 2001).

These activities are among the tenets for Career Pathways. So, how are Career Pathways different from Tech Prep?

Career Pathways Versus Tech Prep

Philosophically, there are no differences between the Career Pathways initiative and Tech Prep. With the passage of the Carl D. Perkins Vocational and Applied Technology Education Act, states were given federal dollars to implement Tech Prep. The Perkins Act, however, did not succinctly define Tech Prep. The lack of a definition in the legislation allowed states to set their own definitions and parameters for Tech Prep. Thus, even though similar Tech Prep activities can be found among the states, the look and feel of Tech Prep differs across the country.

In the spring of 2003, the National Association for Tech Prep Leadership (NATPL) surveyed state Tech Prep directors to determine what Tech Prep activities were taking place in the states.[5] The survey revealed **ten major categories** of activities that were being conducted. These activities were providing a framework for implementing secondary-to-postsecondary transition programs (**Career Pathways**).

The activity categories build on one another, starting with the *strategic planning* (category 1) process and moving on to the *professional development* process (category 2) and the collaboration required to plan and implement both course and program *articulation* (category 3). Collaboration leads to the *program support, development, and enhancement* (category 4) required to provide *student opportunities* (category 5), which include both *school and work-based experiential learning* (categories 6 and 7). These experiences are enhanced by the acquisition of *instructional equipment and materials* (category 8) and must be *promoted* (category 9) through a variety of activities and materials. Finally, the resulting programs must be *assessed and evaluated* (category 10) on an ongoing basis.

---

[5] The survey is posted on the NAPTL website, www.natpl.org.

Tech Prep, as shown by the NATPL report, is working, and these activities provide and will continue to provide a framework for creating and implementing Career Pathways.

Let's examine the Career Pathway tenets as they relate to the ongoing Tech Prep activities being conducted across the states:

Career Pathways	Tech Prep Activities
1. A coherent, articulated sequence of rigorous academic and career/technical courses, commencing in the ninth grade and leading to an associate degree and beyond	1. Tech Prep consortia have established Career Pathways and, in the process, have gained the expertise necessary to develop quality pathways.
2. Career Pathways are developed, implemented, and maintained in partnerships involving secondary and postsecondary education, business, and employers.	2. Tech Prep consortium members include representatives of secondary education, postsecondary education, business, and employers. Their responsibilities are to develop and monitor Tech Prep Career Pathways.
3. Provides foundation and skills in a chosen career cluster	3. Tech Prep consortium members include business representatives and employers who provide input concerning the academic and technical skills necessary for success within a career cluster.
4. Provides opportunities for students to earn college credit through dual/concurrent enrollment and/or articulation agreements	4. Tech Prep consortia are charged with the development of articulation agreements with postsecondary institutions.

Career Pathways	Tech Prep Activities
5. Alignment and articulation with baccalaureate programs where appropriate	5. Tech Prep consortia who have taken the lead in Tech Prep have established articulation agreements with baccalaureate programs.
6. Opportunities for placement in the chosen career cluster at any of several exit points	6. States that have taken the lead in Tech Prep utilize their business partners in finding employment opportunities for students.
7. Empirical evidence is maintained.	7. States that have taken the lead in Tech Prep collect Tech Prep data and use the data in planning and decision-making activities.

In varying degrees, approximately 977 Tech Prep consortia across the nation have conducted these activities. The extent and depth of the activities lie in the respective state's definition and philosophy of Tech Prep.

In many states (e.g., North Carolina, Texas, Massachusetts, and West Virginia) the Tech Prep initiative has become a major change agent in driving education reform. One state in particular, West Virginia, recognizes Tech Prep within its legislated career clusters for all public schools. As a result, Tech Prep has been a leader in establishing Career Pathways that lead to a credential, an apprenticeship, or an associate degree.

> Tech Prep has been a leader in establishing Career Pathways that lead to a credential, an apprenticeship, or an associate degree.

West Virginia's Career Pathways—One Career Pathway Model

In 1996, West Virginia legislators enacted Senate Bill 300. This statute put into law the Career Pathways format for high school curriculum. As a result, all students select Career Pathways that begin in ninth grade.

The curriculum is divided into six occupational clusters: Health, Human Services, Business/Finance, Engineering/Technical, Science/Natural Resources, and I-Humanities/Arts. Each cluster contains Career Pathways. West Virginia has identified twenty-one Career Pathways with three options:

1. Four-year+ degree
2. Associate degree (Tech Prep)
3. Certification or apprenticeship

The curriculum for the Career Pathways consists of:

- The state's graduation requirements (4 English, 4 math, 3 science, 4 social studies, 1 art, physical education and civics) plus 4 required Career Pathway courses,

- A work-based learning experience, and

- A pool of recommended electives for the Career Pathway of choice.

Within each Career Pathway, each student determines his or her postsecondary goal: a credential, an apprenticeship, an associate degree, or a four-year or plus degree. This determination identifies the student's four Career Pathway courses and electives required for graduation.

By law, every West Virginia student is engaged in a Career Pathway. Since the Tech Prep Career Pathway was one of three options for West Virginia students, the West Virginia Tech Prep consortia took the lead in implementing Career Pathways across the state.

Transitioning to Career Pathways

Transitioning career and technical education (CTE) to Career Pathways can best be accomplished through a strong state-level partnership between the Tech Prep and CTE directors. States where this relationship exists have demonstrated great progress in moving to a Career Pathways system. The following are suggested steps in the transition process:

1. Tech Prep and CTE directors develop a state strategic plan for transitioning CTE to Career Pathways. This plan becomes the state's blueprint for Career Pathways.

> **Transitioning career and technical education (CTE) to Career Pathways can best be accomplished through a strong state-level partnership between the Tech Prep and CTE directors.**

2. Utilize established Tech Prep consortia to carry out the strategic plan.

3. Shift from a formula-funded to a competitive, grant-funded system.

4. Provide career development.

Strategic plan — Through a collaborative partnership, the state's Tech Prep and CTE directors would develop an implementation strategy for moving CTE to a Career Pathways system. Each partner would bring expertise to the table that is necessary for the development of high-quality Career Pathways. The plan would include a framework of activities in professional development, articulation, program support, student opportunities, and evaluation.

Tech Prep consortia — Local Tech Prep consortia have been developing Career Pathways for Tech Prep students over the past two decades. They are a valuable resource and have the ability to lead the way in the transition of all CTE to Career Pathways. Consortium activities that are critical to the establishment of Career Pathways exist and have been proven successful in their respective endeavors.

Competitive Tech Prep grants — Moving from a locally formula-funded grant system to a competitive grant system would provide greater synergy for change and implementation of a Career Pathways system. States would set the goals and criteria for establishing Career Pathways. A request for proposals (RFP) would be sent out statewide to Tech Prep consortia. Tech Prep consortia would submit grant proposals outlining the activities they will conduct to meet the specified state goals. Each year, consortia would produce data that reflect success and change in their school systems. The amount of their next grant would be predicated on the success of the previous year.

> Moving from a locally formula-funded grant system to a competitive grant system would provide greater synergy for change and implementation of a Career Pathways system.

Career development—Career development is vital to the success of a Career Pathways system. Career awareness and exploration must take place prior to a student's decision concerning Career Pathways. It is the difference between sound decision making by students and the proverbial "rolling the dice." Choosing pathways and setting goals should be couched within a career development framework. Students who have been engaged in a comprehensive career development system are showing a higher rate of success after high school than those who have not been engaged.

CONCLUSION

Purpose-driven program pathways and structures are required if high school students are to see meaning in their educational experience. It is no accident that Rick Warren's book *The Purpose Driven Life* has become a national best seller. There is an obvious human longing for purpose. One of the driving motivations behind Tech Prep and its logical "next generation," Career Pathways, is recognition of the need for purpose-driven educational programs.

Continuity and purpose in learning, up and down the line, are vital to student success. To be considered well-structured, any educational pathway must enable students to *see* continuity and purpose in what they are doing. Focused learning motivates; unfocused learning does not. Focused learning is what the Career Pathways concept is all about.

APPENDIX 1:
RESEARCH FOUNDATION AND VALIDATION OF THE CAREER PATHWAYS SELF-STUDY INSTRUMENT

Before Career Pathways partnerships can improve, they must have a means of assessing where they are and what goals they should aim for. This is the rationale behind the Career Pathways Self-Study Instrument, which was developed by CORD in consultation with local-, state-, and national-level CTE practitioners and leaders. (The instrument is presented in Chapter 1 of this book.) Using the Career Pathways Self-Study Instrument, CTE practitioners are able to assess their current effectiveness and identify areas in which their partnerships should strive to improve.

The purpose of this appendix is to give the reader a sense of how the Career Pathways Self-Study Instrument came into being, specifically to show that it is thoroughly grounded in up-to-date research and has been fine-tuned through a reiterative process involving experts at all levels of education and educational policymaking.

The Career Pathways Self-Study Instrument grew out of a USED/OVAE-sponsored initiative designed to identify *ideal models* of technical programs of study. Once identified, the programs were then to have been featured as part of an online National Clearinghouse for Career Pathways. The purpose of the clearinghouse was to give the field a comprehensive, web-accessible warehouse of information about successful Career Pathways initiatives from across the country. Admission to the clearinghouse was granted or denied on the basis of a survey filled out by program representatives.

The original USED/OVAE initiative developed a preliminary definition of Career Pathways and recognized five criteria for Career Pathways:

Career Pathway — A Career Pathway is a coherent sequence of rigorous academic and technical courses that prepare students for successful completion of state academic standards and more advanced postsecondary coursework related to their career area of interest.

Criterion 1 — A coherent, articulated sequence of courses, offered to students on a voluntary basis, which begin in high school, include rigorous academic courses as well as career and technical courses, and culminate in an industry-recognized certificate, registered apprenticeship, or associate or baccalaureate degree.

Criterion 2 — The high school academic component must, at a minimum, be made up of the same core courses that have been identified by the state as necessary preparation for enrollment in postsecondary institutions.

Criterion 3 — The career and technical component must be developed in partnership with business and employer groups and prepare students for self-supporting employment in high-demand occupational areas.

Criterion 4 — At the secondary level, Career Pathways must prepare students for both successful achievement of state academic standards and more advanced work related to their occupational area of interest, and should offer opportunities for eleventh and twelfth graders to earn dual/concurrent enrollment credit.

Criterion 5 — At the postsecondary level, programs must be open to enrollment by adults who meet academic prerequisites, whether or not they were enrolled at the secondary level.

The National Clearinghouse for Career Pathways project was discontinued by OVAE after about a year because the project did not yield the anticipated results — *ideal models* of CTE partnerships. But the project had generated considerable momentum that CORD personnel and others carried forward. In January 2004, CORD personnel met with staff and college partners of the College and Career Transitions Initiative (CCTI) to reconfigure the five criteria as a succinct definition of Career Pathways followed by essential characteristics for the secondary and postsecondary components. (This is the definition that appears as Figure 1-1 in Chapter 1.)

Since the National Clearinghouse for Career Pathways was not able to identify any ideal models, project personnel determined that the logical way to move forward with the Career Pathways concept was to provide a means for helping existing CTE partnerships strive to *become* ideal models. But how would those partnerships know how they were already doing? And what goals should they aim for? Those and similar questions led to the development of the first version of the Career Pathways Self-Study Instrument, which appeared in spring 2004.[1] The purpose of the Career Pathways Self-Study Instrument was to provide a means for partnerships to assess where they are (i.e., how successful they are in key areas) and set their sights on achievable goals.

To ensure that the Career Pathways Self-Study Instrument was firmly grounded in educational research, the developers produced a research-based *rationale* for each of the instrument's original ten benchmarks.[2] (The original ten were subdivided into eighteen in the final version, as presented in Chapter 1.) Following are two of the original ten, along with the research-based rationales on which they are based. (The two provided cover concepts addressed by numbers 1, 5, and 6 of the final version.)

I. The secondary-postsecondary partnership has implemented a 4+2 curriculum framework designed to meet postsecondary (college) entry/placement requirements.

---

[1] In its original form the Career Pathways Self-Study Instrument consisted of a one-page survey in which respondents chose 0, 1, 2, 3, or 4 for each of 18 items. In its the final form, the 0–4 has been changed to 1–5, and the one-page document is always accompanied by rating criteria explaining what each selection signifies. (This is more fully explained in the remarks that follow.)

[2] See Appendix B of Dan M. Hull, "Career Pathways: The Next Generation of Tech Prep," *Connections*, vol. 14, no. 5 (http://www.cord.org/uploadedfiles/Vol14No5.pdf).

Rationale—The transition from high school to college can be improved by better cooperation and communication between secondary and postsecondary systems (Bailey, Hughes, & Karp, 2002). Many models of curriculum design seem to produce knowledge and skills that are disconnected rather than organized into coherent wholes. In mathematics, for example, problems are solved not by observing and responding to the natural landscape through which the mathematics curriculum passes, but by mastering time-tested routines, conveniently placed along the path (National Research Council, 1990). The alternative to a "meandering path" curriculum is one of "learning the landscape" (Greeno, 1991), in which there is a progressive formalization framework to teach what is developmentally appropriate at various ages. A systems approach is needed to promote coordination among activities in the design of learning environments (Brown & Campione, 1996).

IV. The secondary component of the secondary-postsecondary partnership provides academic and technical foundation knowledge/skills in a chosen cluster. *Rationale*—Labor market data on America's youth have been viewed by some as an indication of the inadequate preparation of high school graduates for entry-level jobs and decisions about career fields and occupations (as cited in Griffith & Wade, 2001). Young adults between the ages of 18 and 25 years have changed occupations, employers, or jobs on the average of six times (Stern et al., 1995; U.S. Department of Labor, 1993). Young adults 18 to 19 years old also have among the highest rates of unemployment (Stern et al., 1995). One explanation of these statistics is that a lack of preparation by the public educational system has caused graduates to "flounder" after high school, i.e., going from job to job, school to work, or work to school, with little sense of purpose and career direction (Hamilton, 1990; Osterman & Iannozzi, 1993).

During late summer of 2004, the Career Pathways Self-Study Instrument (in its original form) was piloted at Technology in Education Summit II (Plano) and the Model

Schools conference in Washington, DC. It was also reviewed and *endorsed* by a panel of experts comprising college administrators, Tech Prep directors, industry leaders, representatives of state departments of education, and other experienced CTE practitioners. Dan Hull presented the instrument with its current 18 benchmarks at the NTPN conference in Minneapolis in October 2004.

Although the instrument received much positive feedback, many who used it noted that the rating scale (0–4) seemed arbitrary.[3] For any given item, how could the person filling it out know, *precisely*, what selection to choose? In response to this observation, the developers, with the help of an advisory board, added rating criteria that tell the user exactly what each response signifies. As an example, following are the rating criteria for the choices for the first item.

Career Pathways . . .

1. Are guided by one or more 4+2 (+2) curriculum frameworks (*i.e., 6- or 8-year seamless transition plans*).

1 = 10% or less of the Career Pathways in the secondary school have a 4+2 (+2) curriculum framework in place.
2 = More than 10% but less than 40% of the Career Pathways in the secondary school have a 4+2 (+2) curriculum framework in place.
3 = At least 40% but less than 70% of the Career Pathways in the secondary school have a 4+2 (+2) curriculum framework in place.
4 = At least 70% but less than 90% of the Career Pathways in the secondary school have a 4+2 (+2) curriculum framework in place.
5 = At least 90% of the Career Pathways in the secondary school have a 4+2 (+2) curriculum framework in place.

The rating criteria are always provided with the instrument so that the person filling it out can know exactly what each of his or her choices means.

---

[3] In the final version, the 0–4 scale has been changed to 1–5.

The instrument, which reached its final form in late 2004, is fulfilling its purpose, which is to help CTE practitioners identify their strengths and weaknesses. According to the feedback thus far received via the instrument, the areas in which partnerships are strongest and weakest are as follows:

Benchmarks in which partnerships are strongest:

7. The secondary component provides opportunities for students to earn college credit through dual/concurrent enrollment or articulation agreements.

8. The postsecondary component provides opportunities for students to earn college credit through dual/concurrent enrollment or articulation agreements.

10. The postsecondary component provides industry-recognized knowledge and skills.

Benchmarks in which partnerships are weakest:

1. Career Pathways are guided by one or more 4+2 (+2) curriculum frameworks.

13. Business provides student work-based learning experiences after the eleventh grade.

14. Business supports student recruitment and provides ongoing support for the Career Pathways program.

This is extremely valuable information because it tells practitioners exactly where to focus their attention in improving their CTE partnerships.

In summary, the Career Pathways Self-Study Instrument (along with its rating criteria) has been thoroughly reviewed and validated by knowledgeable educators, administrators, policymakers, and businesspeople. It is based on up-to-date research in issues that affect student learning, transitions from secondary to postsecondary, and preparation for the workplace. And, according to people who have used it, it is already producing the kind of information that it was designed to produce — information that they can use to plan for systematic improvement.

The Career Pathways Self-Study Instrument should become an integral of part of the strategic improvement process of every Career Pathways partnership. It provides a way to determine where we are and where we should be, and it provides a common language that will enable Career Pathways practitioners to help one another make their vision a reality.

References

Bailey, T. R., Hughes, K. L., & Karp, M. M. (2002). What role can duel enrollment programs play in easing the transition between high school and postsecondary education? *Journal for Vocational Special Needs Education, 24*(2-3), 18-29.

Brown, A. L., & Campione, J. C. (1996). Psychological theory and the design of innovative learning environments: On procedures, principles, and systems. In L. Schauble and R. Glaser (Eds.), *Innovations in learning: New environments for education* (pp. 289-325). Mahwah, NJ: Erlbaum.

Greeno, J. (1991). Number sense as situated knowing in a conceptual domain. *Journal for Research in Mathematics Education, 22*(3), 170-218.

Griffith, J., & Wade, J. (2001). The relation of high school career- and work-oriented education to postsecondary employment and college performance: A six-year longitudinal study of public high school graduates. *Journal of Vocational Education Research, 26*(3), 328-365.

Hamilton, S. F. (1990). *Apprenticeship for adulthood: Preparing youth for the future.* NY: Free Press.

National Research Council. (1990). *Reshaping school mathematics.* Mathematical Sciences Education Board. Washington, D.C.: National Academy Press.

Osterman, P., & Iannozzi, M. (1993). *Youth apprenticeships and school-to-work transitions: Current knowledge and legislative strategy.* Philadelphia: National Center on the Educational Quality of the Workforce.

Stern, D., Finkelstein, N., Stone, J. R., Latting, J., & Dornsife, C. (1995). *School to Work: Research programs in the United States.* London: Falmer.

U.S. Department of Labor. (1993). *The employment situation. News release.* Washington, D.C.: U.S. Department of Labor, Bureau of Labor Statistics. USDL 93-200.

APPENDIX 2: RATING CRITERIA FOR THE CAREER PATHWAYS SELF-STUDY INSTRUMENT

Career Pathways . . .

1. Are guided by one or more 4+2 (+2) curriculum frameworks (*i.e., 6- or 8-year seamless transition plans*).

1 = 10% or less of the Career Pathways in the secondary school have a 4+2 (+2) curriculum framework in place.
2 = More than 10% but less than 40% of the Career Pathways in the secondary school have a 4+2 (+2) curriculum framework in place.
3 = At least 40% but less than 70% of the Career Pathways in the secondary school have a 4+2 (+2) curriculum framework in place.
4 = At least 70% but less than 90% of the Career Pathways in the secondary school have a 4+2 (+2) curriculum framework in place.
5 = At least 90% of the Career Pathways in the secondary school have a 4+2 (+2) curriculum framework in place.

Career Pathways . . .

2. Include comprehensive student career guidance and counseling. (*This indicates that you see evidence that students, educators, parents, and the community at large understand labor market trends and all the options in a Career Pathway.*)

1 = 10% or less of the students who participate in Career Pathways at the secondary school are provided a system for comprehensive student career guidance and counseling.
2 = More than 10% but less than 40% of the students who participate in Career Pathways at the secondary school are provided a system for comprehensive student career guidance and counseling.
3 = At least 40% but less than 70% of the students who participate in Career Pathways at the secondary school are provided a system for comprehensive student career guidance and counseling.
4 = At least 70% but less than 90% of the students who participate in Career Pathways at the secondary school are provided a system for comprehensive student career guidance and counseling.
5 = At least 90% of the students who participate in Career Pathways at the secondary school are provided a system for comprehensive student career guidance and counseling.

Secondary component . . .

3. Meets academic standards and grade level requirements.

1 = 10% or less of the students who participate in Career Pathways at the secondary school are passing courses appropriate to their grade levels.
2 = More than 10% but less than 40% of the students who participate in Career Pathways at the secondary school are passing courses appropriate to their grade levels.
3 = At least 40% but less than 70% of the students who participate in Career Pathways at the secondary school are passing courses appropriate to their grade levels.
4 = At least 70% but less than 90% of the students who participate in Career Pathways at the secondary school are passing courses appropriate to their grade levels.
5 = At least 90% of the students who participate in Career Pathways at the secondary school are passing courses appropriate to their grade levels.

Secondary component . . .

4. Meets high school standardized testing and exit requirements. (*This indicates that you see evidence that students meet state expectations on standardized tests and graduation rates.*)

1 = 10% or less of the students who participate in Career Pathways at the secondary school meet or exceed high school standardized testing and exit requirements.
2 = More than 10% but less than 40% of the students who participate in Career Pathways at the secondary school meet or exceed high school standardized testing and exit requirements.
3 = At least 40% but less than 70% of the students who participate in Career Pathways at the secondary school meet or exceed high school standardized testing and exit requirements.
4 = At least 70% but less than 90% of the students who participate in Career Pathways at the secondary school meet or exceed high school standardized testing and exit requirements.
5 = At least 90% of the students who participate in Career Pathways at the secondary school meet or exceed high school standardized testing and exit requirements.

Secondary component . . .

5. Meets postsecondary (both 2-year and 4-year college) entry and placement requirements. (*This indicates that you see evidence that Career Pathway students transition successfully to the postsecondary level without having to duplicate courses, receive remedial services, and/or take remedial courses.*)

1 = 10% or less of the students who participate in Career Pathways at the secondary school meet state postsecondary entry and placement requirements.
2 = More than 10% but less than 40% of the students who participate in Career Pathways at the secondary school meet state postsecondary entry and placement requirements.
3 = At least 40% but less than 70% of the students who participate in Career Pathways at the secondary school meet state postsecondary entry and placement requirements.
4 = At least 70% but less than 90% of the students who participate in Career Pathways at the secondary school meet state postsecondary entry and placement requirements.
5 = At least 90% of the students who participate in Career Pathways at the secondary school meet state postsecondary entry and placement requirements.

Secondary component . . .

6. Provides academic and technical foundation knowledge and skills in a chosen Career Pathway (*i.e., begins to build the knowledge needed for college and a career, but the skills are not job-specific at the secondary level*).

1 = 10% or less of the secondary students who participate in Career Pathways at the secondary school are gaining the academic and technical foundation knowledge and skills necessary for success in their Career Pathway.
2 = More than 10% but less than 40% of the secondary students who participate in Career Pathways at the secondary school are gaining the academic and technical foundation knowledge and skills necessary for success in their Career Pathway.
3 = At least 40% but less than 70% of the secondary students who participate in Career Pathways at the secondary school are gaining the academic and technical foundation knowledge and skills necessary for success in their Career Pathway.
4 = At least 70% but less than 90% of the secondary students who participate in Career Pathways at the secondary school are gaining the academic and technical foundation knowledge and skills necessary for success in their Career Pathway.
5 = At least 90% of the secondary students who participate in Career Pathways at the secondary school are gaining the academic and technical foundation knowledge and skills necessary for success in their Career Pathway.

Secondary component . . .

7. Provides opportunities for students to earn college credit through dual/concurrent enrollment or articulation agreements. (*This indicates that you see evidence that students have opportunities to complete portions of their associate degree requirements at the secondary level.*)

1 = The secondary school does not currently provide Career Pathway students with the benefit of dual credit, articulation, or advanced standing agreements.
2 = The secondary school does not currently provides Career Pathway students with dual credit, articulation, or advanced standing opportunities, but the school is communicating with local colleges about establishing articulation and/or dual credit agreements.
3 = The secondary school provides Career Pathway students opportunities for advanced standing through completion of articulated courses. (That is, although students do not receive college credits for Career Pathway courses, they are placed at a higher level when they enter college courses).
4 = The secondary school provides Career Pathway students opportunities to take advantage of articulation agreements wherein the students receive college credit for Career Pathway courses once they become students at the partnering degree-granting institution. (The articulation agreements do not guarantee that the courses will be accepted by other postsecondary schools.)
5 = The secondary school provides Career Pathway students opportunities to take dual-credit and/or articulated courses, for which they receive college credit once the course is complete and requirements are met. Since the credit is given by the college, it is also accepted by other postsecondary institutions.

Postsecondary component . . .

8. Provides opportunities for students to earn college credit through dual/concurrent enrollment or articulation agreements. (*This indicates that you see evidence that students have—and are taking advantage of—the opportunity to complete a portion of their associate degree requirements at the secondary level and that they are performing successfully at the postsecondary level without duplicating courses.*)

1 = The postsecondary component does not currently offer students the benefit of dual credit, articulation, or advanced standing agreements.
2 = The postsecondary component does not currently offer students the benefit of dual credit, articulation, or advanced standing agreements, but the postsecondary institution is in communication with the secondary school regarding the establishment of articulation and/or dual credit agreements.
3 = The postsecondary component offers students who participate in Career Pathways at the secondary school advanced standing as a result of their completion of articulated courses. (That is, although the students do not receive college credit for the articulated courses, they are placed at a higher level when they enter college courses.)
4 = The postsecondary component offers students who participate in Career Pathway programs at the secondary school the benefit of articulation agreements in that they receive college credit for articulated courses once they become students at the postsecondary institution.
5 = The postsecondary component offers students who participate in Career Pathway programs at the secondary school the benefit of dual credit or articulation opportunities, wherein they receive college credit once the course is complete and requirements are met.

Postsecondary component . . .

9. Provides alignment and/or articulation with baccalaureate programs. (*This indicates that you see evidence that students are transitioning to baccalaureate programs with no duplication of courses or remediation at the baccalaureate level.*)

1 = 10% or less of the postsecondary institution's Career Pathway programs offer support and encourage opportunities for alignment and/or articulation with baccalaureate programs.
2 = More than 10% but less than 40% of the postsecondary institution's Career Pathway programs offer support and encourage opportunities for alignment and/or articulation with baccalaureate programs.
3 = At least 40% but less than 70% of the postsecondary institution's Career Pathway programs offer support and encourage opportunities for alignment and/or articulation with baccalaureate programs.
4 = At least 70% but less than 90% of the postsecondary institution's Career Pathway programs offer support and encourage opportunities for alignment and/or articulation with baccalaureate programs.
5 = At least 90% of the postsecondary institution's Career Pathway programs offer support and encourage opportunities for alignment and/or articulation with baccalaureate programs.

Postsecondary component . . .

10. Provides industry-recognized knowledge and skills. (*Career Pathways have been developed using national, state, and/or industry/professional association skill standards and have been reviewed and [when necessary] revised by local business/industry. Local businesses are actively engaged in curriculum/Career Pathway development.*)

1 = 10% or less of the postsecondary institution's Career Pathway programs use curriculum that is based on industry-recognized knowledge and skills.
2 = More than 10% but less than 40% of the postsecondary institution's Career Pathway programs use curriculum that is based on industry-recognized knowledge and skills.
3 = At least 40% but less than 70% of the postsecondary institution's Career Pathway programs use curriculum that is based on industry-recognized knowledge and skills.
4 = At least 70% but less than 90% of the postsecondary institution's Career Pathway programs use curriculum that is based on industry-recognized knowledge and skills.
5 = At least 90% of the postsecondary institution's Career Pathway programs use curriculum that is based on industry-recognized knowledge and skills.

Postsecondary component . . .

11. Provides employment opportunities for high-wage, high-demand careers in the chosen Pathway and provides multiple exit points. (*This item refers to full-time career opportunities following 2-year and 4-year postsecondary programs, not internships.*)

1 = 10% or less of the students who participate in Career Pathways have opportunities to pursue high-wage, high-demand careers via multiple exit points.
2 = More than 10% but less than 40% of the students who participate in Career Pathways have opportunities to pursue high-wage, high-demand careers via multiple exit points.
3 = At least 40% but less than 70% of the students who participate in Career Pathways have opportunities to pursue high-wage, high-demand careers via multiple exit points.
4 = At least 70% but less than 90% of the students who participate in Career Pathways have opportunities to pursue high-wage, high-demand careers via multiple exit points.
5 = At least 90% of the students who participate in Career Pathways have opportunities to pursue high-wage, high-demand careers via multiple exit points.

Business . . .

12. Ensures that students are learning current, in-demand skills. (*This indicates that advisory councils are business driven; their programs of work include activities that ensure that students are learning current, in-demand skills.*)

1 = 10% or less of the businesses in the community are providing activities for students to learn current, in-demand skills.
2 = More than 10% but less than 40% of the businesses in the community are providing activities for students to learn current, in-demand skills.
3 = At least 40% but less than 70% of the businesses in the community are providing activities for students to learn current in-demand skills.
4 = At least 70% but less than 90% of the businesses in the community are providing activities for students to learn current in-demand skills.
5 = At least 90% of the businesses in the community are providing activities for students to learn current in-demand skills.

Business . . .

13. Provides student work-based learning experiences after the 11th grade. (*This indicates that you see evidence of a "progressive" work-based learning system, i.e., one in which participating students begin with simple activities such as tours and job shadowing and progress to internships.***)**

1 = 10% or less of the students who participate in Career Pathways at the secondary school are engaged in a progressive system of work-based learning experiences that culminate in an internship.
2 = More than 10% but less than 40% of the students who participate in Career Pathways at the secondary school are engaged in a progressive system of work-based learning experiences that culminate in an internship.
3 = At least 40% but less than 70% of the students who participate in Career Pathways at the secondary school are engaged in a progressive system of work-based learning experiences that culminate in an internship.
4 = At least 70% but less than 90% of the students who participate in Career Pathways at the secondary school are engaged in a progressive system of work-based learning experiences that culminate in an internship.
5 = At least 90% of the students who participate in Career Pathways at the secondary school are engaged in a progressive system of work-based learning experiences that culminate in an internship.

Business . . .

14. Supports student recruitment and provides ongoing support for the Career Pathway program. (*Business groups believe that student completion of Career Pathways will benefit their firms/companies.***)**

1 = 10% or less of the students who participate in Career Pathways at the secondary school interact with business/industry, either through student recruitment or through some other type of support throughout the school year.
2 = More than 10% but less than 40% of the students who participate in Career Pathways at the secondary school interact with business/industry, either through student recruitment or through some other type of support throughout the school year.
3 = At least 40% but less than 70% of the students who participate in Career Pathways at the secondary school interact with business/industry, either through student recruitment or through some other type of support throughout the school year.
4 = At least 70% but less than 90% of the students who participate in Career Pathways at the secondary school interact with business/industry, either through student recruitment or through some other type of support throughout the school year.
5 = At least 90% of the businesses who participate in Career Pathways are actively involved in student recruitment into Career Pathways and/or make monetary or in-kind contributions to the school.

Partnership ensures a culture focused on improvement by . . .

15. Collecting qualitative and quantitative data on academic and career success, retention rates, dropouts, graduation, transitions, and remediation.

1 = 10% or less of the qualitative and quantitative data on academic and career success, dropouts, graduation, transitions, and remediation is being collected annually for students involved in Career Pathways at the secondary school.
2 = More than 10% but less than 40% of the qualitative and quantitative data on academic and career success, dropouts, graduation, transitions, and remediation is being collected annually for students involved in Career Pathways at the secondary school.
3 = At least 40% but less than 70% of the qualitative and quantitative data on academic and career success, dropouts, graduation, transitions, and remediation is being collected annually for students involved in Career Pathways at the secondary school.
4 = At least 70% but less than 90% of the qualitative and quantitative data on academic and career success, dropouts, graduation, transitions, and remediation is being collected annually for students involved in Career Pathways at the secondary school.
5 = At least 90% of the qualitative and quantitative data on academic and career success, dropouts, graduation, transitions, and remediation is being collected annually for students involved in Career Pathways at the secondary school.

Partnership ensures a culture focused on improvement by . . .

16. Using data for planning and decision-making.

1 = 10% or less of the data that is being collected on Career Pathway students in the secondary school is being used for planning and decision-making.
2 = More than 10% but less than 40% of the data that is being collected on Career Pathway students in the secondary school is being used for planning and decision-making.
3 = At least 40% but less than 70% of the data that is being collected on Career Pathway students in the secondary school is being used for planning and decision-making.
4 = At least 70% but less than 90% of the data that is being collected on Career Pathway students in the secondary school is being used for planning and decision-making.
5 = At least 90% of the data that is being collected on Career Pathway students in the secondary school is being used for planning and decision-making.

Partnership ensures a culture focused on improvement by . . .

17. Providing targeted professional development for faculty, administrators, and counselors designed to improve teaching/learning and integration of technical and academic instruction. (*Training is ongoing and accessible to all appropriate stakeholders; the stakeholders are participating and are showing a high level of satisfaction; data on the effectiveness of the training is being collected.*)

1 = 10% or less of the faculty, administrators, <u>and</u> counselors who serve the Career Pathway students at the secondary school are participating in targeted professional development designed to improve teaching/learning and integration of technical and academic instruction.
2 = More than 10% but less than 40% of the faculty, administrators, <u>and</u> counselors who serve the Career Pathway students at the secondary school are participating in targeted professional development designed to improve teaching/learning and integration of technical and academic instruction.
3 = At least 40% but less than 70% of the faculty, administrators, <u>and</u> counselors who serve the Career Pathway students at the secondary school are participating in targeted professional development designed to improve teaching/learning and integration of technical and academic instruction.
4 = At least 70% but less than 90% of the faculty, administrators, <u>and</u> counselors who serve the Career Pathway students at the secondary school are participating in targeted professional development designed to improve teaching/learning and integration of technical and academic instruction.
5 = At least 90% of the faculty, administrators, <u>and</u> counselors who serve the Career Pathway students at the secondary school are participating in targeted professional development designed to improve teaching/learning and integration of technical and academic instruction.

Partnership ensures a culture focused on improvement by . . .

18. Maintaining ongoing dialogue among secondary, postsecondary, and business partners. (*There is frequent and effective communication involving all levels [administrators, counselors, and faculty]. Secondary and postsecondary faculty meet with their subject-matter peers at the next higher or lower level [e.g., secondary math meet with postsecondary math].*)

1 = 10% or less of the individuals involved in the Career Pathway programs have quarterly, ongoing dialogue with their counterparts at the secondary, postsecondary, and/or business partner level.
2 = More than 10% but less than 40% of the individuals involved in the Career Pathway programs have quarterly, ongoing dialogue with their counterparts at the secondary, postsecondary, and/or business partner level.
3 = At least 40% but less than 70% of the individuals involved in the Career Pathway programs have quarterly, ongoing dialogue with their counterparts at the secondary, postsecondary, and/or business partner level.
4 = At least 70% but less than 90% of the individuals involved in the Career Pathway programs have quarterly, ongoing dialogue with their counterparts at the secondary, postsecondary, and/or business partner level.
5 = At least 90% of the individuals involved in the Career Pathway programs have quarterly, ongoing dialogue with their counterparts at the secondary, postsecondary, and/or business partner level.

APPENDIX 3: EXAMPLE INTEGRATED CURRICULUM STANDARD (ICS) FOR *TEAMWORK*

Excerpted from CORD's *Curriculum Integrator*. For more information on *Curriculum Integrator*, contact CORD at 800-972-2766.

ICS Statement

Participate as an effective member of a team by contributing to the group effort of accomplishing goals. Identify and employ the appropriate role within the group. Use effective communication, interpersonal skills, and learning techniques while working with others of diverse backgrounds. Participate in group decision-making processes incorporating the appropriate role within the group. Evaluate the team's efforts.

Rubric

Component 1 of 4—*Contribute to the group effort of accomplishing goals.*

Performance Criteria	Level of Performance			
	World-Class Learner	Proficient Learner	Developing Learner	Emergent Learner
Exhibits concern and encouragement for each team member and team goals.	Consistently	Usually	Occasionally	Rarely, if ever

Component 1 of 4—Contribute to the group effort of accomplishing goals.

Performance Criteria	Level of Performance			
	World-Class Learner	Proficient Learner	Developing Learner	Emergent Learner
Accepts tasks set according to team-established procedures.	Completes all... in an exceptional manner	Completes all... in an adequate manner	May not complete all...if so, may not be according to established procedures	Does not complete tasks

Component 2 of 4—Shows sensitivity to diverse backgrounds through communication, interpersonal skills, and learning techniques.

Performance Criteria	Level of Performance			
	World-Class Learner	Proficient Learner	Developing Learner	Emergent Learner
Considers cultures and how they differ when working with and for others.	Consistently considerate of all cultures	Usually considerate of all cultures	Occasionally considerate of most cultures	Little if any consideration for other cultures

Component 2 of 4—Shows sensitivity to diverse backgrounds through communication, interpersonal skills, and learning techniques.

Performance Criteria	Level of Performance			
	World-Class Learner	Proficient Learner	Developing Learner	Emergent Learner
Takes ownership of one's own culture and values while tolerating and appreciating different cultures and values of others.	Remains so with high levels of sensitivity	Remains so with adequate sensitivity	May or may not remain with little sensitivity	Is unaware of his own or that of others
	├──┼──┼──┼──┤			
Exhibits consideration through positive, clear, and sensitive communication, appropriate personal contacts, and learning opportunities between parties.	High levels of…	Adequate levels of…	Very little…	No…
	├──┼──┼──┼──┤			

Component 3 of 4—*Participate in group decision-making processes incorporating the appropriate role within the group.*

Performance Criteria	Level of Performance			
	World-Class Learner	Proficient Learner	Developing Learner	Emergent Learner
Cooperates with team members to reach realistic, attainable goals.	Consistently	Usually	Occasionally	Is not able or is unwilling
	├──────┼──────┼──────┼──────┤			
Works toward resolving conflict, constructing compromises, and building consensus.	Consistently and skillfully	Usually and skillfully	Occasionally	Does not and may even weaken the team instead
	├──────┼──────┼──────┼──────┤			

Component 4 of 4—*Evaluate team's efforts.*

| Performance Criteria | Level of Performance | | | |
	World-Class Learner	Proficient Learner	Developing Learner	Emergent Learner
Participates in observing team's efforts and completing follow-up activities to evaluate team's goals.	Consistently	Usually	Occasionally… may or may not complete tasks	Rarely…does not complete tasks
	|—|—|—|	|—|—|—|	|—|—|—|

A Sampling of Supporting Elements

(KSA = knowledge, skills, and attitudes. Abbreviations such as ABT and HMT refer to the published standards that went into the *Curriculum Integrator* database.)

Ref No	Employability	Bus/Ind	Academic	KSA	Elements
10	NCDG-1.02.b			S	Demonstrate interpersonal skills required for working with and for others.
218	SCANS-C9-Interpersonal			S	Participates as a Member of a Team – Works cooperatively with others and contributes to group efforts with ideas, suggestions, and effort.
373		ABT-15A.14		A	Recognize the necessity of being a team member.
379		ABT-15B.05		K	Explain the concepts of group trust and systems orientation, within and between teams.
381		ABT-16B.07		K	Develop understanding of individual roles and responsibilities in groups.
705		BS-M-07		S	Participate as a member of the research team

Ref No	Employability	Bus/Ind	Academic	KSA	Elements
1019		CLT-36.04		S	Work with team members to set goals and divide the work to be done.
1364		HMT-13.03A		S	Perform as a team member on an emergency-response team.
1617		HMT-27.04		A	Sociability: Demonstrate understanding, friendliness, adaptability, empathy, and politeness in new and ongoing group settings by being able to: assert self in familiar and unfamiliar social situations; relate well to others; respond appropriately to situations; take interest in what others say and do.
1637		HPM-21.CT.01		K	Identify interpersonal characteristics of a team player.
1642		HPM-22.CT.06		S	Apply group dynamic principles to manufacturing situations.
1645		HPM-22.CT.09		S	Select appropriate communication methods.
1648		HPM-23.CT.12		K	Identify components of group dynamics.
2353		V701-F.3.1		S	Resolve conflict.
2545		CADD-ES.2.2		SA	Interpersonal: Participate as member of teams (e.g., following instructions, providing feedback, cooperating with established team goals)
2547		CADD-ES.2.4		A	Interpersonal: Maintain professional respect for coworkers and customers without prejudice
2762		ELEC-1.B.07		A	Treat people with respect
2767		ELEC-1.C.03		S	Adapt as necessary to complete the team task
2953		ELEC-4.B.05		S	Interact with co-workers and customers in a logical, clear and understandable manner
3467		V705-E.1.6		SA	Recognize the accomplishment of others.
3470		V705-E.1.9		SA	Cooperate with peers, employer, and customers.
5676			ELA-3.9	KA	Students develop an understanding of and respect for diversity in language use, patterns, and dialects across cultures, ethnic groups, geographic regions, and social roles.

Ref No	Employability	Bus/Ind	Academic	KSA	Elements
5871			AAAS-173.07F.1	K	Conflict between people or groups arises from competition over ideas, resources, power, and status. Social change, or the prospect of it, promotes conflict because social, economic, and political changes usually benefit some groups more than others. That, of course, is also true of the status quo.
6009			AAAS-275.11C.3	K	Things can change in detail but remain the same in general (the players change, but the team remains; cells are replaced, but the organism remains). Sometimes counterbalancing changes are necessary for a thing to retain its essential constancy in the presence of changing conditions.
6043			AAAS-297.12D.6	S	Participate in group discussions on scientific topics by restating or summarizing accurately what others have said, asking for clarification or elaboration, and expressing alternative positions.
6469			CG-108.2D.4	S	Evaluate, take, and defend positions on issues in which fundamental values and principles may be in conflict.
6664			SS-033.I.e	K	Demonstrate the value of cultural diversity, as well as cohesion, within and across groups.
6933			NGS-203.10a	S	Compare the role that culture plays in incidents of cooperation and conflict in the present-day world
8794		MS1-78.4.1		S	Social Skills – Identify and demonstrate the appropriate social skills and related personal qualities in the performance of major duties requiring cooperative relations with supervisors, team leaders, and team members.
9321		AWS-EX.1.1.3d		S	Behavior (teamwork, negotiation, interpersonal delegation, motivation, coaching, counseling)
9875		V706-V.2		S	Develop team trouble shooting techniques
9876		V706-V.3		S	Develop team metrics for measure of effectiveness (i.e., tracking, reporting)
9882		V706-V.8		S	Match team members' skills and group activity
9883		V706-V.9		S	Demonstrate ability to work with team members as a group or individually

Ref No	Employability	Bus/Ind	Academic	KSA	Elements
9900		V706-V.22		K	Contrast the role of a team player with the role of an individual
9902		V706-V.24		S	Demonstrate productive relationships within workgroup
10005		V706-Z.4.14		S	Evaluate team performance
9	NCDG-1.02.a			S	Demonstrate effective interpersonal skills.
96	NCDG-A1.02.a			SA	Demonstrate appropriate interpersonal skills in expressing feelings and ideas.
222	SCANS-C13-Interpersonal			S	Negotiates to Arrive at a Decision – Works toward an agreement that may involve exchanging specific resources or resolving divergent interests.
223	SCANS-C14-Interpersonal			S	Works with Cultural Diversity – Works well with men and women and with people from a variety of ethnic, social, or educational backgrounds.
245	SCANS-F15-Personal			S	Sociability – Demonstrates understanding, friendliness, adaptability, empathy and politeness in new and on-going group setting; asserts self in familiar and unfamiliar social situations; relates well to others; responds appropriately as the situation requires; and takes an interest in what others say and do.
375		ABT-15B.01		S	Develop and use listening skills.
376		ABT-15B.02		A	Develop objectivity.
377		ABT-15B.03		S	Demonstrate understanding of team planning, problem solving and how communications processes and individuals contribute to the group.
378		ABT-15B.04		S	Develop conflict resolution and consensus building techniques.